ORIGINAL PAPERS ILLUSTRATING THE HISTORY OF THE APPLICATION OF THE ROMAN ALPHABET TO THE LANGUAGES OF INDIA

ORIGINAL PAPERS ILLUSTRATING THE HISTORY
OF THE
APPLICATION OF THE ROMAN ALPHABET
TO THE
LANGUAGES OF INDIA

EDITED BY

MONIER WILLIAMS

GYAN

Published by

GYAN

Gyan Publishing House
5, Ansari Road
Daryaganj, New Delhi-110002
Phone: 011-47034999, 9811692060
E-mail: books@gyanbooks.com

Distribution Network
gyanbooks.com
India, USA, Canada, UK, Australia, France

ISBN : 978-81-212-3863-2 (PB)
First Published, London, 1859

2nd Impression 2020

Printed at: Gyan Press, Delhi.

Original Papers Illustrating the History of the Application of the Roman Alphabet to The Languages of India
Editor: Monier Williams

ORIGINAL PAPERS

ILLUSTRATING

THE HISTORY

OF THE

APPLICATION OF THE ROMAN ALPHABET

TO THE

LANGUAGES OF INDIA.

EDITED BY

MONIER WILLIAMS, M.A.

OF THE UNIVERSITY OF OXFORD:

LATE PROFESSOR OF SANSKRIT AT THE EAST INDIA COLLEGE, HAILEYBURY.

LONDON

LONGMAN, BROWN, GREEN, LONGMANS, AND ROBERTS.

1859

PREFACE.

THE following papers were intrusted to me for publication by Sir Charles Trevelyan, the present Governor of the Madras Presidency, on his departure from England, under the conviction that the first germ and subsequent growth of what now seems destined to become a mighty movement should be placed on permanent public record. My task has been very simple. I have merely arranged the various documents in chronological order, and left them to speak for themselves. Even the errors in orthography, which I might have corrected with little trouble, have been allowed to stand. My duty has been to lay before the public a series of original papers and articles, in such a shape as to present a complete history of a great enterprise; and I have acted on the principle that even inaccuracies of scholarship, when regarded as historical, become interesting and instructive.

The intelligent reader will, of course, bear in mind that more than a quarter of a century has elapsed since the date of the first of these papers, and that the state of things under the pressure of which they were written is greatly changed. We live now in an age of toleration and conciliation. Controversy in these days is conducted with less party-spirit, less prejudice, less asperity; and men bring to the discussion of disputed questions a more disciplined taste, greater logical precision of argument, and more judicial calmness of mind.

We have also the advantage of greater accuracy of information, and a better acquaintance with the niceties of scholarship. Moreover, every moot-point is now subjected to the salutary ordeal of a thorough "ventilation" (according to the modern phrase) in the public press, and especially in the columns of that mighty organ of public opinion, the "Times" newspaper. Whatever be the topic of debate, it is there agitated in the fresh air of free discussion; and, if it survive a long exposure to the storms of controversy, its whole aspect becomes purified and invigorated. Such has happily been the case with the investigation into the respective merits of the Eastern and Western alphabets. For a long period the idea of applying the Roman character to the Indian languages struggled doubtfully for existence. Nevertheless, gradually but surely, amidst much contempt and opposition, it gathered strength, till at last, in the healthy atmosphere of open and liberal inquiry, this grand conception has acquired a force and a vitality which nothing can now extinguish.

In introducing, then, to the notice of the public, the interesting papers which describe the course of this movement from its earliest commencement to the present time, it may justly be expected that I should prepare the way by an outline of its most prominent features. Great discoveries which have worked stupendous changes, and conferred incalculable benefits on the human race, have had insignificant beginnings.

The lifting of the lid of a boiling kettle suggested the notion of the first steam-engine. In like manner the idea of applying the Roman letters to the languages of India, which promises to act like steam-power on the progress of Eastern civilisation, had its origin in a very simple circumstance. It happened on this wise. More than twenty-five years ago Mr. Thompson, a missionary, at the instigation of Mr. Trevelyan, then a youthful and active member of the Bengal Civil Service, wrote an English and Urdú Dictionary in the Roman character. This somewhat crude offspring of Mr. Thompson's brain stood in need of a sponsor to recommend it to the notice of the Committee of the Calcutta School-book Society; whereupon the Rev. Dr. Yates stood forth in this capacity, and in a letter to the Committee submitted the book to their notice, and advised their subscribing for 200 copies.

It might have been supposed that a request so modest, preferred by a man like Dr. Yates, would have met with immediate favour; and probably no objection would have been raised, had not the book been entirely printed in Roman type. Here, then, was a barbarous innovation which shocked the orthodox notions of two great Oriental scholars, Messrs. Prinsep and Tytler. In two contemptuous minutes they record their protest against what they consider the ultra-radicalism of the author of the Dictionary.

This opposition was, it must be confessed, quite natural in these gentlemen, and withal excusable. Some of us may remember what happened when it was proposed to disturb the classic shades of Oxford by the introduction of the broad gauge. The cassocked Dignitaries of Christchurch stood aghast. They were slow to discern the signs of the times, and little suspected that sooner or later the broad gauge must come to their very doors, and be welcomed as a boon. Let us not to be too hard, then, on Messrs. Prinsep and Tytler. As scholars, they only did what most other scholars would have done twenty-five years ago. They opposed a doubtful innovation, and did their best to crush the too audacious author of it. In the double grasp of these two learned giants the meek unpresuming missionary had like to have been annihilated. But, happily for him, succour was at hand. All Englishmen are lovers of fair play. An uncontrollable impulse prompts us to take the part of the weaker side; and this feeling would probably have led Mr. Trevelyan (who was even then noted for his liberal views) to enter the lists and do battle for the oppressed, even if he had not been in a manner committed to the defence of Mr. Thompson, by having originally suggested the compilation of his Dictionary. Here, then, may be said to terminate the First Act of the history. Messrs. Prinsep and Tytler are seen bearing down the unresisting missionary, when a champion appears in the person of Mr. Trevelyan, who in true knightly style advances to the rescue.

The Second Act opens with the actual combat, and right valiantly does Mr. Thompson's champion quit himself in the field. The tilt may be said to commence at Paper 4, by a long thrust from Mr. Trevelyan, and the contest is carried on by alternate lunge and parry to the end of Paper 8. Though the odds are against him, no one can read the particulars of this encounter without feeling that Mr. Trevelyan has the best of it. His defence of Mr. Thompson marks an important epoch. It is the first recorded vindication of the Roman system as applicable to the languages of India.

The Third Act brings another combatant on the arena, who not only declares for the champion of the Roman alphabet, but turns out himself to be a mighty man of valour — no less a person, in fact, than the now noted Dr. Duff. Let any one read his Papers (signed Alpha, and numbered 9, 10, 11), and say whether he does not fight on the winning side, and by his hard knocks contribute to the victory. The warmth of his zeal may betray him now and then into tedious amplification, but the accumulated weight of his arguments is irresistible, and the shrewdness with which he exposes Mr. Tytler's fallacy in confounding the Roman alphabet with English so-called orthography is worthy of all praise. The conclusion of this period sees an offensive and defensive alliance entered into between Mr. Trevelyan and the four Baptist missionaries, Messrs. Duff, Yates, Pearce, and Thomas. A regular scheme is then promulgated for the printing and circulation of useful vernacular books in the Roman character, the first book printed being the "Sermon on the Mount" in Romanised Hindústání.

The Fourth Act of the history presents to our view Mr. Trevelyan carrying on the contest in conjunction with the three remaining Baptist missionaries, after the departure of Dr. Duff for England. The most noticeable feature in this period is the controversy which takes place between Mr. H. T. Prinsep and Mr. Trevelyan; the former advocating the adoption of Dr. Gilchrist's system of Romanising, the latter defending in an able paper the method of Sir William Jones. (See pp. 138—161.) Further allusion will be made to this subject before concluding the Preface. During this period also two or three interesting episodes occur. The four champions of the Roman alphabet (Messrs. Trevelyan, Yates, Pearce, and Thomas) meet together, and address a circular letter to missionary students in the United States, inviting their aid in support of the cause. They also draw up a series of resolutions with the object of establishing a permanent fund for the publication of books, and the promotion of the Roman system generally. These resolutions are given at p. 175, and are followed by an enumeration of fifty-seven useful books in Hindústání, Bengálí, Uriya, &c., printed in Roman type, which were either published or in the press at the end of 1836, only three years after the commencement of the movement.

In the year 1838 Mr. Trevelyan leaves India for England, and here occurs an interval of no less than twenty years. This chasm, however, is bridged over by the letter of the Rev. R. C. Mather to Mr. (now Sir Charles) Trevelyan, describing the progress made in the application of the Roman alphabet to Indian languages up to the great mutiny in 1857. (See p. 202.)

The Fifth and concluding period of the history embraces the revival of the controversy in the columns of the English press during the past year, and includes nearly all the articles and letters which have appeared in various journals, whether in favour of or in opposition to the scheme, up to the commencement of 1859. (See pp. 210—274.)

Having thus sketched a rough outline of the five principal stages which mark the progress of the movement, it remains to draw attention to one or two points which have suggested themselves to my mind in perusing these remarkable papers.

The first observation I have to make is, that it must strike a casual reader as very curious, that Mr. Tytler and other controversialists of his school should have run their heads against the fallacy of confusing the Roman letters with the English alphabetical system. They will have it that the advocates of the Roman letters want to warp and distort the Indian languages, by forcing them into conformity with our so-called English orthography. The reverse, however, as Mr. Trevelyan shows, is the case. It is the Roman system, and not the English abuse of it, that is advocated. The Sanskrit and Latin languages are, as every scholar now knows, derived from a common source. Their alphabets (though one has been carried to an excess of elaboration, the other to an extreme of simplicity) are capable of mutual adjustment and assimilation, both as regards the powers of the letters and their classification. Our English alphabet, on the other hand, is an entire perversion of the proper powers of the Latin letters, and especially of the vowels, to the confusion of all sounds. Nothing can possibly be imagined more irregular and systemless, than our use, or rather abuse, of the Roman vowel symbols. We take the symbols a, i, u, e, o, and instead of making each the fixed representative of one invariable sound, we allow each to stand for almost any sound. Thus *a* represents five different sounds in the words *tape*, *tap*, *tall*, *tar*, *mortar;* and each of the five vowels may stand for the sound of *u* in *gun*, as in the words *organ*, *sir*, *gun*, *her*, *son;* and the sound of *a* in *tall* may be equally represented by *o*, *au*, *oa*, *ou*, and *eo*, in the words *nor*, *taught*, *groat*, *thought*, *George*.

Any attempt, therefore, to bring the Oriental vowel system into conformity with the English must fail, for the plain reason that in English we have no system. But why is our contempt of all method to be laid at the door of an alphabet which is capable of the most regular and methodical adjustment? If we have perverted that alphabet to the subversion of all order, and made a Balaklava out of what might have been systematised, that is merely the result of our usual careless habit of letting matters take their course. Let us not confound two things which are as distinct as light from darkness,—the simple, flexible, symmetrical Roman alphabet, and the pseudographical perversion of it called by a delicate euphemism English orthography.

Even the great Dr. Gilchrist fell into this mistake. His system of Romanising Oriental words is a partial attempt to write them according to the more common English pronunciation of the Roman vowels, and especially of the vowel *u*. This plan, however attractive to the eye of an Englishman, is radically unsound. That of Sir. William Jones on the other hand, which is a symmetrical system of *transliteration* (see the Table at p. 162), is now universally acknowledged to be the only successful adaptation of the Roman alphabet to the expression of Indian languages.

Another point which deserves notice is, that the controversialists have perhaps dwelt with unnecessary prolixity on the advantages to be derived from substituting the simple Roman for the complicated Eastern symbols. These advantages are patent to all sensible people. It cannot for a moment be doubted that both Europeans and Asiatics would save themselves enormous trouble, and gain enormous benefits, by using the same common alphabet to express their respective languages. The great question is, whether the force of association and the inveteracy of habit in the Hindú mind are too strong to be overcome by any considerations of advantage;—whether, in other words, the Hindú, whilst admitting the superiority of our alphabet, as he does of our religion, will not still regard his own system of writing as a sacred institution, inherited from his forefathers, hallowed by their use, and therefore not to be abandoned. This point is forcibly treated by some of the advocates of the Roman letters, and it is well shown that, as the Hindús have already accepted a totálly new alphabet from their Musalmán rulers, so, *a fortiori*, they will not hesitate in due course of time to adopt that of their English masters. But more stress might perhaps have been laid on this aspect of the question. It might, I think, have been shown that the Hindús are more utilitarian in their views, and greater worshippers of expediency, than we are apt to imagine. After all, a Brahmin and an Englishman are offshoots from the same Indo-European stock, as their languages can testify. Many of their household words are the same; and although climate and the force of circumstances have caused vast diversities, yet their national characters have features of similarity, and there is much common ground on which they can take their stand. A Brahmin thinks a great deal about caste and social distinctions; so does an Englishman. Your true Saxon, however, is rarely disposed to permit his pride of caste to stand in the way of any prospect of advantage or profit to himself. Nor does the most bigoted of Brahmins yield in this respect to the most exclusive of Englishmen. When his interest is concerned he holds religiously to his caste; but drops it without the smallest compunction when it suits his convenience. He has a horror of leather, and shrinks from leather-dressers as from polluted objects. But leather shoes are found to be very convenient things, and he uses them accordingly. He abominates animal fat, and is up in arms at the bare notion of being asked to use a greased cartridge; yet the very Sepoys who make this a pretext for revolt think nothing of biting the same cartridges when they want to shoot their masters. It was thought that the severity of caste regulations would seriously affect the passenger traffic on Indian railroads. High caste and low caste, it was said, would never consent to travel by the same train. But what is found to be the fact? The natives of India of all classes have as keen an appreciation of the convenience of railways as Europeans, and throw their pride to the winds under the levelling influences of steam and the locomotive engine. In much the same spirit have they adopted all the improvements which the industry and ingenuity of Englishmen have introduced into India. Railroads, electric telegraphs, gasometers, postage stamps,—nothing comes amiss. With the utmost complacency they are ready to acquiesce in any innovation, provided it holds out a prospect of profit or advantage which they can appropriate to themselves or in any way turn to account. And so will it be with the Roman alphabet. We have only to convince them that their interest is involved in its introduction, and they will be eager to adopt it.

One more remark, and my task is ended. Let all who desire the welfare of the people of India join heart and hand in this good cause, without waiting for the Government to take the lead. It is the glory of England that, unlike other great empires, its government is moved by the community, and not the community by the government. Though the Queen be supreme, the will of the majority rules the land. Public opinion, therefore, must be brought to bear on the Executive, ere that power can accord the weight of its sanction to the introduction of changes. But let the public will once be unmistakably expressed, and the Executive authority must bend to its decision. It is but little that the advocates of the Roman alphabet solicit. All they ask of the Government of India is that their system shall be allowed fair play and perfect toleration. If this be conceded, if there be no unfair preferences, no undue truckling to prejudices or caprice, no uncalled for patronage of antiquated customs, it is not too much to predict that the general adoption of the Roman alphabet, as a common medium of expression for the Indian vernaculars, must soon take its place amongst the "accomplished facts" of this wonder-working century.

MONIER WILLIAMS.

Cheltenham: March, 1859.

CONTENTS.

TO THE BINDER.

Extract from Map of the Dooab to face page 144.

ORIGINAL PAPERS

DESCRIPTIVE OF THE HISTORY OF

THE APPLICATION OF THE ROMAN ALPHABET

TO THE

LANGUAGES OF INDIA.

(1.)

LETTER OF THE REVEREND W. YATES TO THE PRESIDENT, VICE-PRESIDENTS, AND COMMITTEE OF THE CALCUTTA SCHOOL-BOOK SOCIETY, SUBMITTING TO THEIR NOTICE MR. THOMPSON'S ENGLISH AND URDŰ DICTIONARY IN THE ROMAN CHARACTER.

Dear Gentlemen,

I have the pleasure to submit to your notice an English and Oordoo Dictionary, prepared by Mr. Thompson of Delhi* at the request of Mr. Trevelyan, who from acquaintance with his talents considered him well capable of executing such a work. It is designed to assist natives in the Upper Provinces in the acquisition of English, and Europeans in the study of Oordoo. It was expected that the work, if approved, would be printed at the expense of the Society, and as usual 150 copies allowed to the author as a remuneration for his labour; but from a private letter of Mr. Thompson's it appears that 1000 rupees is the least he would expect if the Society accept the work, and that he thinks he could realise considerably more than this by printing it himself. Under this view of the case, Mr. Trevelyan and myself think it would be best for the Society to subscribe for 200 copies, and let Mr. T. print for himself. It seems, however, desirable

* Mr. Thompson's widow and daughters were killed in the recent massacre at Delhi.—*M. W.*

that this subscription for two hundred copies should be made on the express condition that, while the Society consent to Mr. Thompson's receiving the benefit of any edition he may print, he shall allow them to print for themselves if they deem it necessary. Past experience has proved that it is not an eligible plan to employ the resources of the Society in the patronising of works over which they can have no control, and after the adoption of which into their depository list they cannot pledge themselves for a regular supply. It is better not to adopt, than after having adopted, to be obliged to discard. Should the book be generally approved, and should Mr. T. be willing to submit to these conditions, then I suppose he may be left at liberty to print it where he pleases, stipulating only that it shall be on good English paper, in cloth covers, and not exceeding four rupees a copy.

I remain,

Dear Gentlemen,

Yours very sincerely,

(Signed) W. YATES, *Secretary.*

Calcutta School-Book Society's Depository,
20th November, 1833.

(2.)

MR. JAMES PRINSEP'S FIRST MINUTE, OBJECTING TO MR. THOMPSON'S DICTIONARY.

Mr. Thompson's work will doubtless find a ready sale among Europeans, but I trust that none of our colleges has it in contemplation to teach Arabic, Persian, or Hindee words in Roman characters. This would, indeed, be ultra-radicalism, and I cannot therefore vote for any sanction being given by the School-Book Society, even in receiving a dedication from the author, unless the words "for the use of European students" be inserted in the title-page. Besides, before giving countenance to such an important work as a Dictionary, we should have a report on its execution from some competent person.

(Signed) J. P.

(3.)

MR. J. TYTLER'S FIRST MINUTE, OBJECTING TO MR. THOMPSON'S DICTIONARY.

We shall compromise our character very much, particularly with European scholars, in whose eyes the Oriental literature of Calcutta does not, I fear, stand very high at present, if we go back to the old system of printing Oriental books in Roman characters. This is, indeed, "to mistake the infancy of science for its maturity," and I cannot give my vote for doing so. I am aware that a *School-Book Society* is not to publish books of too high an order, but the present appears to me even below our general run of publications, and I am at a loss to see for what class of pupils it can be intended, as it appears ill calculated for any. It is a mere naked vocabulary destitute of every principle of scientific philology, in which the words are thrown together in a heap, and full of mistranslations and misapprehensions. A hundred instances might be picked out in a few minutes. In this state it can only serve to puzzle beginners, and will certainly be thrown aside by those who have made the least advance. I think on the whole that the encouragement of such works is a mere waste of funds, and therefore vote against it.

(Signed) J. TYTLER.

(4.)

MR. C. E. TREVELYAN'S FIRST MINUTE IN SUPPORT OF MR. THOMPSON'S DICTIONARY AND OF THE APPLICATION OF THE ROMAN ALPHABET TO HINDÚSTÁNÍ.

I owe an apology to the Committee for having suffered a proposition with which my name was connected to be submitted for their decision unaccompanied by any explanation on my part, for I am convinced that if this precaution had been taken, the objections which have been brought forward to Mr. Thompson's work would have been obviated, and the scope and motives of it would have appeared to the members of the Committee in a clearer point of view than has actually been the case. It will now be my endeavour to supply the deficiency as far as it can be done at this late period of the discussion, and I am encouraged to adopt this course by observing that several gentlemen for whose opinions I entertain a high respect, are inclined to view the proposition with favour, while our highly honoured President has suspended the expression of his opinion until the question shall have received more complete elucidation. I shall now proceed to consider each of the objections in the order in which they have been brought forward.

Mr. Prinsep "trusts that none of our colleges has in con-"templation to teach Arabic, Persian, and Hindee words in "Roman characters. This," he observes, "would indeed be "ultra-radicalism." This is the sole objection assigned by this gentleman to the plan, that it would be "ultra-radi-"calism." Let us consider therefore what ultra-radicalism is. It means an *entire* change. Now change is a relative term which may be either good or bad according to the circumstances of each particular case. If the change is good, it is of course desirable that it should be radical; and if it is bad, it were better that it did not take place at all.

This is not the first ultra-radicalism in the department of education which has emanated from Delhi.

At Calcutta scarcely any encouragement is offered to the Mahomedans to study English, while they are bribed at an expense of more than 30 rupees a month for every student to cultivate Arabic *; the consequence of which is that there is scarcely a single Mahomedan to be found at Calcutta who has received a tolerable education. At Delhi equal encouragement is held out to Mahomedans and Hindoos to prosecute

* The following description of this Monkish institution is taken from a note of the Secretary to the Committee of Public Instruction:

"I deem it my duty to notice that the Madrissa has only 74 students, all of whom it supports by pecuniary allowances, and that (without taking into consideration the heavy items of printing) the board and tuition of each student costs 320 rupees per annum, a rate greatly exceeding the expenditure on the pupils of any other institution. It is possible the excess may be counterbalanced by great public advantages."

the study of English literature and science, and the youth of both denominations are pursuing it there in nearly equal numbers and with equal success. This is an ultra-radicalism.

At Calcutta the division of society into castes is carefully cherished and perpetuated by maintaining separate institutions for Christians, Mahomedans, and Hindoos. At Delhi the youth of every religion and caste pursue their studies together in the same institution. This is another ultra-radicalism, and so little was it anticipated by Mr. Wilson that at the first formation of the Delhi College, among other branches of study proposed by him for the new institution, one was the "scheme of castes" in all its complicated ramifications. Happily this kind of propagandism did not take there. Benares has always been more under the influence of Calcutta, and the institutions at that place present an exact counterpart to those at the capital.

I have now submitted to the Committee two instances of ultra-radicalism, and I fearlessly allege that they are both good and contain in themselves the seeds of great prospective improvement. A third has now been produced emanating from the same place, and before Mr. Prinsep can justly call upon the Committee to condemn it, he is bound to show that it is of a bad and not of a good description. This he has omitted to do, and as yet he has not favoured us with a single reason against the more general introduction of the Roman letters to which he so strongly objects. The subject, however, is of so much importance that I cannot suffer it to be thus cursorily passed over, and I will proceed to answer, as briefly as possible, all the difficulties with which the change can be supposed to be attended.

Perhaps it may be thought that the Roman letters are so strange and foreign to the people of this country, that the extensive use of them in writing the Indian languages cannot reasonably be anticipated. To this I would reply that these letters, which were at first used only for the Latin tongue within the limits of the little territory of Latium, have gradually been adopted to express all the languages of Europe, America, Australia, and part of Africa and Asia. The Greek, the German, and the Russian characters are the sole exceptions to the general uniformity in the mode of writing in Europe, and at least two of these are rapidly falling into disuse. The old German text is now almost entirely abandoned, and few new books are published in Germany except in the Roman character. In Greece the revival of letters has been marked by the simultaneous adoption of the universal written character of the civilised world, and Romaic or modern Greek School-Books, Testaments, and, I believe, newspapers also, expressed in Roman letters, are daily becoming multiplied. Both in North and South America, whether the language be English, French, Spanish, or Portuguese, the Roman characters prevail, without any exception, and the same in the Australian continent, which is in progress of being peopled as yet by Englishmen only. The letters which have been adopted to express the languages of the South Sea islanders are also the Roman, with only such modifications as are necessary to denote the sounds peculiar to their tongues, and numerous printing-presses are at this moment employed in spreading these universal harbingers of civilisation throughout the great Southern Archipelago. The same plan has been pursued in Java, the Celebes, and wherever else the Dutch have had authority, and, as a specimen, I have the honour to submit to the Committee a Testament in the Malay language and Roman character.

The Roman letters have actually been adopted to express the popular languages of India. The plan was introduced by Sir William Jones and zealously followed up by Mr. Gilchrist, and had the latter gentleman been supported by a Society like ours, the system would no doubt by this time have been fully established. Unfortunately, however, for the cause of popular education, the Oriental rage was, at the period when Gilchrist laboured, at its height, and he was overborne by a host of learned Orientalists, who, in making knowledge simple, foresaw the ruin of their craft. Everybody must be aware that when the popular languages of the East are once disencumbered of their Persian or Sanskrit dress, the gentlemen who are the depositories of Asiatic lore will no longer be looked up to with the same degree of wonder and admiration as they are at present, and they will greatly sink in the estimation of their learned brethren in the West.

The Roman system of letters has now been adopted in India for the third time under happier auspices. The exclusive taste for Oriental studies never extended in its full force to the extremities of the empire. The focus of this influence was at Calcutta, where its intensity was concentrated by a profusion of honours and rewards in the shape of professorships both for Natives and Europeans, secretaryships to Oriental colleges, moonsheeships, Arabic translationships at the rate of 750 rupees per 50 pages, studentships in the Arabic College at an expense to the state of more than 30 rupees a month, &c. &c. There was nothing of this kind in the Upper Provinces. Occasionally, indeed, a stray Orientalist made his appearance there, but unfortunately for the profession, his qualifications in other respects did not always sufficiently correspond with his attainments in the science of words to gain many admirers for the system. In the Upper Provinces, therefore, there were no predilections to stand in the way of the new letters, and there was no danger of their being strangled as soon as they were born, as they had formerly been at Calcutta.

Another circumstance which augurs very favourably for the success which is likely to attend the reproduction of the old system, is, that the measure has not been adopted until the necessity of it became self-evident. Great numbers of the youth of Delhi, who are brought up at the English College, have no acquaintance whatever either with the Nagree or Persian character. They know English as their language of education, and Hindoostanee as their vernacular tongue, but the only character with which they are acquainted is the Roman, and this they employ to write both languages. For their use, therefore, (and they are a very intelligent and annually increasing class,) an English and Hindoostanee Dictionary was indispensable. Under these circumstances Mr. Thompson undertook the compilation of a small vocabulary, which met with such eminent success that he was encouraged to apply himself to the task of preparing the larger work to which the patronage of the Committee is now solicited. The vocabulary is circulated herewith, and it is deserving of attention as the first fruits of a system of letters which will eventually become universal throughout the East, and will contribute in a high degree to hasten the period when India will possess a national literature of her own equal to any other in the world.

The plan which the Committee is requested to support is, therefore, anything but an uncertain experiment suggested by the expectation of probable advantage. It is a measure called for by urgent necessity, and proved to be advantageous by the result of a trial which has been already made. If there was anything of speculation in the matter, it was in the original essay made by Mr. Thompson, and not in the measure now adopted to follow up a plan the soundness of which has been fully established.

I beg leave to call the attention of the Committee to the commentary furnished by the facts which have been stated upon the cry now raised of ultra-radicalism. The first great change was effected when the Roman letters surpassed the ancient limits of the territory of Rome, and, since that time, by a succession of ultra-radicalisms, they have been adopted by one nation after another, until at last they bid fair to become the universal written character of the whole world. Every one of these changes was, no doubt, condemned by the lovers of ancient lore of the day; and, if their advice had been attended to, every nation would to this day have had its own separate character, as well as language, and one more barrier would have been added to those which already stand in the way of the general fraternisation of the human race, and the general enlightenment of the human mind. In England the Roman letters did not acquire their present well established ascendency until after several struggles; and the lovers of the Saxon, Norman, Old English, court hand, &c., no doubt, each in their day, strenuously maintained that their own way of writing English was the only one in which the force and beauties of the language could be properly expressed. The ultra-radicalism has actually been perpetrated in this country. The Roman letters have taken their place in Indian literature, and, notwithstanding the opposition which may be raised by learned Orientalists, I am convinced that they will continue to advance by a slow, but sure, progress, until that day shall arrive when the curse of Babel will be removed, and all mankind will be united in the enjoyment of a common language and a common mode of expressing it.

The Roman is not the first foreign character which has been adopted to express the popular language of India. The Persian and Arabic characters are equally foreign, and they are not nearly so distinct or so easy to be used in printing as the Roman. The Nagree character also, although quite foreign to the languages of Persia and Arabia, is used to express words of pure Arabic and Persian origin.

The Roman letters are capable of being adapted to the popular languages of India in a much more complete manner than they have been to that of England. Nothing can be more preposterous than our English system of *writing*, for it is not deserving of the name of Orthography. For instance, *hare, hair, heir, were, pear*, are all written differently, although the vowels have precisely the same sound; but in adapting the Roman letters to the popular languages of India, whether Sir Wm. Jones's, Mr. Gilchrist's, or Mr. Thompson's scheme ultimately come into general use, an exact correspondence between the writing and the pronunciation will be preserved.

In the different schemes of letters which have been devised, the varying sounds of the Indian consonants which are not represented by a corresponding letter in the Roman alphabet have been distinguished by some peculiar mark, or by some modification of the kindred letter. I know that the lovers of Arabic and Sanskrit will reply to this, that if any modifications of the Roman alphabet are admitted for the purpose of denoting sounds peculiar to the Indian languages, the system of letters which it is proposed to bring into more extended use will then be neither one thing nor the other, neither Roman nor Indian. I rejoin by asking whether the Persian character, as used in writing Hindoostanee, is more pure? It is far from being so. In order to adapt the Persian characters to the language of Hindoostan it was necessary to invent signs to distinguish the different variations of sound in the Sanskrit consonants, and the letters peculiar to the Arabic (ain, ghain, toe, zoe) were introduced without any alteration in the forms in which they are used in writing the original language. The Persian alphabet, therefore, as used in writing the Hindoostanee language, is as great a mongrel as ever the Roman letters can be when they are applied to the same purpose, being made up, partly of pure Persian characters, partly of letters introduced from the Arabic, and partly of certain modified forms of Persian letters which have been invented by the Fort William philologists to represent those sounds of the Sanskrit letters which are not to be found in the Persian. This adaptation was not completed until of late years, when the subject was taken up by the learned Orientalists of the College of Fort William. They might just as well have modified the Roman as the Persian characters to express the language of this country. They are both equally foreign, and equally applicable to it with some slight alterations.

We are not such pedants as to desire to sacrifice both sense and usefulness in the attempt to attain an ideal uniformity. The basis only of the Indo-Roman character is Roman, as the basis of the Indo-Persian character is Persian, and where additions or modifications are required they have been made. So far as the languages agree, the pure Roman character is used for both; and, so far as they differ, a modification of it has been devised suited to meet the exigency of the case. The particulars in which the languages coincide are made evident to the student from the similarity of character, and the points in which they differ are rendered plain to him by the peculiar marks. This, it must be admitted, is a great assistance both to the Englishman learning the Indian, and to the Indian learning the English language; and besides this, by clearly pointing out the discrepancies between the tongues, a tendency has been created to produce a more exact correspondence between them.

If it were to be asked what advantages are to be expected from adopting the Roman letters as the medium for expressing the Indian languages, I would answer as follows:—

First. The Roman character, whether it be written or

printed, is more distinct than any other which can be adopted for expressing the languages of India, whether they be derived from the Sanskrit, Arabic, Persian, or English source, or whether they be mixed and compounded of the whole or any number of these tongues. The superiority of the Roman letters may be inferred from the circumstance of their having gradually been adopted, in spite of every opposition, to express the language of so many different nations in different parts of the world; and, notwithstanding the continuance of the same opposition, they are still spreading to a degree far exceeding any other character. One main cause of the superior distinctness of the Roman character is that the vowels are expressed, instead of being either entirely omitted, or distinguished by diacritical points, which are continually liable to be misplaced and left out; and, even when every precaution is taken, it is more difficult to read Hebrew, Arabic, or Persian, in which the vowels are represented by minute points, placed above or below the line, than any language printed in Roman characters in which they are denoted by a separate letter standing in its place in the line. Another reason is the extreme neatness of the printed Roman character. The art of printing has been carried to a far higher degree of perfection in these letters than in any others. As they are the universal character of the civilised world, they have been more extensively used in printing than any other, and, from the first invention of the art to the present day, they have been gradually elaborated and improved in the manner which has been found by experience best adapted to meet the difficulties which from time to time have suggested themselves. They have the result of nearly three hundred years' experience in their favour, and I put it to the Committee whether it be more desirable to adopt the Roman character, thus perfected and improved, or to go on with the tedious process of elaborating Nagree and Persian by a succession of changes, which must be carried through a long series of years before we can hope to arrive at the same degree of perfection.

Secondly. Printing can be carried on in Roman characters much cheaper and more expeditiously than it can either in

Persian or in Nagree. For instance, Mr. Pearce informs me that it would cost one third more, and take up double the time, to print Mr. Thompson's manuscript in Roman and Nagree and Persian characters united, as it would to print it in Roman characters alone; and, after all, it would not be so perfect, if Persian characters formed part of the design, on account of the liability of the numerous vowel and other points used in writing that language to break, to be misplaced, to be omitted, or not to be correctly ascertained; their application varying according to the authority of different dictionaries. In laying the foundation of a national literature, it is of great importance to select a character which will cause as small an expenditure as possible of the time and money of the nation. It is not easy to imagine how much of these important elements of human affairs might be saved in the course of one hundred years, by having all our books printed in Roman characters only, which cost one third less, instead of Persian or Nagree, which cost one third more. To make knowledge cheap and bring books down to the level of the means even of the poorest class of people, it must be admitted, is an object of some importance.

Thirdly. A still greater advantage which will be gained by the plan will be, that the adoption of the Roman characters in India will lead to the gradual disuse of the Nagree and Persian and Arabic, and we shall thus have three characters less than we had before. Need I point out the advantages of such a consummation? Next to the multiplicity of languages, the intellect of India is oppressed by the multiplicity of letters; and it is shocking to think how much human time, which might be directed to the best purposes, is wasted in gaining a knowledge of the many barbarous characters with which the country abounds. The student of Hindoostanee now has to learn both the Nagree and Persian characters, and, if he would commence the study of English, he must learn the Roman also; but, under the new plan, the Roman characters will do for all. The infancy of every nation in the pursuit of knowledge is always marked by a diversity of languages and letters, and, as it improves in civilisation, they gradually become assimilated and ultimately merge in one common character and tongue. The natural and just tendency of everything is to simplicity.

Fourthly. It is generally admitted that our endeavours should be mainly directed to the gradual formation of a national literature embodying in itself the selected knowledge of the whole civilised world, and it forms a strong recommendation of the plan now under consideration that it will greatly tend to facilitate the accomplishment of this highly important object. When the languages of England and of India shall become expressed in a character common to both, the obstacles which stand in the way of their assimilation will be materially diminished. The path from one language to the other will be in a manner smoothed to every student, as he will have the words only to learn and not the symbols whereby they are expressed. The person who knows English will be more easily induced to cultivate a tongue embodied in a character with which he is already acquainted, and into which he can introduce pure English words without any glaring impropriety; thereby gratifying his literary taste at the same time that he will be able to convey his meaning with greater readiness and precision in terms taken from the more scientific and cultivated language; while, on the other hand, the Hindoostanee scholar will, for the same reason, enter with greater ease upon the study of English, and draw from it, in like manner, stores of expressive words for the improvement of his native dialect. In either case, whether the English scholar descend to Hindoostanee, or the Hindoostanee scholar ascend to English, the transition will be made much easier to them both by the use of a common character; and the certain result of this intimate connexion between the two languages will be, that the national literature will be enriched by plentiful supplies of words and ideas derived from the English source. The words of the English language are so generally indeclinable that their introduction into the Indian dialects may be accomplished with peculiar ease. How desirable would it be to engraft upon the popular languages of the East such words as *virtue, honour, gratitude, patriotism, public spirit,* and some others for which it is at present difficult to find any synonyme in them!

Lastly. By means of the assimilation proposed, the mutual good understanding between the two races will be greatly promoted. When their languages shall be expressed in a character common to both, the English will learn more Indian, and the Indians will learn more English. If Latin were to be written in Hebrew, and French in Greek, characters, is it likely that we English should know so much about those languages as we do?

Mr. Prinsep observes: "Mr. Thompson's work will doubtless find a ready sale among Europeans. I cannot vote for any sanction being given by the Society even in receiving a dedication from the author, unless the words *for the use of European students* be inscribed on the title-page;" from which we must infer, that, in Mr. Prinsep's opinion, the circumstance that it will also be of use to European students constitutes a ground of objection to the book. For my part, I entertain exactly the contrary opinion, and that it will be equally useful to all classes appears to me to be a clear indication that the work is founded on sound principles. If, through the medium of our Society, books can be provided which shall not only facilitate the acquisition of the English language by the natives of India, but shall also assist the natives of England in acquiring a knowledge of the Indian languages, surely no wiser or nobler application could be made of our patronage. This appears to me to be the exact point of union towards which we should direct all our efforts, as far as mere language is concerned.

It is asked what class of people will make use of such a Dictionary as Mr. Thompson's. I reply briefly:

First. Those native students of the English language who, like the Delhi youths, are not acquainted with any character except the Roman.

Secondly. Every native who is engaged in studying the English language. In order to acquire even the slightest knowledge of English, every student must learn the Roma character; and it is obvious that the same degree of acquaint ance with it which enables him to read English imperfectly, would enable him to read his own language fluently. It will be a good way for children to begin to learn the Roman character by reading their own language in it, since a familiarity with any written character is more easily acquired through the medium of one's own than through that of a foreign language. If we wished to teach an English boy the Roman character, we should first set him to read English, and not Latin.

Thirdly. Every person, whether Indian or European, who is already acquainted with English and wishes to obtain an acquaintance with Hindoostanee.

In short, every Englishman who wishes to learn Hindoostanee, and every Indian who wishes to learn English, will take the first four rupees he has to spare to Mr. Thompson's stall.

In his love for Oriental hieroglyphics, Mr. Prinsep has overlooked the fact that to use *any* Hindoostanee and English Dictionary *a native must understand the Roman letters,* unless indeed that gentleman, in his ultra-toryism, would express our English words in Sanskrit, Arabic, or Persian characters. The Roman letters must be used and understood, *at any rate,* and why, therefore, should we increase the price of our Dictionary and puzzle the brains of our readers by the addition of barbarous Persian?

Before I conclude this part of the subject, I may as well observe, that it is not expected that the Roman letters can be generally introduced at once. Their complete establishment throughout India, to the exclusion of every other character, must be a work perhaps of several generations. The principle I advocate is the one which is understood to form the leading maxim of our Society, viz. that we should prepare books of a kind suited for every class of readers, and leave it to the popular taste to determine which shall be ultimately adopted and which rejected. I have shown that there are at present large classes of people to whom a Hindoostanee Dictionary printed in the Roman character would be highly acceptable, and, having done so, I conceive that I have made out a sufficient claim for the patronage of the Committee. If the demand for books printed in the Roman character spreads, so much the better; and, if not, we shall only have done our duty in supplying an actual call for the means of instruction. Although, therefore, the change of which I am the humble advocate may some day become radical, in the meantime it will only be gradual.

I shall now proceed to answer the objections brought forward by Mr. Tytler. The learned gentleman is of opinion that we "shall compromise our character, particularly with European scholars, in whose eyes the Oriental Literature of Calcutta does not stand very high at present, if we go back to the old system of printing Oriental books in Roman characters."

To this I reply that our Committee was not established for the purpose of raising the reputation of Calcutta as a seat of Oriental Literature, but for the purpose of providing the means of cheap and easy instruction for the people of the Bengal Presidency. These two objects have heretofore been too much confounded, or to speak more correctly, the latter, which is by far the more important, involving the intellectual and moral welfare of about sixty millions of people, has in a lamentable degree been sacrificed to the former. So long as we remained engrossed in the pursuit of the higher branches of Oriental lore, the education of the people was almost entirely lost sight of by us. The rage for Orientalism commenced in the time of Marquis Wellesley. The object which that nobleman had in view was to educate Europeans in the languages of the East. Our object is to educate Asiatics in the sciences of the West. The means adopted by Marquis Wellesley, therefore, whether they were well adapted or not for the ends which he had in view, are totally unsuited to forward the design of our society.

If Lord Wellesley's Oriental system had been confined within its proper limits, although it might not have done any good, yet it would not have done much harm; but, instead of this, it soon exceeded all due bounds and deluged the country with such an inundation of Sanskrit and Arabic, as had not been seen since the time of King Bhoj or Muhmood of Ghuznee. Instead of a revival of sound learning, it was only a revival of antiquated errors, and our Orientalists fondly imagined that, while they were propagating the long-exploded absurdities of Avicenna or the profligacies of the Sanskrit dramas, they were promoting the cause of public instruction.

This era of the history of India affords a curious instance of the natural tendency of the human mind to attach an undue degree of importance to those particular pursuits with which it happens to be conversant. The study of Sanskrit and Arabic is unobjectionable as a curious branch of inquiry, to be pursued by men of leisure and literary curiosity who happen to have a turn for the study of different languages, but it is absurd to suppose that the spread of true knowledge and the elevation of the morals of a nation can be promoted by such means.

For about thirty years, all the influence of the state was employed in directing the talent of the country towards the exclusive cultivation of the three dead languages, Sanskrit, Arabic, and Persian *, and a high standard of acquirement in any of them formed a certain avenue to civil employ. There

* The languages of Arabia and Persia, as known in India, are dead languages. If we except a few Arab and Persian merchants, they are the living spoken languages of no one class of people; and, when the natives of the country wish to cultivate them, they are under the necessity of commencing the study of them from the beginning, as they would of any other disused tongue. There was a time, no doubt, when they were the living languages of large classes of people in India. But that period has long since passed by, and English has taken the place which they once occupied. The spoken languages of India are the Hindoostanee, Bengalee, &c., which are the languages of the many, and English, which is the language of the few; but, although it be the language of the few, English possesses an importance far out of proportion to the numerical amount of the people by whom it is spoken, arising, as well from the superior influence inseparable from our situation in India, as from the superior stores of learning which our language contains. The English language is the source from which we must draw for the improvement of Native literature, and we might as well separate the stream from the fountain or the bread from the leaven which leavens it, as the vernacular dialects from the English language. The two will go on together through successive generations till they meet in a common language, equal for variety and power of expression, and for the amount of knowledge which it contains, to any of which the world can boast.

was also another, and a still more powerful, motive to encourage the taste for Orientalism, particularly among the English portion of the community. This is the one alluded to by Mr. Tytler. By means of the three dead languages, an *European* reputation was to be acquired. Here was a meed worthy of the most aspiring ambition! By the successful study of Sanskrit, Arabic, and Persian, a person not only becomes well known in England, but his name is familiarised to the "European scholars" of France and Germany and almost every other European country, for there is none which does not boast of some Orientalist.

This would be very well in an Antiquarian Society of European gentlemen, but it will not suffice for our Society, which has in view the improvement of an intellectually ignorant and morally degraded people. Let Mr. Tytler continue to pursue his Arabic studies, in the prosecution of which I wish him every success; but let us not suffer ourselves to be persuaded by him that we are instructing the Indians, while we are only gratifying the peculiar literary taste, and I fear, too generally, the vanity, of a few European scholars who happen to have turned their attention to the Sanskrit and Arabic languages. Our business is not with Europe, but with India; and our object is to instruct the people of India by the united means of English and of the popular languages, and not to gain a reputation in Europe by a patronage of the learned few who have leisure and inclination to devote themselves to the study of Sanskrit and Arabic. The objection that we shall fail to acquire for ourselves an European reputation, and that the bounds of the continent of India will also form the limits of our fame, can therefore have no influence with us. We never meant to aspire to the honour of knighthood, nor did the prospect of filling the Oriental chairs in the universities of England ever enter into our imaginations, and when we travel abroad, we shall not feel mortified if we pass unrecognised by the literati of Paris, Bonn, and Vienna, never having expected any attention from them. These honours are the rewards of encouraging Sanskrit and Arabic lore. But we shall enjoy the humble satisfaction of having done good in our day and generation, and I am sure that there are some gentlemen on our Committee whose souls are susceptible of being influenced by such a motive. We desire not to claim fraternity with Messrs. Bopp and Schlegel, but we recognise the duty of providing for the mental cultivation and moral improvement of millions of our fellow-subjects, and to this cause we are ready to devote time and talents and property, and all we possess that can be spared from other claims.

It may be thought that I have exaggerated the extent to which the instruction of the many has been sacrificed to the literary taste of the few. I beg leave to assure the Committee that such is far from being the case. A statement is annexed of the entire sum which has been expended by the General Committee of Public Instruction, from the date of its institution up to the 30th April, 1832, in the printing of Oriental works, or in assisting the authors to print them, by taking a certain number of copies off their hands. From an examination of this document it will be seen, that the patronage of the General Committee has been bestowed in the following proportions up to the above-mentioned date:—

Sanskrit	13,000	volumes.
Arabic	5,600	ditto.
Persian	2,500	ditto.
Hindee	2,000	ditto.

Not a single Bengalee or Oordoo book has been printed by the General Committee, nor has one translation been made through their medium into the popular languages. It is true that four Hindee works have been published by them (Sabhá Bilás, Rájníti, Chhatraprakása, and Dáyabhága), but none of these convey any European information. Not one of them is a translation of any European book, but they are either reprints of original Hindee books or of old Hindee translations from Sanskrit books; and they are all classical works, formed on an exclusively Sanskrit model, without a knowledge of which language they are almost unintelligible, and are therefore quite unfit to be used as a medium of popular instruction.

Will it now be said that I have exaggerated? These books were printed at the expense of a fund consecrated by the Parliament of Great Britain to the cause of *popular education*, and they form the result of twelve years' labours of the Committee of Public Instruction in that highly important branch of their duty which consists in the provision of Oriental books for the instruction of the public. Some of these books are of such a nature that the members of the General Committee would at once repudiate the idea of their being intended for the instruction of youth, or even of their being at all put into their hands. The Sanskrit drama called the Mricchhakati, or Toy Cart, for instance, is all about a prostitute. The Sanskrit poem called Naishadha, or Nala Damayanti, now reprinting at a great expense in twenty-two cantos, is another of this nature. The whole object of the poet appears to be to display his critical acquaintance with the Sanskrit language and his exquisite taste for sensuality. At times the author positively revels in licentiousness, and Don Juan is a tyro compared with him. The Committee will be able to judge of the character of the work when I inform them that the plot of the poem is as follows. Nala is rendered invisible and introduced by the god Indra into the harem of Damayanti to make love on his behalf to the beautiful mortal, but, as might have been expected, Nala fell in love himself and married the lady. A large portion of the poem is taken up in the detail of all that Nala observed in the interior of the harem in the most unguarded hours of its inmates, while he himself preserved his invisible form. Repasts of this kind may contribute very much to the gratification of the Oriental scholars of Europe and India. The book was of course intended exclusively for their perusal, and I strongly disclaim the idea of supposing that the members of the General Committee ever intended to pollute the minds of the youth of this country by teaching them lechery under its most seductive forms. These two books are only specimens of a great variety of the same character that might be named. If the sum which has been employed by the General Committee of Public Instruction in providing books for the amusement of Oriental scholars in Europe had been devoted to the supply of books of popular instruction, there would now be scarcely a school in the country which might not have been provided with some easy tracts of sound knowledge and pure morality. With the exception of the Sanskrit dramas, the works referred to are almost all quarto volumes of seven hundred or eight hundred pages each; and, for the same cost at which one of these great books is got up, twenty or thirty, nay sometimes eighty or a hundred, school-books might be supplied.

Among other honours with which the administration of Lord William Bentinck will descend to posterity, it will not be the least that in his time the Oriental mania, which broke out under Lord Wellesley's Government, advanced under Lord Minto's, was in the height of its career under Lord Hastings, and began to flag under Lord Amherst's, has completely exhausted itself. Orientalism has, at length, ceased to be considered the exclusive test of merit, and the public mind has completely awoke to the fact that the shortest and most effectual way of communicating knowledge to the people of this country is by educating the youth in English literature, and, where this is impracticable, by providing them with translations of books on European science in their own languages. All classes now concur in the expediency of opening in India the pure fount of English literature, and, where the parent source happens to be inaccessible to the student from the existence of other claims upon his time, he may at least be enabled to imbibe sound knowledge, though to a more limited extent, by means of translations in his native tongue.

According to the best of my judgment the truth lies in this opinion; but, whether this be the case or not, it is certain that in proportion as the public have advanced towards this point, the majority of the Committee of Public Instruction have receded from it. By referring again to the annexed statement, it will be seen that in 1832 and 1833 seven Sanskrit and the same number of Arabic books were printed by the Committee and only one Hindee (which, like the others, was on an exclusively Sanskrit model), and none in Bengalee or Oordoo; while on the 2nd November last, when the return was furnished, there were four Sanskrit and ten Arabic books in the press, and none in Hindee, Oordoo, or Bengalee. A change, therefore, has taken place, but it is all on the side of the learned languages and against popular instruction; and while Sanskrit used to be the principal object of the Committee's patronage, the tide has since turned in favour of Arabic. These learned languages seem to have just changed places in the estimation of the General Committee, and as there were 25 Sanskrit and 12 Arabic books published by them up to the end of 1831 and 1832, so there are now 10 Arabic and 4 Sanskrit books in the press; that is to say, while Sanskrit was formerly twice as much encouraged as Arabic, so now Arabic is twice as much encouraged as Sanskrit. In the years 1832 and 1833 the two languages were treated with equal favour, there having been exactly seven books published in each in that year. It will also be seen from the return that there are at this moment a number of translations into Arabic going through the press for the purpose of *popular* instruction, but there is no account of what they cost.

Compared with the limited use which can be made of them, owing to the small number of persons in India capable of reading and understanding Arabic books, the expense of these translations is very heavy. Indeed it is the rarity of acquirements like Mr. Tytler's which is supposed to confer such a high value upon his labours. He is said to be the only person in India who is qualified for the task of translating English science into Arabic, from which we may form some conception of the limited number of individuals who possess such a practical acquaintance with this language as to render it easier for them to acquire knowledge through its medium than through that of any other. The Committee of the Agra College have for months past been advertising for a native professor to fill the vacant chair in the department of Arabic Grammar, and no person possessing the necessary qualifications has yet made his appearance. The following is a statement of Mr. Tytler's receipts, as Arabic translator general, from September 1829 to March 1833: —

Works translated	From what date.	Remuneration for Translation.			
Hooper's Vade Mecum - -	Sept. 1829 -	1,000	0	0	
	Oct. „ -	1,000	0	0	
	Nov. „ -	1,000	0	0	
	Feb. 1830 -	1,000	0	0	
	March „ -	1,000	0	0	
	April „ -	1,000	0	0	
	May „ -	1,000	0	0	
	July „ -	1,000	0	0	11 months at 742 Rs. per month.
		8,000	0	0	
Hutton's Mathematics, vol. 1st -	Sept. „ -	1,000	0	0	
Crocker's Land-Surveying - -	Oct. „ -	1,000	0	0	2,000 Rs. 2 months at 1,000 Rs. per month.
Crocker's Land-Surveying - -	Nov. „ -	1,000	0	0	
	Jan. 1831 -	1,000	0	0	2,000 Rs. 3 months at 666 10 8 ditto.
	May „ -	1,000	0	0	
Hutton's Mathematics - -	Sept. „ -	1,000	0	0	2,000 Rs. 5 months at 400 ditto.
Medical Books -	Ditto 1832 -	750	0	0	
	Nov. „ -	750	0	0	
	Feb. 1833 -	750	0	0	
	March „ -	750	0	0	3,000 Rs. 7 months at 428 9 ditto.

Abstract.

Remuneration received by Dr. Tytler for translating
Hooper's Ana. Vade Mecum 8,000
Ditto one half Hutton's Mathematics, vol. 1st . . . 2,000
Ditto Crocker's Land-Surveying 4,000
Ditto Hooper's Physician's Vade Mecum 3,000

Rs. 17,000

Being 42 months at 400 Rs. a month.

This new light only lately broke in upon the majority of the General Committee, and it never seems to have been imagined before, that translations into Arabic were good for public instruction. The prevailing taste used to be entirely on the side of Sanskrit. Brighter days, however, have at length begun to dawn upon India, and both Sanskrit and Arabic, after many a hard-fought battle, are slowly retiring from the field of popular education. The Arabic translations have been put a stop to, with the exception only of about 3,000 rupees which were saved out of the fire, on the ground that Hooper's Anatomist's Vade Mecum was still incomplete. *At the period when this change took place* 65,000 *Rs. remained to be expended in completing Arabic translations of only six books, that is* 32,000 *Rs. for five Medical works, and* 33,000 *Rs. for the untranslated part of Hutton "with something extra for diagrams."* This is according to Mr. Tytler's own estimate.

I am far from wishing to discourage the prosecution of Oriental studies within their proper limits. If it be the duty of Government to preserve the knowledge of Sanskrit and Arabic as a branch of curious literary inquiry, after the public voice has decided against them as a medium of national instruction, let professorships be established, and a certain portion of the public revenue set apart for this particular purpose; but let us not give out that we are instructing the people of India, while we are really only endeavouring to support our own reputation for Oriental learning. If we were real *Orientalists*, we should make the welfare of *the East* the main object of our efforts, and should endeavour to draw from the ample stores of Western learning intellectual food for the improvement of our Asiatic brethren, but our conduct is really exactly the reverse of this. Nothing effectual is done for popular education in the East. No efforts are made to naturalise in this country the knowledge which we have so largely to bestow, and a considerable portion even of the scanty fund which has been assigned by the British Parliament for the purpose of Indian popular instruction has been alienated by us, to cater for the taste of the lovers of Oriental learning in Europe. It seems to have been overlooked, that the annual lakh of rupees was assigned by Parliament *for the education of the youth of India*, and that it was never intended from this source to provide matter for the lucubrations of Messrs. Bopp and Schlegel, or even to gratify the taste of the professors to the English Universities. However it may have been recognised elsewhere, I trust that the principles of the Orientalists will not be admitted into our Committee, and that a book of popular instruction will not be rejected, because it is suggested that its publication may "compromise our character with European scholars."

Mr. Tytler further observes that Mr. Thompson's book appears to be "even below our general run of publications," and he adds that "it is a mere naked vocabulary destitute of every principle of scientific philology." These remarks afford a singular illustration of how diametrically opposite different people may think on the same subject. The very reasons for which Mr. Tytler objects to the book form the ground on which I have presumed to recommend it to the notice of the Committee. All the English and Oordoo Dictionaries which have yet been published are above both the comprehension and the purses of the people, and they are too scientific for their edification. They are inaccessible to the poor and unintelligible to the unlearned and to children. The lowest price at which Gilchrist's, Shakespear's, and the other existing English and Oordoo Dictionaries are to be obtained, places them beyond the reach of any except the highest class of the people; and they are often so much crowded with synonymes drawn fresh from Arabic and Sanskrit, and quite unknown in common parlance, and contain such a profusion of learned etymologies, as to puzzle and confound the minds of the uninitiated. Under these circumstances Mr. Thompson designed the plan of his "School Dictionary," intending to make it so cheap as to be within everybody's reach, and so popular in its character as to be universally intelligible. The work has now been completed, and it is submitted to the Committee in the hope that the author may be enabled through their assistance to bring it before the world. The price of each copy will be 4 rupees, which is only one fifth part of the cost of the Dictionaries hitherto published, and great care has been taken in the compilation of it to explain the meaning of the English words only by such synonymes as are in general use.

The existing Dictionaries have all been formed more or less upon the Sanskrit, Arabic, and Persian models, and their authors appear to have taken a pride in displaying their intimate acquaintance with barbaric lore. Their columns are swelled with foreign words taken wholesale from Richardson and Wilson, without in the least considering whether or not they form part of the language of the country; and the general tendency to fall into this error has been greatly aggravated by the pedantic spirit of the native assistants of the lexicographers, who were almost always learned Mouluvees and Pundits puffed up with literary pride, and more conversant with musty volumes than with the spoken language of the land. Mr. Thompson's Dictionary, on the contrary, has been drawn up strictly on the popular model, and it has been steadily kept in view, as the main principle of the undertaking, to admit no word which is not in familiar use in the towns and villages of Upper India. "Scientific Philology" has been discarded from the work, *on principle*, and "popular philology" has been adopted in its room; and it is therefore as reasonable to expect that it should fail to conciliate the regard of the "man of letters," as that it should be accepted with pleasure by every one who considers the instruction of the many as an object of superior importance to the literary celebrity of the few. The education of the natives at large has too long been made a sacrifice to the exclusive taste of our Orientalists; and philology, which is only one out of many branches of science, is the only one which has yet received any considerable cultivation in this country. We do not want a Babel of dead languages, but the living languages of the English and Indians. We do not want an ocean of words, but an influx of ideas.

In a late series of letters, signed with a German T, and published in the *India Gazette*, those persons who wish to encourage the Indians in their laudable endeavours to acquire our language were taunted with the "extraordinary fact, that, amidst all the zeal at present manifested for teaching English, no one step has been taken, either by individuals or Societies, however much they profess to have the object at heart, for compiling either an English Grammar or Dictionary for the use of the natives." An effort has now been made to supply one of these requisites; the step, the absence of which was lamented by the gentleman who designated himself by the German T, has been taken, and it was therefore reasonable to expect that Mr. Tytler, who evidently belongs to the same school with his German namesake, would have hailed the event with satisfaction, and congratulated our Committee upon having provided a Dictionary which, although it did not come up to his standard of perfection, at any rate brought the means of learning English down to the level of every native, however narrow his circumstances might be; but, instead of this, he condemned the work because it is "below our general run of publications," and because it would "compromise our character, particularly with European scholars."

The same letter contains Mr. 𝕿's notion of a popular Dictionary, which it will be useful to transcribe, as it furnishes a happy illustration of the motives which have induced his learned friend to reject Mr. Thompson's performance. "The Grammar must be accompanied by a copious Dictionary, comprising not a list of mere vocables, with a string of Oriental words thrown after them in a random heap, but *a philosophical account of each word, explaining its etymology, its radical and metaphorical meanings* IN ALL THEIR SHADES, *its synonymes and cognates, its modes of construction, and the various idioms with which it is connected,* which in English are so numerous and so capricious, yet so necessary to be understood; the whole to be clothed in a simple style of *the native language which is that of* THE SCHOLARS, and *the points of similarity and difference between the English and Oriental phraseology pointed out as they occur.*" The letter also contains a curious prospectus of a popular Grammar, but as it does not immediately relate to the subject before us, I will not allude to it further than by observing that it is worthy of perusal. A copy of the *India Gazette* containing Mr. 𝕿's letter is annexed to this paper.

Mr. Tytler states that the School Dictionary is a "mere naked vocabulary destitute of every principle of scientific philology," to which I fully assent, in the sense and for the reasons above stated; but then the learned gentleman goes on to say, "in which the words are thrown together in a heap" and "full of mistranslations and misapprehensions," which I deny. The term "thrown together in a heap" would lead one to suppose that the Dictionary is of a complex character, and that it is burdened with a number of useless synonymes, whereas the opposite to this is really the case. The plan of the work is of the simplest kind, and, as no word has been introduced which is not in general use, the synonymes are very few. Generally speaking there is only one, and there are seldom more than two or three. Any recourse to the Sanskrit or Arabic Dictionary was expressly excluded by the plan of the work, and there was, therefore, no source from which synonymes could be drawn except popular parlance.

The assertion that the book is "full of mistranslations and misapprehensions," could only be completely met by challenging an examination of it by a Committee of unprejudiced persons, which I should not hesitate to do if the copyright belonged to me, which it does not. The book is the property of Mr. Thompson, who depends in a great measure upon the produce of his literary labours for the means of providing for a numerous family, and I do not know how far he might be disposed to subject it to the risk of being condemned. He might think that the object to be attained by success would not compensate the loss which might ensue from defeat, because he could only gain the patronage of the School-Book Society if the book were to be approved of, whereas he might lose not only their patronage, but the patronage of the public also, by its formal condemnation. Perhaps also he might not place sufficient confidence in the gentlemen who have hitherto acquired a reputation as "great Orientalists," to trust them with passing a decision upon the value of his property. It would at once occur to him that they would be likely to judge of his work by a standard which he does not acknowledge; and the language of Hindoostan is as yet so unfixed, that, if a work were ever so perfect, it might be condemned, according as one or another criterion might be adopted as the rule of decision. A lover of Sanskrit might condemn it, because it did not sufficiently approach to the Sanskrit model. An Arabic scholar might object to it, because many highly expressive words, which are probably in daily familiar use between the scholar and his Moonshee, are omitted; while others are used in a sense in which they are not to be found in the original Arabic: and in the same way the Persian scholar might condemn it, because the *thent* Hindee is sometimes preferred to a more elegant Persian synonyme. That such is not unlikely to be the case, we have already had a convincing proof, since the moment the book came to Mr. Tytler he condemned it, because it had not been formed upon *his* model of "*scientific philology*." There is a great difference also in the kind of Hindoostanee spoken at different places, and although the work might be perfectly identical with the language spoken at the majority of places and by the majority of persons in Upper India, it might differ greatly from that which is spoken at some places and by some persons. Sometimes Sanskrit, and sometimes Arabic and Persian, predominate in the language of different places, and even of different persons in the same places; so that, if Mr. Thompson did not happen to hit off that particular modification of the language with which the members of the examining Committee were familiar, he might be condemned, though entirely without fault, to lose the reward of all his labours. The Arabian Hindoostanee, which has grown up at Calcutta under the fostering patronage of Government, and is spoken by the Moonshees of the College of Fort William, and the Mouluvees and students of the Mahomedan College, is quite a different language from that which prevails in any other part of India.

In judging of a work of this kind, a great deal must depend on the qualifications of the author and the character which he has at stake. Although he may not be known to all the members of the Committee, Mr. Thompson is a person of tried ability for the task which he has now brought to completion. He has resided for so many years in the Upper Provinces, and has been brought by the nature of his duties into such frequent and familiar intercourse with people of all classes both in town and country, that he possesses a thorough acquaintance with the popular language; and, besides this, he has had great experience in the preparation of books for the instruction of the people, through his connexion with the Serampore Mission. One of his last works was the Vocabulary to which the attention of the Committee has been already called. This little book is exactly on the same plan as the School Dictionary, only on a much smaller scale, and, as before stated, it was the success attending this publication which encouraged Mr. Thompson to undertake the larger work. Owing to his reduced circumstances, he has not now the means of paying the expense of printing his Dictionary, and he therefore requests the assistance of the School-Book Society, which, by taking a certain number of copies, may enable him to print the work; at the same time that the Society itself cannot be a loser by the transaction, as all the copies taken by it will readily sell at the price agreed on, or four rupees a copy, and the assistance given to him will therefore really be of the nature of an advance, to enable a deserving man to bring out a work of great popular utility. Mr. Thompson's letter is annexed, which will throw some additional light on the above remarks. For my part, I have spent some years in different parts of Upper India in constant communication with all classes of the people, and I can assure the Committee that the School Dictionary contains the nearest approximation to the popular language which I have yet seen. No doubt it has some faults, like every other human production, but these may be rectified and great improvements may be made in subsequent editions.

(Signed) C. E. TREVELYAN.

Calcutta, January, 1834.

Appendix to Mr. Trevelyan's Minute, showing the Number of Books printed by the Calcutta School-Book Society in the Native Characters up to the 30*th April,* 1833.

SANSKRIT.

	Copies.	
Mugdabódha	500	
Laghukáumudi	500	
Bhatti Kávya, in 2 vols. 500 copies each .	1000	
Siddhánta Muktávali and Bháslia Pari-chhéda	500	
Nyáya-Sútra Vritti	500	
Sáhitya Darpana	500	
Védánta Sára	500	
Dáya Tatwa	500	Of these 250 copies each were given to the Editor for correcting proofs and collating.
Vyaváhára Tatwa	500	
Dáya Krama Sangraha	500	
Dáyabhága	500	
Mitákshara	560	
Manu Sanhitá, in 2 vols. 500 copies each	1000	

	Copies.	
Mrichchhakati	500	Of these 100 copies each were given to the Editor for correcting proofs and collating.
Uttara Ráma Charitra	500	
Vikrámorvasi	500	
Málatí Mádhava	500	
Mudrá Rákshasa	500	
Ratnávalí	500	
Sanskrit and English Dictionary	500	
Lilávatí	500	
Raghu Vánsa	500	
Mahábhárata, vol. 1st	500	
	13,060	

ARABIC.

		Copies	
Majaz ul Qánún		300	
Sudídí		300	
Tashríh ul Qalb		500	
Fatáwá Alamgírí, vol. 1st		500	
Ditto	ditto 2nd	500	
Ditto	ditto 3rd	500	
Ditto	ditto 4th	500	
Kifáyah	ditto 3rd	500	Of these 250 copies each were given to the Editor for correcting proofs and collating.
Ditto	ditto 4th	500	
Ináyah	ditto 3rd	500	
Ditto	ditto 4th	500	
Hidáyah		500	Of this 100 copies as above.
		5600	

PERSIAN.

	Copies
Lilávatí	500
Mulukhkhas ut Tuwarikh	500
Majmua Shamsi	500
Persian Miscellany	500
Esop's Fables	500
	2500

HINDI.

	Copies
Sabhá Vilás	500
Rájníti	530
Chhatra Prakása	500
Dáyabhágga	500
	2030

ABSTRACT PRINTED.

Sanskrit	13,060
Arabic	5,600
Persian	2,500
Hindi	2,030
Total copies	23,190

In the Press.

SANSKRIT.

Mahábhárata, vol. 2nd.	500	
Susruta	500	
Rája Tarangini	500	
Naishadha	500	

ARABIC.

Fatáwá Alamgírí, vol. 5th.		
Anís ul Musharrihín, Arabic Version of Hooper's Anatomist's Vade Mecum	500	
Ustugisat, a Treatise on Geometry	500	
Jawámiá ilm-ur Riází, Arabic ditto of Hutton's Mathematics	500	
Jawámiá ilm-ul Masáhat, Arabic ditto of Crocker's Land Surveyings	500	
Bridge's Algebra, Arabic ditto	500	

PERSIAN.

Harington's Analysis	500	
Khazánat ul Ilm	500	Of this 100 copies ditto.

List of Books printed in 1832—33.

SANSKRIT.

Mahábhárata, vol. 1st.
Rája Tarangini.
Ratnávalí.
Naishadha.

ARABIC.

Fatáwá Alamgírí, vols. 4. and 5.; vol. 5. in the press.
Hidáyah.
Sadídí.

HINDI.

Dáyabhága.

PERSIAN.

Khuzánat ul Ilm.

In the Press.

SANSKRIT.

Lílávatí.
Susruta.
Sanskrit and English Dictionary.

ARABIC.

Anís ul Musharrhín.
Jawámiá ilm-ur Riází.
Jawámiá ilm-ul Masáhat.

Statement of Printing Charges.

Total charges of Printing from 1824-25 to 1829-30 - -	69,347	2	4			
Deduct received from Mr. Pearce, by transfer of the printing materials - - - - -	9,218	0	0			
				60,129	2	4
Total charges in 1830-31 - -	19,363	8	9			
Ditto ditto 1831-32 - -	16,653	6	3			
Ditto ditto 1832-33 - -	7,103	11	9			
				43,120	10	9
				103,249	13	1
Add charges for printing Bridge's Algebra in the Bishop's College Press - - - - -				2,176	0	0
Total				105,425	13	1

(5.)

MR. JAMES PRINSEP'S SECOND MINUTE.

When on the first circulation of the proposal for subscribing to Mr. Thompson's Dictionary I recorded the minute which has been made the subject of so lengthened a reply from Mr. Trevelyan, I certainly never contemplated the probability of its forming the text of a voluminous disquisition in the *India Gazette*. In the ordinary business of a Committee consisting of about twenty members, little more than a vote or a brief remark could be allowed to each, or discussions would become interminable and real business would stand still. The broad questions and principles on which the education of the country should be conducted may form very proper themes for those who have the time and talent to write volumes upon them out of Committee. In it I think a contest of opinion would be very inconvenient, and I shall therefore merely trouble my brother Committeemen with a brief explanation of my former minute lest its purport should be misunderstood.

I said that a Vocabulary like Mr. Thompson's, of Hindoostanee in Roman character, would be much sought after by European students. I learned the spoken language thus myself, and I know how difficult it is, when such a text is available, to keep the eye upon the native character. This was one motive for my objection. We print or purchase books (I presume) for schools of *Native youth*, not for European *educated adults*. In childhood it is equally easy to master either system, and it seems to me to be particularly desirable not to lose that opportunity of imprinting upon the pliable mind of the pupil, a thorough habit and facility of writing and reading his Native tongue; not to thwart his knowledge of it by keeping it out of sight, and pushing prominently forward a system which must keep him in comparative ignorance of the construction and orthography of his mother tongue. The only plea upon which Mr. Thompson's scheme could be upheld for *Native education*, is the eventual general substitution of the Roman character; which to me appears as chimerical as the establishment of an universal language, or the "removal of the curse of Babel." At any rate, a School-Book Society of the present generation must conform to existing things, and give such books and such education as shall prove in after life to be most useful to its scholars. To a large class the knowledge of Persian, and to a larger that of the Hindee, is essential for the business of their lives; and it appears to me to be of much greater importance to ground them well in the *writing* of those languages (the speaking of them being their birthright cannot be eradicated though it may be systematised and purified), than even to introduce them to much vaunted English with all its moral and scientific advantages. The instruction of the country, as well as the business, and eventually the literature, must be in the vernacular, and our aim ought to be to foster that, and transfuse into it the substance of our own advanced knowledge. Those whom we instruct in English are to be the pioneers and interpreters of this peaceful and insensible innovation, not the uncompromising guerillas of a violent and *ultra-radical* subversion of all that now exists. What would the parents of a boy at the Calcutta Anglo-Indian College say, if we turned out his son "a finished youth" without a knowledge of the Bengalee Alphabet? Have we yet seen a Bengalee Dictionary in the Roman character?

As for the superiority of English orthography I never heard a mother who did not complain of the difficulty of teaching a child the difference between C and S, and I will ask whether a Native child is more likely to learn the identity and the pronunciation of the word for "Town" from the unchangeable نگر or नगर, or from the delightfully variable nagar, nugur, nagore, nuggur, naghur, nigurh, nogor, and nugre, which will be naturalised by the introduction of the system Mr. Trevelyan advocates. For my part I think the urchin would as readily recognise the "City of God" (*Allahabad*) in the "isle of bats" and the Palace at Ghazeepore in "Chelsea tune" (*chuhul sitoon*).

(Signed) J. PRINSEP.

2nd January, 1854.

(6.)

MR. J. TYTLER'S SECOND MINUTE.

In all this I fully CONCUR, and feel much obliged to Mr. Prinsep for having expressed my sentiments so fully.

(Signed) J. T.

(7.)

MR. TREVELYAN'S SECOND MINUTE.

I think it hard in Mr. Prinsep not to allow a large body of the youth of India the same advantage of learning Hindoostanee through the medium of the Roman letters, which he gratefully acknowledges in his own case. I repeat that there is a numerous class of Native youth rising in Upper India, who are acquainted only with the Roman characters; for their use Mr. Thompson's Vocabulary was prepared, and so highly was it appreciated by them, that the more extended plan of the dictionary was shortly after commenced upon. In assisting in the publication of Mr. Thompson's Dictionary, therefore, we are only conforming our operations to "the existing state of things" which is correctly stated by Mr. Prinsep to be the ruling principle of our Society. Mr. Prinsep's mistake consists in his taking the last generation for the present, and he will not be persuaded that the people of this country have made such a considerable advance towards correct ideas as they really have.

But Mr. Prinsep would have them learn the Persian and Nagree characters at any rate, for the sake of enabling them to study *Hindoostanee literature.* I should like to know where this literature is to be found. I have never been able to discover it, unless such trash as the Kalaila Dimna and Bagh-o-Bahar, which are translations from the Persian got up by the Orientalists of Fort William, and a few popular songs can be called such. Miss Bird's books and a very few others which have been published in Hindoostanee of late years represent the whole body of the Hindoostanee literature, and I am prepared to have editions of them all printed in the Roman character, as soon as Mr. Thompson's Dictionary is out. The truth is that we have to *construct a literature for Upper India from the beginning,* and the more we shut our eyes to the broad glare of this fact, the less disposed shall we be to enter upon our task with the zeal befitting its magnitude and importance.

Mr. Prinsep admits that in childhood it is *equally easy to master either system* of letters, and why, therefore, of the two systems, should we choose, in order to express the new literature, that which is the least perfect, and which will always render school-books one third dearer than there is any necessity for, owing to the superior cost of printing in Persian and Nagree? In my former minute, I endeavoured to prove that, as far as the Hindoostanee language is concerned, every object of "construction and orthography" is more effectually answered by the use of the Roman than of the Persian letters, and that with regard to the question between the Roman and *Nagree* letters, these ends are at least equally answered by both, but, without replying to my arguments, Mr. Prinsep has now made a contrary assumption.

But "construction and orthography" are only a very insignificant part of the question. The object of language is to impart knowledge, and whence is this to be derived, for the Hindoostanee language does not contain it at present in any recorded shape? Mr. Prinsep would marry the Hindoostanee to the Persian language by maintaining the Persian character for both, and encouraging the study of the Persian language; while I, on the other hand, would form a close union between the *English* and Hindoostanee by using the English character for both, and encouraging the study of the English language. The beau ideal of a place of education, according to the gentlemen who think with Mr. Prinsep, is the Mahomedan College, where the youth of India are bribed, by the offer of excessive emoluments, to imbibe systems of error which we all know have been exploded and their falsehood demonstrated ages ago. The astronomy of Ptolemy, the medicine of Galen and Hippocrates, and the logic of Aristotle! Although we should scorn the idea of English youth being even permitted to waste their time upon such studies, yet the children of this country are not only allowed to do so, *but extraordinary advantages are offered to those who can be induced through the influence of such motives to devote the best years of their lives to them.* A system of education which we should never for a moment think of using ourselves is considered quite good enough for our Indian fellow-men and fellow-subjects. I will never cease to protest against this wilful murder of the minds and time of the youth intrusted to our charge. Was there ever such a thing heard of in any other country in the world, as that *rewards should be held out for the propagation of falsehood far exceeding in liberality any that are offered for the cultivation of truth?* At the Mahomedan College the youth are seduced into the study of Ptolemy's Astronomy by a bribe which costs the state more than 30 Rs. a month, while at the Hindoo College they get nothing for studying Newton and have to pay besides! I have often admired the good sense of the Hindoo community of Calcutta, who long ago rejected the absurd system of education which the then existing Government held out for their acceptance, and established the Hindoo College at their own expense.

Mr. Prinsep says, with great propriety, "those whom we instruct in English are to be the pioneers and interpreters of this peaceful and insensible innovation." The natives of the country, those whose mother tongue the vernacular idioms are, must be the translators, the noble artificers of the literature which will hereafter constitute the medium through which the treasures of knowledge will be laid open to the mass of their countrymen. A moderate acquaintance with a foreign tongue suffices to enable a person to collect the sense which is to be translated; but a far more perfect knowledge of a language than a foreigner is generally able to acquire is necessary to write successfully in it.

So far Mr. Prinsep and myself are quite agreed, but then comes the question, how the future translators are to acquire such a taste for science, and such an acquaintance with its principles, as will qualify them for the great work in which they are to be engaged. Mr. Prinsep would have them *all taught Persian*, but, unless it be intended to contaminate the popular languages with such polluted streams as the Mahomedan College youths are taught to rejoice in, which is not the case, I cannot imagine how this plan can forward the end in view. The youth cannot learn *two* foreign languages. Even in England, where the state of society admits of more leisure and consequently of education being carried further than is the case in this country, not one young man in a thousand obtains a tolerable acquaintance with more than one foreign language, and in India, where fathers are generally anxious to put their sons out in life at 16, it is quite out of the question. They cannot be expected to learn both Persian and English. To which, therefore, are they to be encouraged to give their attention in preference? Mr. Prinsep says Persian. I say English. Translations of books on European science are every day put forth by the young men who have been educated at the Hindoo College, and let Mr. Prinsep point out a single such translation which has been accomplished by a person educated principally at the Mahomedan College, where Persian and English are joined in monstrous connexion. As Persian and Arabic literature form the principal subject of their studies, this class of people do not possess the necessary qualifications to become translators of European science. They are only able to propagate the corrupt and erroneous Persian system by means of such translations as the Kalaila Dimna and Bagh-o-Bahar.

It is quite a mistake to suppose that a knowledge of Persian is "essential for the business of the lives" of the rising generation. The only reason why English does not at once take the place of Persian in the Courts of Justice and other offices of Government is, because a sufficient number of persons qualified in the English language are not at present procurable. Those fathers who are so besotted as to teach their children Persian will hereafter lament the inferiority of their own offspring to the children of their neighbours who had sense enough to perceive the signs of the times and to give their sons an English education, and they will grieve at the recollection of the invaluable years, never to be recovered, which have been thrown away in studying a language the learning of which is a system of error; the style of which is so depraved and servile as to be quite unfit to form an habitual medium for the expression of the sentiments of British subjects; and in favour of which the utmost that can be said is that it is spoken in Persia, and contains some pretty poetry, which for the most part is very immoral. The recommendation that it is necessary for the transaction of business only applies to those who are now practising in the Courts. Five years hence the case will be very different, and instead of being considered as a qualification, the very reverse will be the case. It will be regarded as a strong presumption against the general fitness of a person for office that he has had a Persian education, and I should not wonder if *fársee-dán* (a knower of Persian) were to grow into a by-word and stigma before ten years pass over our heads.

I beg leave to call the attention of the Committee to what Mr. Prinsep calls "the unchangeable نگر." Now let us consider in how many ways this unchangeable combination of letters can be pronounced نُگِر نَگَر نِگُر نُگُر نِگَر نِگر نَگَر

nugur, nigar, nugir, nugoor, nigoor, noogur, noogir, and so forth. I contend that *nugur* deserves the epithet of "unchangeable" much better than this. From a reference to Mr. Thompson's scheme of vowels it will be seen that in his book *u* is *invariably* used as in *purse,* and, when the system comes more into vogue, the same uniform plan, or another equally good, will be pursued. The Sanskrit is a better character than the Persian, but it is much less known to the class of Native youth in Upper India who will use Mr. Thompson's Dictionary than the English is; besides which, I must recall the attention of the Committee to the strange and unaccountable notion of forcing another character besides the Roman into the Dictionary, when it is not in the least required for the assistance of the student. He must read the English column in Roman characters at any rate, and if he has a sufficient acquaintance with them to be able to do this, he will of course be able to read his own language in the same characters with much greater facility.

An apology is due from me to the Committee for taking up so much of their time. The serious importance of the subject is my excuse, and I hope it will be deemed sufficient.

(Signed) C. E. TREVELYAN.

February 4th, 1834.

(8.)

MR. TYTLER'S REPLY TO MR. TREVELYAN.

To the Editor of the India Gazette.

Sir,—I am not fond of professed newspaper controversy. I engage in it now, as thinking that, besides what is due to myself, something also is due to the Committee of the School-Book Society in explanation of that minute of mine respecting Mr. Thompson's English and Oordoo Dictionary, which is commented on at so much length in your papers of January 28th and 29th. Had this comment been confined to my opinion given in to the Society, I should have replied to it only in the regular circulation of the Society's box, but as it has a reference also to my employments under the Committee of Public Instruction, and to a variety of extraneous matter besides, it becomes necessary for me to adopt another mode of communicating my sentiments. Want of time prevented my doing this sooner.

I shall begin by observing that the minute in question was communicated by me to the members of the School-Book Society in confidence: I had not the least idea of its ever going further, and do not see what advantage can accrue to any party from its publication.

I shall not enter here into the merits of Mr. Thompson's work, but confine myself to a brief consideration of a few of the other topics touched on in Mr. Trevelyan's minute.

The first of these is the revival of the old project for printing Oriental books in Roman characters. Most people, I believe, supposed that after the ponderous volumes on this subject with which Dr. Gilchrist so long afflicted the public the subject had been pretty well set at rest, and that the worthy Doctor had fully succeeded in demonstrating the utter impossibility of his own system. As, however, it appears that the plan is proposed to be revived, and the School-Book Society are called upon publicly, and upon principle, to grant their approbation and patronage to works thus formed, it becomes my duty, as a member of the Society, to inquire how far they are likely to advance their own reputation, or to benefit the public by so doing.

I shall admit thus much, that a short Vocabulary of the kind may be useful enough to a fresh-arrived Griffin in enabling him to give a few common orders to his servants; but surely this is not a want which the School-Book Society was instituted to supply.

The printing of Oriental books in Roman character must be either to enable Europeans more easily to learn the Oriental languages, or to enable Orientals to read them with more facility.

As to the first of those objects: I should ask, upon what

principle can it rationally be expected that a person who has not perseverance enough to learn the *letters* of a language should ever be able to learn *the language itself?* We might as reasonably propose carrying a student through the Principia who declared himself unable to master the multiplication table. The letters are most assuredly the easiest part of every language, and he who declares himself willing to learn the rest, though he cannot or will not learn these, in truth declares that, though he is not able to lift five seers*, he is yet quite willing and capable to lift five hundred.

Next, as to the advantages which the Orientals are to derive from this scheme. It is certain that of all the parts of our language its alphabet is the most unfortunate to select as fit for transplantation to the East; since, however much and however justly we may admire the other properties of the English tongue, it is utterly impossible to admire its orthography. Our alphabet is at once so redundant and deficient, so barbarous and unscientific, that its substitution for the Arabic or Sanskrit, far from being an advance in intellect, would be a decided retrogression. For this the reason is easily assigned. The European alphabets have not, like European sciences, been formed and successively improved through a long course of ages of increasing intelligence: they were formed in times of the darkest ignorance, and have remained unchanged and unimproved since then. They are, as might be expected, radically imperfect; and to add to the confusion, while the pronunciation of European languages has gone on altering, the orthography for the last three hundred years has remained nearly unchanged. The consequence of all is, that the spelling of English and French, at least, is so capricious, and the words written bear so little resemblance to the words pronounced, that no one could tolerate our orthography but those to whom it has been familiar from their cradle; and in fact any unprejudiced person taking up Walker's Dictionary and comparing the written with the pronounced words, will find scarcely a single letter in all our Christ-Cross-Row of which the sound is ascertained, and will

* An Indian weight nearly equivalent to two pounds.—*M. W.*

be apt to think our system more allied to Chinese arbitrary marks than to alphabetic spelling.*

It is certainly extremely difficult to see what advantage the natives can derive from having a system forced upon them so imperfect and so much less precise than their own.

Besides, there are a number of sounds in the Oriental languages which no Roman letters and no combination of Roman letters can express, and which no two persons will agree in their mode of representing. The whole question, then, may be dismissed as an unprofitable discussion, till it be decided according to what system the Oriental words are to be written. Without this it is odds that if twenty different books were printed by as many persons, almost each word would be found spelt in twenty different ways, not one expressing the true sound. The sum of the whole is, that our letters were never intended for their languages, and therefore cannot express their sounds.†

* Instances of this are too familiar to require enumeration, but we may take as an example the words rite, write, right, wright, which all have the same sound, but whose spelling sets system at defiance.

† I shall here support myself by the authority of the "master of thirty legions." In a list of native names now before me, issued from the Adjutant General's Office, I find the simple appellation علی expressed in the following modes, Ali, Allee, Ullee, Allie; and in the same way another word thus, Shekh, Shaickh, Shaick, Sheick, Shaikh, Shaik: which of these is to be adopted in our Roman Oriental alphabet? Not one of them expresses the right sound except the last but one, Shaikh, and that will only do so by giving kh a sound which it never has in English, that is of ch in the Scotch Loch, Buchan, or in the German Buch, and which no doubt is that of the Greek χ. I shall also mention another authority, who is not, I think, altogether to be despised. Not knowing whether Mr. Trevelyan ranks French in the class of barbarous and unintelligible languages, I shall venture to leave it untranslated. "On s'est fié à l'oreille, en apprenant les noms de la bouche des naturels du pays; mais l'oreille saisit mal les sons d'une langue inconnue. Ensuite on a voulu exprimer ces sons par la valeur que les lettres Latines ont dans la langue Anglaise; et c'est là une entreprise *impossible et contradictoire en elle-même.* L'orthographie ou plutôt la *scoliographie* Anglaise n'a rien à démêler avec la prononciation; elle est historique, elle désigne la prononciation d'un autre temps, altérée depuis. Beaucoup de lettres ne sont pas prononcées du tout; plusieurs consonnes ont un son différent selon les mots où elles sont employées. Deux voyelles homogènes signifient souvent une voyelle différente, et des voyelles simples une diphthongue; d'autres diphthongues ou voyelles longues sont exprimées par la réunion d'une voyelle et d'une semi consonne. D'ailleurs la langue Anglaise d'aujourd'hui abonde en voyelles qui n'ont pas de place bien fixe dans l'échelle musicale des sons articulés."—*Schlegel's Reflexions sur l'étude des langues Asiatiques adressées à Sir James Mackintosh.*

In what Mr. Trevelyan says of the Greek and German and Russian alphabets, he confounds two things essentially different,—the shape of the letters and the system of the alphabet; the one a matter of very little importance, the other the whole basis of the dispute. The English printed and written characters, their capitals and their small letters, are all different; yet it will not be affirmed that they are different alphabets; they are all formed on the same system and represent the same sound. In the same manner, though the Roman, the German, and the Greek (I am not acquainted with the Russian) are a little different in shape, the principal and by far the majority of sounds in all are the same; and it is a matter of little consequence whether to express the same sound we employ P, 𝔓, or Π; L, 𝔏, or Λ. The same parallelism, however, by no means exists in the European and Oriental alphabets. The Oriental alphabets are not, like the European, *literal,*—they are *syllabic;* that is, each element expresses not a simple sound, but a syllable. In English, for example, no consonant can be pronounced without the addition of a vowel. In Arabic and Nagree, on the contrary, each letter is a consonant with a vowel inherently combined: to use it as a simple consonant a mark must be added, indicating that the vowel is taken away. Which of those two systems is the best, is a question that would admit of long discussion: each, no doubt, has its advantages and disadvantages. It is plain, however, that we are not to take it for granted that ours is the best, merely because it is that to which we are accustomed.

Mr. Trevelyan asserts that "the old German text is now almost entirely abandoned, and few new books are published in Germany except in the Roman character." On what he founds this assertion I am at a loss to know. I certainly was not aware of the fact as he states it: I have now before me (not a very old nor unpopular book) Goëthe's Wilhelm Meister, published in the usual German character at Stuttgard in 1816, and by going into another room I could collect forty or fifty volumes of the same kind; while, I believe, I have not above two or three in the Roman: Mr. Trevelyan will also find abundance of modern German periodicals in the Asiatic

Society's Library. To settle this point, however, at once, I shall bring forward a more satisfactory authority than any in this country can be. "For this reason, many German works have, in more recent times, been printed in Roman type: that practice, however, is hitherto not become general, and the greatest number of publications continues to appear in the ancient habit; and it is to be doubted whether that innovation would be of any advantage, if generally adopted. By disaccustoming the eye from the old type, many valuable productions of literature, unless reprinted, would be rendered less easy to read, and might be prejudiced in their general utility. Of late years, however, the disposition of disusing the character, and substituting for it the Roman letter, instead of increasing, has considerably diminished; and I believe I am right in asserting, that *now by far the greatest number of German books is printed in the old type*."—*G. H. Noehden's German Grammar* (5th edition, 1827), pp. 18, 19.

A few miscellaneous observations are to be made on the advantages which it is stated would result from using Roman characters. One is, that the vowels are expressed "instead of being either entirely omitted, (in the Oriental alphabets) or distinguished by diacritical * points." This is the case only to a very partial extent. It is but the short vowels that are omitted in Hebrew, Arabic, and Persian, the long are all expressed. Both long and short are very accurately expressed in the Nagree and its derivative alphabets. On the other hand, the Roman alphabet labours under the great disadvantage that it has no distinction between long and short vowels, and this in the accurate writing of words, far more than counterbalances all the difficulties of the Oriental orthography.† I omit the perfectly capricious and unaccountable manner in which the vowels and diphthongs and triphthongs

* Strictly speaking, *diacritical* points are the dots which distinguish several letters of the Arabic and Persian alphabets. The marks for the short vowels zubur, zer, pesh, are *vowel* points.

† What, for example, must a native medical student think of our orthography when he is taught to pronounce the *o* in Camphora and Cinchona so differently, or the *i* in Serratus Anticus, and Flexor Pollicis? If, to remedy this, we employ the prosodial marks of longs and shorts, this is the system of diacritical points which Mr. Trevelyan so much condemns.

are pronounced in English, as these must be obvious to every one, and are past defending.*

With respect to the superior distinctness of the Roman letters, I must say this advantage appears to me wholly imaginary. No doubt in the books printed twenty or thirty years ago the characters were very indistinct, chiefly, I believe, from an injudicious wish of closely imitating the written hand. Since, however, that idea has been abandoned † and our books have been printed in the niskhee character, they have every year improved, and I cannot be persuaded that any one can find the least difficulty in reading the Arabic and Nagree typography of Mr. Pearce. He who cannot learn these must, I think, be unable to learn any characters at all. Besides, there is no reason why we should not go on if necessary in our improvements in the Oriental *printed* letters, and form, in comparatively a very few years, a set of characters even more distinct than we have now.

Again: Mr. Trevelyan states that printing can be carried on in Roman characters much cheaper and more expeditiously

* English, it is known, wants the sound of the Italian and German u, that is the Persian peshe and the 5th Nagree vowel; this is a great defect which our attempts to remedy have been very unsuccessful. We employ at least ten different combinations of vowels to express a sound in itself perfectly simple. Thus o, u, eu, ew, oe, oo, ou, ough, ue, wo, as in these words: to, flute, feud, new, shoe, too, soup, through, sue, two. There may be more that I don't recollect: the pronunciation of *e* defies all classification.

† The chief supporter of this plan was Dr. Lumsden; at least he mentions it, seemingly with approbation, in his preface to his edition of the first volume of the Shah Nameh. Of its disadvantages any one may convince himself in a moment, by comparing the broken and confused letters in that volume, with the distinct and elegant typography in Captain Macan's noble edition of the same work.

I may observe, that for this great improvement in typography, I mean the distinction between the written and printed character, we are, I imagine, mainly indebted to the meritorious exertions of Dr. Rind. The honour of establishing the first Lithographic Press in India belongs to that gentleman. Before his time we had no cheap way of giving any idea of the written character except through types, which it was necessary therefore to make so as to resemble manuscript: but that invaluable invention enables us now to copy any characters we please; and we can accordingly employ Lithography when it is necessary to publish works in the *written* character, reserving our types to express the niskhee or printed.

‡ The natives consider some of Mr. Pearce's types so beautiful that, as he has informed me, they declared nothing should be printed by them but the Koran.

than in Persian or Nagree. This would be incontrovertible did the same number of Roman as of Oriental letters serve to express a given word. Every one, however, who has tried, knows that to express a given Oriental word requires many more Roman than Oriental letters; and conversely, to express the generality of European words, more Oriental than Roman characters are necessary. This is a general principle through all parts of language: every translation comprehends more words than its original. The letters of one language will not answer for those of another formed on a different system, and the words are never precisely parallel, to render them so, something explanatory must always be added. In attempting to write an Oriental language then in Roman letters, a great deal of room must be taken up, and the compositor's work increased. I am not prepared to say that this will actually make the Roman books dearer than the Oriental, but it will certainly much diminish their cheapness.*

It is easy no doubt to call the Nagree and Arabic characters "barbarous:" that is an epithet with which all nations have been in the habit of honouring each other since the beginning of time, and generally those who have most deserved it have been most liberal in its application.† The Mouluvees and Pundits have only to bestow, as no doubt they do, the same

* To show this I shall take the first book that comes in my way—the opening sentence of Syud Auzumooddeen's English Grammar.

چون ظاهر است که در زمانِ قلیل زبان فارسي از تمام
هندوستان رخصت خواهد شد لهذا ٭

Choon zauhir ast kch dur zumaun e quleel zoobaun e Faursee az tumaum e Hindoostaun rookhsut khwahid shud lehauza.

"As it is self-evident that in a short time the Persian language is to bid good-bye to the whole of Hindoostan, therefore."

I cannot be accused of having employed too many characters; yet on counting it will be seen that to express 60 Persian, 94 Roman must be employed; that is more than one and a half for one. An inspection of this book will show that, to complete the scheme, it seems proposed to teach the natives English in the *Persian* character, so that each language is to be disguised interchangeably in the letters of the other. This will no doubt be a vast step in the march of intellect.

† "God curse these dogs, what a strange barbarous language they speak!"—*Gibbon*, chap. 51, A.D. 638. Such was the judgement of a conqueror on the language of Homer. The old Sclavonians, not understanding the language of foreigners, modestly concluded that all mankind but themselves were dumb.

appellation upon our alphabets, and the argument is equal on both sides. But these surely are unfit expressions to be brought into a literary discussion: they do little honour to the party using them, and are not likely to produce much conviction in the mind of his antagonist. No one who contemplates the ingenuity of the Arabic and Sanskrit orthography, will be induced to bestow such an epithet on the noblest invention of the human mind.

Leaving this, however, as a matter of taste in argumentation, I shall go on to notice that Mr. Trevelyan speaks of "the many barbarous characters with which the country abounds." He surely must know that, with the exception of Arabic, they are all derived from Nagree, and in most cases with so little variation that any one who has mastered that (which he may do in a week) may learn any other he chooses in three days; and at any rate, no one, I presume, unless he likes, need learn them all. One or two are generally sufficient for useful purposes. The difference between the various Hindoo alphabets is certainly not much greater than between our Roman and Italic, Writing and Old English characters*, Capitals and Smalls, to say nothing of Greek, which altogether compose eight distinct and very dissimilar alphabets as far as the shapes of the letters go.

To use Mr. Trevelyan's own words, "it is shocking to think how much human time, which may be directed to the best purposes, is wasted in gaining a knowledge of the barbarous characters with which the British islands abound,"—with this additional grievance, that in Europe our unfortunate infants are compelled to learn them all, while the happier youth of Hindostan have seldom to learn more than one.

Admitting, however, the inconvenience to be as great as Mr. Trevelyan states, it is difficult to understand how this would be remedied by adding to the number, and bringing in

* The reading of all these is not to be considered a matter of no moment: it is recorded to the honour of Johnson's first schoolmistress that she could do so. "He was," says Boswell, "first taught to read English by Dame Oliver, a widow, who kept a school for young children in Lichfield. He told me she could read the black letter, and asked him to borrow for her, from his father, a Bible in that character."—*Boswell's Life*, in the beginning.

upon the natives a set of new characters totally incongruous and immiscible with the old. Mr. Trevelyan will not, I suppose, go the length of saying that the natives are to be prohibited, by a regulation of the Governor-General in Council, from using their own alphabets in their letters and private concerns; and as long as they continue to do so,—which will, in all probability, be longer than any of the present generation will have an opportunity to witness,—so long will the Roman printed books, instead of diminishing, add inconceivably to the confusion.

It is not to be denied, however, that diversity of alphabets is, to a certain extent, an evil which it would be desirable to remedy, and the plan which the Committee of Public Instruction have gone upon, is as rational as any that can be devised. It is, to fix on some well-known, distinct, and easily learnt character and employ that universally in printing. The Deb Nagree immediately suggests itself as that which of all others possesses these characteristics, and it is in that accordingly that the Committee's books are printed. This imposes on the Bengal, Tamool, or Orissa readers a task no greater, nor even so great, as to an Englishman that of learning the German letters after knowing the Roman or Italian, and this is surely not much to be complained of.

Still, the whole subject has, I think, been invested with a disproportionate degree of importance, and the mole-hill in some measure exalted into a mountain. After all, the letters, as was said before, are the easiest part of every language: he who will not learn them, certainly will not learn the rest, and I cannot be persuaded that the bare learning of an alphabet is such a heavy imposition on youths of common capacity. On the contrary, I think a knowledge of different alphabetic systems is *primâ facie* likely to be very beneficial in enlarging their views and improving their capacity.

Mr. Trevelyan thinks that it would be desirable "to engraft upon the popular languages of the East such words as *virtue, honour, gratitude, patriotism, public spirit,* and some others, for which it is at present difficult to find any synonyme in them." To me, on the contrary, it appears that the bare engrafting of these words would be a matter of very little moment; it would only be a part of the system of teaching words instead of things, which unhappily prevails so much throughout Indian education. If, indeed, we could infuse into the breasts of the natives the *ideas* expressed by these words, this, I am willing to allow, would be a real benefit*, but the bare teaching them the words is a very short step towards this object. Could we really succeed in teaching the virtues, we might safely leave the invention of the proper terms to the natives themselves; and whether in this case they were taken from a European or Oriental source, is scarcely worth while to consider.

It may be right that I should here take some notice of the Delhi College which is spoken of so highly. Having no knowledge of its constitution, except what Mr. Trevelyan's minute affords, I can, of course, only speak from what appears there. I think it might be prudent to be moderate in its eulogiums till we see what sort of scholars it produces, and this more especially as the Allahabad School, of which we heard so much some time ago, has been, I am told, a complete failure. If it be really the case, as Mr. Trevelyan informs us, that the pupils of the Delhi College "have no acquaintance whatever either with the Nagree or Persian character," and that "they know English as their language of education and Hindostanee as their vernacular tongue, but the only character with which they are acquainted is the Roman, and this they employ to write both languages," one can scarcely conceive more helpless members of society than they must ultimately turn out, nor a system of education less likely to benefit its alumni. What would be thought of a proposal at home to teach English through the medium of the Persian characters? Yet this, disguise it from ourselves as we will, is the plan on which, by Mr. Trevelyan's account, the Delhi College is proceeding. No doubt its success is possible, but the best disciple of De Moivre would be puzzled to calculate the infinitely small chances in its favour. All

* I say this to avoid the appearance of cavilling, but to confess the truth, there are more than one in Mr. Trevelyan's list of virtues which appear to me very suspicious. For the whole I would venture to substitute, The Love of God and the Love of Man.

we can do is to hope that the pupils steal a march on their teachers, and learn in secret the characters which are prohibited to them publicly, so that at their coming out into the world they may be able to read and write like their countrymen.

Mr. Trevelyan tells us that the vernacular language of the Delhi students is Hindostanee. It would be desirable to know what that language is: the natives are quite unacquainted with it, — *they know no such language as Hindostanee.* It is a word entirely grown up among Europeans, to supersede the old and elegant appellation of Moors, which is still to be found in the mouths of some Indians of the olden time. What Europeans mean by it is, I believe, the Rekhtu or Oordhoo. Now this Rekhtu is composed (like English) from three sources, Arabic, Persian, and the old Hindee, which last may be the mother, sister, or daughter of Sanskrit. But there is this difference, that Arabic and Persian enter into Rekhtu in a much greater proportion than either Latin or French into English. To talk, then, of using Hindostanee and abandoning Arabic and Persian, is a plain contradiction in terms; and if Rekhtu be the language (as no doubt it is) of the Delhi students, they must be, at this moment, using a large proportion of those very languages which Mr. Trevelyan pronounces dead, barbarous, and unintelligible.*

* I draw this conclusion chiefly from Mr. Thompson's book, which Mr. Trevelyan tells us is intended for the Delhi pupils. A large proportion of its Vocables are pure Persian and Arabic. I do not mention this as matter of blame. From the nature of the language it must be so.

In general, in Hindostanee, the substantives are purely Persian and Arabic, and the verbs derivations with some alterations from Sanskrit. To give an idea of how those are combined, I shall take the first and most simple of the "Pleasant Stories" contained in the first volume, p. 344, of the Hindostanee Selections used at the College of Fort William, and substitute in it French words for Persian, Latin for Arabic, and mark the Sanskrit derivatives by printing them in capitals. The story (and its style cannot be called very complicated) is as follows:

It is UNDERSTOOD that A *quidam* WENT to a certain *monarque* and BEGAN to MAKE *prætentionem de l'inspiration. Le monarque ordonna* that *opus est miraculi* to *un prophète.* Do thou SHEW one. HE REPLIED, I WILL DO whatever you TELL me, for I am *prophète.* At that *tempus* there was an IRON *claustrum* in the HAND of *le monarque.* He SAID, *Si* thou art *prophète*, OPEN THIS. HE REPLIED, I MADE *prætentionem de*

It is worthy of remark, also, that the plan of having one vernacular and one language for education is by no means well calculated for mental improvement; because it completely separates the objects of education from the affairs of common life. It was this, by universal confession, that kept

l'inspiration and not *d'être forgeron*. At this saying he BEGAN to LAUGH, and having GIVEN (a present) MADE *missionem*.

Can it, I would ask, be reasonably said, that such a composition as this could be understood by those utterly ignorant of French and Latin, or that either of these languages was dead in a country where such a dialect formed the vernacular speech. Yet such is exactly the case with what is called Hindostanee.

In the same manner, to show the connexion between Bengalee and Sanskrit, I shall take a paragraph from the translation of the abridgement of Dr. Goldsmith's History of Greece by Khettro Mohun Mookerjea, which having been printed under the patronage of the School-Book Society, and excessively praised by all the newspapers of the time, is to be considered, I suppose, quite classical: the passage I have taken is this:

"To counteract, however, the influence of a popular assembly, Solon gave greater weight to the Court of Areopagus, and also instituted another council consisting of four hundred. Before his time the Areopagus was composed of such citizens as were most remarkable for their probity and wisdom. But Solon now ordained that none should be admitted into it but such as had passed through the office of Archon."

The following is a re-translation of the Bengalee into English, in which Latin words are substituted for Sanskrit: it will appear that they are, if possible, even of more frequent occurrence than the Arabic and Persian in Oordhoo:

Sed thus *potentia* of the *populus* could not receive *magnam augmentationem**, with this *consilium* Solon bestowed *ingens onus administrationis* on the *conventus judiciarius nomine* Areopeg; and beside this he caused *alter conventus consiliarius* to be *constitutus*, in which there were four hundred *consiliarii*. *Ante tempus administrationis Solonis, universi cives*,* who on account of their *fidelitas* and *sapientia* had obtained *famam*, composed *conventum* of the Areopeg; *sed tempore administrationis Solonis* this was the *mos** that none but those who had performed the *munus* of Archon could be *conjunctus* with this *conventus*.—p. 24.

Such is the style of the Bengalee translations, which it is said are to be encouraged as being simple and intelligible. He who can understand the above without Latin will understand Bengalee without Sanskrit. It is worthy of remark, that short and easy as is this passage, there are in it three mistranslations markèd by asterisks. The first is directly opposite to the original, which implies that there was danger, lest the power of the people should become too great: the Bengalee translation implies that it could not become great enough. In the second, the original is, that the members of the Areopagus were chosen out of those eminent for probity and wisdom. The translation is, that all the men of probity and wisdom that could be found in the city formed the Areopagus. In the third, the original has it that Solon made a law: the translation states that a custom existed in Solon's time. How can we expect the natives to learn from works so incorrect as this?

Europe so long in a state of ignorance during the middle ages: all science was taught in Latin, while the people were speaking the modern tongues. The consequence was, no knowledge ever diffused itself among them, and whatever existed, remained shut up in the walls of the college.

The great objections indeed to the exclusive use of English in education is, that it necessarily discourages the natives from the cultivation of their own tongues. It puts an end to native composition and indigenous literature, and confines their whole efforts to a wretched and servile imitation of English models, than which nothing can possibly have a greater tendency to prevent improvement. As long as European literature was confined to Latin, the attempts of our ancestors at composition, the far greater part of which are now deservedly forgotten, were forced imitations of the classics. Their philosophy was nothing more than a jejune commentary on the imperfect system of the ancients, and their poetry a cento in which the lines and half-lines of the classical masters, taken from their original situations, are forced into new and unnatural combinations. So it will be with the English productions of the natives of India: their prose will be a mere patchwork of sentences extracted from the common-place English books with which they are acquainted, destitute of any effort of original thought, and their verse a bald imitation of Thomas Moore and Lord Byron. Such productions Europeans may now agree to praise and call wonderful specimens of native poetic talent, but the next generation will assuredly reject them with astonishment that they were ever esteemed. All this, so far from enlarging the ideas, is the most effectual means of cramping the intellect and keeping it in perpetual trammels.

I now come to that part of the Minute which more especially applies to myself; and to prevent all misapprehension and appearance of self-contradiction, shall here endeavour to state clearly my opinion of Oriental literature, and the uses to which it may be applied.

The first part of my literary creed, then, is this. Without denying that occasional scintillations of genius appear in the poetry and romances of the East, still I hold that they are greatly inferior to those of the West, and I also hold that Eastern sciences bear scarcely more proportion to those of Europe, than the first lispings of an infant to the ratiocinations of a man.

If it then be inquired, what is gained by the study of Oriental literature? the answer divides itself into two parts: first, the speculative; next, the practical. The speculative advantages are those which a person of a contemplative and inquiring turn of mind derives from that most delightful of all purely mental pleasures, an increase of knowledge. In the present case the student of the Oriental languages enlarges his views as to the structure of language, the history and antiquities of nations, the sentiments of mankind in different ages and under different circumstances. As long as human nature is what it is, these subjects will continue to be interesting; and he who attempts to blot them out from our view, so far from improving, does what he can to degrade and dishonour, our species.

Besides this, though Oriental science is very inferior, I am by no means disposed to admit that it is worth nothing at all; many valuable hints may be gained from the labours of our predecessors, and many useful lessons learnt from their mistakes. The history of science is in many cases almost as useful as science itself. "There is no part of history so generally useful as that which relates to the progress of the human mind, the gradual improvement of reason, the successive advantages of science, the vicissitudes of learning and ignorance, which are the light and darkness of thinking beings, the extinction and resuscitation of arts, and the revolutions of the intellectual world."—*Rasselas*, chap. 30.

All this must be lost, if we be determined to blot out from the world every vestige of ancient science, and monument of ancient-learning.

But the practical and great use of studying the Eastern languages is to communicate with, and to instruct, the inhabitants of the East. It is not what we find, but what we are to transfuse into these languages, that is valuable; and it may be regarded as axiomatical in native education, that *European knowledge cannot be extensively diffused among the natives of the East, unless it be translated into, and taught in their native tongues, and that their vernacular dialects cannot be understood thoroughly, nor used with propriety, without a knowledge of their learned languages.* That instances may be given of a few particularly clever individuals, such as the late lamented Rammohun Roy, who, with good opportunities, have acquired a considerable or even very perfect knowledge of English, and used it as a means of acquiring information, is not to be denied; but such rare exceptions take away nothing from the truth of the general rule.

I shall make little reply to what is hinted of my aspirations after European reputation and a Professor's chair. Neither of these objects would be dishonourable if I had them in view, but it is not usual, I believe, nowadays, to support a literary discussion by the imputation of what are supposed to be improper motives to an opponent. Such imputations are, no doubt, always easy, but experience proves that little is gained by this mode of argumentation. Upon this head, however, it is, if necessary, easy to clear myself: a twelvemonth ago undoubtedly I did cherish the idea that after an absence of twenty-five years I might return to my native country, and then make what honest efforts were in my power to remain. Recent events have effectually cut off this prospect, and there is little likelihood that I shall ever have the power of interrupting the canvass of any candidate for the chairs to which Mr. Trevelyan alludes.

It is not easy to understand the sense in which Mr. Trevelyan so repeatedly asserts that Persian is a dead language in India. If that be a dead language the words of which are in every one's mouth, and in which a vast proportion of literary composition, periodical publication, and epistolary correspondence is carried on, and which almost all ranks above the very lowest speak and understand, then, no doubt, Persian may be ranked as such, but on no other terms. I will venture to say that for one native letter written in the Rekhtu, which we call Hindostanee, there are at least fifty written in Persian, containing a large proportion of Arabic.*

* One can scarcely suppose the editors of native newspapers so blind to their own interest as to publish in a dead unintelligible language; yet

According to Mr. Trevelyan's views, English and Hindostanee are "to go on together till they meet in a common language." Without inquiring too curiously what is meant by two languages going on together, the result is supposed to be that a new language is to be formed out of English, Bengalee, Hindee, &c., in the same manner as English itself was formed out of the various European dialects, or Spanish out of Latin, Gothic, and Arabic. I do not say that in the various combinations of mundane affairs such an event is not possible, but it appears to me nearly as improbable as any can well be. Admitting, however, that it actually does take place, still little advantage will be gained unless the whole inhabitants of the British empire can be prevailed on to unlearn their present language, and to learn Hindostanee in exactly the same proportion as Hindostanees learn English. Without this the languages must still remain distinct, and the speakers unintelligible to each other. The transposition even of thousands, perhaps tens of thousands of words, from one language to another, is not enough to render it intelligible. Thousands of words are common to French and Italian, to English and German, yet a Frenchman will not understand an Italian, nor an Englishman a German; and by Mr. Trevelyan's account, Arabic and Persian are unintelligible in Hindostan, though tens of thousands of their words are used in the common language.

This result, however, Mr. Trevelyan allows is not to take place "till after successive generations." What are we to do in the meantime? Are we to sit idle till, perhaps after Herschel shall have performed some centuries of revolutions, this amalgamation of languages actually takes place. Miss

all the Mohammedan newspapers are invariably in Persian, mixed with a very large quantity of Arabic. What would be thought of a project at home for publishing a newspaper in Latin or Greek? yet this is what the native editors, by Mr. Trevelyan's account and to use his expression, are besotted enough to do here. To accumulate authorities in proof of the common use of Persian by the inhabitants of India is, in fact, like accumulating them to prove that they commonly use rice for their food or cotton for their clothes. I may, however, mention just one more. The pupils of the Native Medical Institution,—persons certainly of no very high education,—keep a case-book of the symptoms and treatment of the sick on the establishment. The language of this is left entirely to their own choice, and they uniformly write in Persian.

Martineau furnishes an answer in her last publication—"Nature is slow in her workings; and since the life of man is short, his business is to work with her, not to wait for her." —*Homes Abroad.*

So it is here; we are not to wait for new languages that may possibly spring up,—it is our business to make use of those at present existing.

I shall not undertake to defend the licentiousness of Sanskrit literature, except to observe that it is a fault unfortunately common to it with the literature of many other nations, which it is rather a violent remedy to propose curing by absolutely abolishing the Sanskrit language. These are not the measures by which morality is to be advanced: it is not the destruction of Sanskrit literature, but the eradication of impure affections, at which we ought to aim, and as long as these are suffered to exist there will never be wanting immoral books in all languages. Upon Mr. Trevelyan's principle, French should be strictly prohibited, as that language contains abundance of immoral books. The plan of getting rid of Sanskrit immorality by the destruction of the whole of Sanskrit literature and language, is like that said to be practised in the Papal dominions for the extermination of robbers: when they are suspected to be residents in a town, they are not themselves sought out for punishment, but orders are given for the destruction of the whole town altogether.

I now come to the statements made respecting my translations: it is true that I have translated into Arabic Hooper's Anatomist's Vade Mecum; that I have also translated his Physician's Vade Mecum; that I have also translated Crocker's Land-Surveying (though this was not a work of my choosing, but that of the Committee); and it is also true that I have translated the half of the first volume of Hutton's Course of Mathematics, and would have translated the whole had I been allowed. All this is true, and I am proud to think that it has been in my power, under Providence, to execute works, certainly not dishonourable to myself, and so useful to the Oriental world, and to enrich their languages with such a valuable fund of knowledge. Committees may alter, Governments change, and Colleges decay, but a well translated book, when once given to the world, can never lose its value or cease to be useful.

My remuneration, however, has by no means been 400 Rs. a month: from this is to be deducted the expense of Moulu-vees (which were always the best in my power to procure), copyists, writers, books, paper, and numerous et cæteras, the minimum of all which was 150 Rs. a month, leaving me never more than 250; and this cannot be called a very exorbitant sum for a labour which they only can judge of who have tried it, and by which I nearly ruined my health at first commencing.

If it be asked why no more Oordhoo or Bengalee translations have been made, the answer is short: because no adequate measures have been taken for the purpose. No European can undertake to translate without incurring a monthly expense of from 100 to 150 Rs. for native assistants: if he calculates on less, he only deceives himself and deceives his employers. It is not natural to suppose that any one would make this outlay without some prospect of remuneration. Where this does not exist the business has been left chiefly, if not entirely, to natives, who look for remuneration to the printing of their own works at their own presses, and the sale of a certain number of copies to the Committees connected with native education. How translations thus undertaken have been executed has been explained in the letters of 𝕿, which need not therefore be repeated here. No one, I believe, has ever praised, except those who have not read them.

The labourer is worthy of his hire. Good translations, like everything else that is good, to be had, must be paid for. He who pretends to undertake gratuitously a task that requires so much previous study, so many qualifications, and so much labour, acts like the Sircar who professes himself willing to serve Master without wages, purely for the honour of doing so. This kind of service is too well known to be infinitely the dearest of all. To have good translations, the Committee should make up their minds as to the books which they require, the languages in which they want them made, and the remuneration they are willing to give. They should then ascertain that the person who undertakes the work has a sufficient knowledge, first, of the science which forms the subject of the book; secondly, of the language which he is to translate into; thirdly, of the principles of translation, and the art of adapting English books to Oriental readers; and, lastly, they should require from him a moderate specimen of the manner in which he is to execute the work. This should be examined by a qualified Committee, who should be requested to give their opinion unbiassedly after *an actual perusal* of the specimen and comparison of it with the original; it being understood that they are to have full liberty of speech, and that the opinions of the individual members are to be confidential and *not liable to be published to the world without their consent.* These restrictions would no doubt diminish the quantity of Bengalee and Oordhoo translations with which the Calcutta presses now groan, but most assuredly they would greatly improve the quality.

As my notions respecting the principles on which an Oriental Dictionary should be compiled are (as Mr. Trevelyan justly remarks) identical with those of 𝔗,* it would be needless to repeat them here, and I shall make no further observation on Mr. Thompson's book except that, without the least wish to derogate from its merits, I cannot think it (as Mr. Trevelyan seems to do) sufficient for the use of the natives. In my opinion, the labour of a whole life of the profoundest study would scarcely suffice, and might be well employed in such an undertaking; and I shall assert, even at the risk of the imputation of whatever motives my readers may choose, that no measure could be more creditable to Government nor more useful in itself, than the employment of a body of well qualified men in the compilation of such a work.† To expect a

* This T is not *German*, as Mr. Trevelyan supposes, but black letter, or *Old English*. There is not, probably, a real German T in any of the Calcutta printing-presses, and I am not therefore able to exhibit the difference; but there are still some books extant printed in the barbarous hieroglyphics of that language, and, if Mr. Trevelyan will take the trouble of looking into any of them, he will see the true figure of a German T.

† I need not on this occasion mention the national dictionaries compiled in Italy, France, and Spain, as instances in which Governments have not thought works of this kind unworthy of their notice. Barbarous as we may think the Chinese to be, and perhaps as they are, it is certain they have shown themselves no barbarians in this respect, having long

private individual to undertake this is quite absurd: he would ruin his fortune and health before getting through the first letter.

I may here notice a publication of this kind that does indeed deserve commendation, that is the Murathee and English Dictionary by Captain Molesworth and Lieutenants T. and G. Candy, lately published at Bombay. A perusal of the 16th and 17th pages of its preface will give some idea of the labour which these gentlemen have gone through so successfully and so meritoriously.

To conclude this long discussion; a good translation of the circle of the sciences into Arabic and Sanskrit would be a boon of inestimable value to the Oriental world, and, till we have accomplished it, all our other efforts in native education will be maimed and imperfect. With whatever honour, to use Mr. Trevelyan's expression, the name of Lord William Bentinck may descend to posterity, I shall venture to assert that these honours would suffer no diminution, were it recorded that his administration had presented the natives with the key to the unbounded treasury of knowledge in the shape of this compilation, and widened the intercourse between the Eastern and Western worlds, by the formation of a scientific system of the philology of their respective languages.

I am, Sir,

Your obedient servant,

JOHN TYTLER,

Member of the Committee of the School-Book Society for the examination of works in the Mohammedan languages.

P. S.—Since writing the above I have seen in your paper of the 8th instant Mr. Trevelyan's observations on Mr. Prinsep's

been in possession of the Imperial Dictionary of their language, of which, as a national work, it appears from the accounts of it, they may justly be proud. In all probability the great Arabic Dictionary of the Qaumoon was compiled under the auspices of the well-known Timoor or his rival Bajazét. The Indian Government would not be disgraced by imitating these barbarians.

second minute. It may be as well to make a few remarks on these, to avoid having to write on the subject again.

One of the first of Mr. Trevelyan's observations is, that "we have to construct a literature for Upper India from the beginning." This matter, I confess, appears to me in a different light. It is not our business to *construct* a literature, but *to assist and encourage the natives to construct one for themselves*, —and this can only be done by the cultivation of their own language. A national literature made by foreigners in a foreign language is a contradiction in terms; English, I admit, ought to be an object in native education, but a national literature they must construct for themselves in their own languages.

I think Mr. Trevelyan should make further inquiries before speaking contemptuously either of the medicine of Hippocrates or the logic of Aristotle. If he does, he will perhaps find that the medicine of Hippocrates is a very different thing from that with which he seems to confound it, — the physiological theories of Galen. However low we may value the latter, the former will lose its value among medical men only when the human constitution shall cease to be what it is. The Madrasah would have little to fear from its critics could they accuse it of nothing worse than the study of the medicine of Hippocrates. I shall not pretend to be very profoundly versed in Aristotle's logic, but suspect Mr. Trevelyan has not distinguished between the art of syllogistic reasoning, as invented by that philosopher, and the useless subtleties added to it by his commentators. Had he done so, he might perhaps have agreed in the opinion expressed by Fielding's Dr. Harrison, "that Aristotle was not so great a blockhead as many persons think who have never read him."

Mr. Trevelyan informs us that the Delhi College youths cannot learn *two foreign languages* *; and therefore of the

* This is no very high compliment to the Delhi College, and it would have perhaps been better had Mr. Trevelyan (to use an expressive Scotch phrase) "keepit his thoomb upon it." Boys at a common school at home learn Latin, Greek, and French, and they find no difficulty in adding to these, when required, Italian or German. Both French and Italian are, as a matter of course, learnt by every young girl of tolerable

two he recommends English instead of Persian. I have already examined in what sense Persian can be called a foreign language in India, and shall therefore add only, that even supposing (though by no means allowing) that Persian is foreign, still Mr. Trevelyan's conclusion cannot be allowed without the most violent strain upon the meaning of that word. Strictly speaking, French and Chinese are both foreign languages in England, but can it be maintained that they are both equally foreign and equally difficult to acquire, and that an English schoolboy will find it equally easy to master either? A little trial would show that while a few months' study will make him a very respectable French scholar, the labour of half his life might be hardly sufficient to gain even a moderate acquaintance with Chinese. So it is with Persian and English here: a twelvemonth will be enough to enable a native to gain a very serviceable knowledge of the former, — eight or ten years will give but a broken and imperfect acquaintance with the latter. The one already composes three fourths of their vernacular tongue, and its idioms and trains of metaphor are those to which they are accustomed; the other has not the slightest association with any of their ideas.

I cannot see any mistake in Mr. Prinsep supposing "that Persian is essential to the business of the lives of the rising generation." Admitting the case to be as Mr. Trevelyan states, that "the only reason why English does not at once take the place of Persian in the Courts of Justice and other offices of Government is because a sufficient number of persons qualified in the English language are not at present procurable," (though this be evidently a petitio principii,) still it is certain that Courts of Justice and Government Offices are by no means the greatest, and by no means the most important, part of human affairs. Hundreds of thousands and millions pass their lives very happily without any intercourse with either. Could the mass of private correspondence and private transactions be collected, the records of Govern-

education. Nay, however shocking Mr. Trevelyan may think it, I have heard of some young ladies actually learning Latin besides, and helping their younger brothers to make their quotas of hex- and pentameters.

ment and of Courts of Justice, voluminous as they may appear, would shrink before it into insignificance. All this among the Mohammedans, and a large proportion among the Hindoos, is carried on in Persian, without a knowledge of which a native at all above the lowest ranks must be quite helpless. Limited as my transactions are, I yet could manage to furnish Mr. Trevelyan with a large drawer full of letters and *arzees* on all sorts of subjects, of not more than three years old, written in Persian *by choice* from persons who know that I am equally ready to receive them whatever may be their language or character. There may be two or three Hindoostanee pieces in the collection, but so few as not to be worth mentioning; and even these are so full of Persian words and phrases, that the difference between the two languages is more nominal than real.

As to the word *Nugur*, there is no doubt that it *might* be written and pronounced in all the ways Mr. Trevelyan points out, just as our village *might* be written vallage, villuge, vollige, vulloge, and a dozen others. The only abatement is, that in Oriental characters it never *is* written or pronounced in any way but one, and that no native will hesitate for a moment in giving to it one invariable pronunciation, whereas its Roman representative actually *is* subject to all the capricious variations of spelling and pronunciation which Mr. Prinsep represents.

Of the general run of the Bengalee translations which issue in such numbers from the Calcutta press, I have given my opinion in two or three places, and need not repeat it here. I shall therefore only say that I think they should be *read* before they are printed; or if this be too hard a condition, at any rate before they are *praised*.

In spite of all that is written and said on the subject, it is lamentable to find the public in general still so ignorant of the real state of native education. A writer in the *Literary Gazette* of February 15th, 1834, in describing the want of adequate editors to Oriental books, seriously informs us that "the Hindoo College is rapidly bringing forward scholars who will unite a critical knowledge of their own language to a very considerable skill in those of Europe." Had the writer of this article inquired, he would have found that the scholars of the Hindoo College learn no Sanskrit, and are unable even to read its alphabet. So far from having a critical skill in Bengalee, they declare they know nothing of its grammar, and don't understand the language so well as English. It is not very likely, therefore, they will ever give the important assistance to philologists, which the writer of the article appears to think they will be able to do.

The other parts of Mr. Trevelyan's minute have been answered in the course of the present long letter. I shall therefore here take leave of the discussion, and trust he will pardon me for doing so, in a line and a half of a dead, barbarous, and unintelligible language:—

ἐχθρὸν δέ μοί ἐστιν
Αὖτις ἀριζήλως εἰρημένα μυθολογεύειν.

(9.)

THE REV. A. DUFF ON THE POSSIBILITY, PRACTICABILITY, AND EXPEDIENCY OF SUBSTITUTING THE ROMAN IN PLACE OF THE INDIAN ALPHABETS.

(*A paper in favour of Mr. Trevelyan's scheme: extracted from the* CALCUTTA CHRISTIAN OBSERVER *for April,* 1834.)

The discussion respecting the substitution of the Roman in place of the Indian Alphabets has recently been revived, in consequence of the publication of Mr. Trevelyan's Minute on the proceedings of Education Committees in Calcutta. Mr. Trevelyan advocated the substitution: Dr. Tytler opposed it. The Minute of the former is the exposure and appeal of a sweeping reformer and ardent philanthropist: the rejoinder of the latter, with the exception of a few awkward attempts at sarcasm, is the production of a sober-minded gentleman and accomplished scholar.

It is not my present intention to follow the remarks of either of these. Long before the recent discussion arose, the subject in dispute was forcibly brought home to my own mind, in connexion with various plans for the amelioration of the people of India. And the result of my own inquiries was a decided conviction in favour of the views that have been so ably propounded by Mr. Trevelyan.

The subject I conceive to be one of far greater importance, in the *present* stage of native improvement, than most people are willing to admit, or rather than those who have not made it an object of study are capable of comprehending. On this account, I should rejoice to see the whole question traced in all its bearings,—to see it agitated in the public press, and presented in every possible form to the public mind. With the view of adding my mite to the general cause, I shall now furnish a few facts, and offer a few cursory observations.

I. *Is the proposed substitution possible?*

One party replies, yes; and another, no. Those who answer in the negative dwell chiefly on the circumstance that in the Oriental languages there are *peculiar* sounds, i. e. sounds *unlike* any which occur in the languages of the West. How, then, ask they triumphantly, *can* these sounds be represented by Roman characters? Now, it must be owned that if these characters were of the nature of pictorial delineations, like the Mexican paintings now to be found in the Bodleian library; or of the nature of expressive symbols, similar to the Egyptian hieroglyphics; or of the nature of verbal representations, like the encyclopædic letters of China; it would not be easy to divert them into *new* channels. But the case appears totally different when we find that alphabetical characters, like the Roman, are merely *arbitrary or conventional signs of sounds;* i. e. any character, bearing as it does no resemblance to the sound itself, may become the sign of any sound. All that is required is, that there be a mutual understanding amongst those that employ a letter of any figure, as to the sound which such letter is intended to represent.

Since then all letters are, or ought to be, the arbitrary signs of certain *elementary sounds,* and since in *all* languages the *greater part* of the elementary sounds are the *same,* it follows that the *greater part* of the alphabetic letters of any language may be *directly* represented by Roman characters. Next, as to *peculiar* sounds, it may often be found, as in the Indian languages, that they are not *radically diverse* from all that find a place in the languages of the West. That which is said to be *peculiar* in the former, may be only *some particular modification of an elemental sound that* enters essentially into the latter. The difference, instead of being a radical one, may be only a difference in the tone, time, or mode of enunciating the same elementary sound. In this case, the Roman character, with some mark above or below it, would, if agreed on by mutual consent, sufficiently distinguish the peculiarity.

This was the deliberate opinion of Sir William Jones; and as his authority ought to weigh much with even the profoundest Orientalists, I shall here quote his words. "*By the help*," says he, "*of the diacritical marks used by the French, with a few of those adopted in our own treatises on fluxions, we may apply our present alphabet so happily to the notations of all Asiatic languages, as to equal the Deva Nagari itself in precision and clearness; and so regularly, that any one who knew the original letters might rapidly and unerringly transpose into them all the proper names, appellatives, or cited passages, occurring in tracts of Asiatic literature.*"

So positive and unhesitating an opinion, delivered by such a man, may be reckoned decisive of this part of the subject. But, if any lingering doubt still remain as to the possibility of representing all *peculiar* sounds by means of Roman letters with diacritical marks, there is still the expedient of effecting this end by *particular combinations of letters.* Without reverting to the excessive simplification of Wachter, who maintains that *ten* distinct characters would suffice to express all the elementary sounds that belong to the human organs; or to the more moderate opinion of Harris, who declares that "to about *twenty* plain elementary sounds we owe that variety of articulate voices which have been sufficient to explain the sentiments of such an innumerable multitude of all the past and present generations of men;" let us adopt what some would reckon the still more reasonable conclusion of Bishop

Wilkins, that 34 separate characters would be requisite for the purpose, and what follows? That the Roman alphabet, being both defective and redundant, could never be made to express the sounds *not peculiar* to it? No such thing. Let any one consult the Bishop's alphabetic table, and, if not satisfied with the extension of Roman letters with diacritical marks to denote *all* peculiar sounds, he cannot fail to be convinced that the object can be fully and satisfactorily accomplished by an appropriate combination of two of the existing letters.

It is a mere fallacy to talk of the inadequacy of simple Roman letters to express *certain peculiar* sounds. No one has said that, barely and nakedly by themselves, unaccompanied by any mark or uncompounded, they can. What has been alleged is, that the majority of Indian letters can be represented *directly* by corresponding Roman characters, and that the remainder can be *adequately* represented by Roman characters with diacritical marks, or Roman characters suitably combined.

And after what has now been advanced may I not fairly conclude that *such* representation is in all respects *possible?*

II. Admitting the *possibility* of substituting Roman characters, under certain prescribed conditions, in place of all the Indian letters, the next question is, can such substitution be held to be *practicable?*

Those who regard it as *impracticable* generally ask in a tone of defiance, Has such a thing ever been done? has such a thing been known or heard of?

Now, I may surely assert that, though we could not appeal to a single example in the history of the past, this would be a sorry argument. While I hold the maxim to be a sound one, that "what man *has* done, man *may* do again," I must hold it to be at once unsound and injurious to lay down the principle that "what man *has not* done, man *cannot* do." And yet this is the principle on which, in the present instance, much of the opposition on the score of impracticability rests. The argument put in plain terms amounts to this: 1st, "No people ever employed the characters of a foreign language to express the ordinary and extraordinary sounds of their own:

therefore, the attempt to accomplish this is not practicable." 2nd, "No person ever substituted the appropriate characters of another language in place of those peculiar to their own: *therefore,* the attempt to accomplish this is not practicable." This is palpably very bad reasoning, since, if allowed to be valid, it would lay an arrest on all possible improvement. Applied to the inventor of the steam-engine, it would stand thus: "No people ever made use of steam as an impulsive force; *therefore,* the attempt to do so is not practicable." And so of every other invention in art, and every discovery in science. In all these cases, and in all alike, would not the proper course of procedure be: "Is the thing in itself possible? is it, as to its object, desirable? If so, let us make it practicable."

But we have conceded too much to our opponents. Past history is *not* wholly a blank in respect of examples. And as *facts* seem to weigh with them more than arguments, or abstract possibility and desirableness, I shall indulge them with a few statements of facts.

First. As to the employment of letters of one language to express the peculiar sounds of another.

The language of the Tongan Islands has various peculiar sounds, and yet these have been successfully represented by a judicious application of the Roman letters.

The old Celtic or Gaelic language, which is nearly the same as the old Irish, and is still spoken universally in the Highlands of Scotland, has several *peculiar* sounds, i. e. sounds to which there are none perfectly similar either in the English, or in any other of the European languages, and yet these sounds have been successfully expressed by Roman letters. No diacritical marks have been used. Only 18 of the Roman letters have been selected, and by a skilful employment of these, not only the common, but all the *peculiar,* sounds in the language have been represented in a way that is perfectly intelligible to every Highlander.

Ought not these facts to demolish the bugbear of impracticability on this head?

Second. As to the national substitution of one set of characters in place of another widely dissimilar in form.

In Europe, these substitutions have been notoriously frequent from the earliest ages.

Before the conquest of Gaul by Cæsar, the old Gaulish letters, which somewhat resemble the Gothic, were alone used in that country. After the subjection of the Gauls to the Roman yoke, the letters of the conquerors, though extremely dissimilar, were universally introduced, and substituted in place of their own. Towards the close of the 6th century, the Roman Gallic letters were again changed by the Francs into what was called the Franco-Gallic, or Merovingian. This was succeeded, a few centuries afterwards, by the German mode of writing, which had been improved by Charlemagne. In the 12th and 13th centuries, the modern Gothic, the most diversified, complicated, and barbarous of all alphabets, supplanted the German letters. And at the time of the Reformation, the Roman once more usurped the place of the existing alphabet, and has ever since maintained its ground.

In England the changes were not less numerous. At one time the German mode of writing prevailed; at another, the Saxon; at another, the modern Gothic, &c.; and finally the Roman.

In different parts of Ireland and Scotland similar dialects of the old Celtic language have been spoken for at least 18 centuries. There were peculiar letters, of a form distinct from that of other alphabets, to express all the elementary sounds of this ancient language. These letters, having been used chiefly by the Irish Celts, are commonly known under the designation of the "old Irish character." Now, when, about a century ago, great efforts began to be made to improve the condition of the Scottish Celts, the alphabet that contained appropriate letters to express the ordinary and peculiar sounds of their language was set aside, and the Roman notation of letters universally adopted. And in that character have all works ever since, without one single exception, been printed.

Whether the practice be as yet uniform I cannot tell, but I have also seen translations of the Bible and the confession of faith into the Irish dialect, published in the Roman character.

In Spain, during the earliest period of its history, letters were used somewhat similar to the Greek. After the Romans became lords paramount of the soil, they introduced the general use of their own letters. When the country was overrun by the Visigoths, they abolished the Roman and substituted their own very different form of writing. In the 11th century, by the decree of a synod held at Leon, the alphabet of the Visigoths was superseded by the restoration of the Roman characters.

In Italy, from the vicissitude of its fortunes, the mode of writing was often changed. At one time the Lombardic mode of writing entirely set aside the use of the Roman letters, being adopted even in the Bulls of the Popes; at another, the modern Gothic, &c.

Though in most of these cases the forms of the letters were as widely different as can well be imagined, it may still be objected, however absurdly, that they all belong to the languages of the West. Of the people of the East, their languages, manners, customs, &c., unchangeableness has been predicated!

In removing even this cavil, the following *facts* may be of some service:

Who more tenacious of everything Jewish, than the descendants of Abraham? And yet it is generally allowed that the old Hebrew character, now known under the name of the Samaritan, was abandoned during the time of the Babylonish captivity, and that the Chaldaic form, which is vastly different, was substituted in its place, and has been ever since retained.

Originally the Arabic alphabet, as asserted in the learned Dr. Hales' Analysis of Chronology, was the same as the Syriac, which differs as much from the modern Arabic alphabet as it does from the Chaldaic and old Hebrew. This total change in the order and form of the Arabic letters took place about the commencement of the Mohammedan era.

The old Persian or Zend, which is said by Jones to approach to perfection, was superseded by the Arabic alphabet, which has been adopted by all nations that have embraced the religion of Mohammed.

But, what some may think still more to the purpose, has not the Persian character been often practically employed in representing Indian words, particularly in the Upper and Western Provinces? And, *vice versa*, has not the Nagari character been employed in expressing Persian and Arabic terms? The Oordoo, which is a compound of Persian and Indian words, has been represented indifferently by Persian or Nagari letters. And if so, why not this and other Eastern languages by the Roman?*

Rather, if so many and such radical substitutions of one form of letters for another totally dissimilar have actually taken place in the West and in the East, does not the voice of history loudly and emphatically protest against the baseless notion, that to substitute the Roman in place of the Indian letters is impracticable? Does not the testimony of experience, as it rolls along different ages and different countries of the world, perfectly demonstrate that such substitution is, and must be pronounced to be, in every point of view *practicable?*

III. On the supposition of the possibility and practicability of the proposed change, is it *expedient* to substitute the Roman in place of the Indian letters?

Those who oppose the expediency of the substitution often argue thus: "Look at the English orthography; Jones himself pronounces it to be disgracefully, and almost ridiculously,

* I have been told by a friend, who has derived his information *direct* from M. Alexander Csoma de Körös, the celebrated Hungarian who has thrown so much light on the language and literature of Thibet, that the *general structure* of the Hungarian language is so *very unlike* the parent stock of any of the dialects of the West, and so *exactly like* the Sanskrit, that he doubts not the Hungarian and Sanskrit are essentially connected as to their *original source*, if not as Primitive and Derivative. And this conclusion, deduced from the striking *similarity of structure*, is greatly confirmed by the equally striking *similarity* in the *names* of the *most common objects*. M. Körös is of opinion that the Huns had undoubtedly an original alphabetic character of their own when they first invaded Europe, and that it was retained by them till their conversion to Christianity, when *they adopted the Roman character*.

If this be the case, and the peculiar philological attainments of M. K. render his opinion worthy of the highest possible respect, what a remarkable *corroboration* does it afford of all that has now been advanced! A language possessing originally a peculiar alphabetic character of its own — and what is more, *a language radically Indian in its structure and terms — has for ages been successfully represented by Roman characters?*

imperfect: look, on the other hand, at the Indian orthography; its precision, clearness, and regularity cannot well be surpassed:—would it not then be most inexpedient to disturb the beauteous order of the latter, by introducing the irregularities of the former? And this sort of reasoning is backed by what some account a few good jokes and pithy sarcasms at the expense of our poor English orthography. But it will not do to pass off this subject by mere orthographical jokes and sarcasms. There is a radical fallacy in the reasoning of these gentlemen. They suppose that we really wish to introduce the absurd anomalies of English orthography into the East, and without this supposition their argument is good for nothing. Now this *supposition* is a *most barefaced assumption. It cannot be conceded, because it is not true.* We do *not* wish to see the anomalies of *English* orthography incorporated with the languages of the East. Neither do we wish to see superfluous Roman characters employed. If, in the East, one alphabetic letter uniformly represents one elementary sound, *let the Roman letter substituted in its place be invariably appropriated to the expression of that sound.* This is what we propose: and, in this way, I should like to know where a corner can be found for a single anomaly; or how the greatest possible clearness, precision, and regularity may not be attained. In this view of the case, the potent arguments of our learned Orientalists must fall with deadly effect on *their own false premises.*

If then the reasons usually urged *against* the expediency of the substitution be utterly *groundless,* let us now state a few reasons *in favour* of it.

1. The substitution is expedient, because thereby we should obtain an alphabet more perfect than any of our Eastern alphabets, more perfect even than the Deva Nagari.

This may startle the idolisers of Sanskrit; but, nevertheless, it can be proved to be true. What are the requisites of a perfect alphabet? Without specifying the whole, I may remark that, by the common consent of the soundest philologists, the following are of the number:—As every separate elementary sound ought to have a separate character to express it, so none but separate elementary sounds ought to have separate characters. Elementary sounds, radically the same, but differing somewhat in the tone, time, or mode of enunciation, ought not to have representative characters wholly different in form.

Now, in *both* these respects, the Deva Nagari is exceedingly imperfect.

Consonant sounds, such as the two *d*s and the two *t*s marked by Jones *d* and *d'*, *t* and *t'*, though radically the same, and differing in the *tone* of pronunciation, are represented by characters totally different.

Vowel sounds, such as the long and short *a*, the long and short *i*, &c., which of course differ only in the *time* of their pronunciation, are expressed by separate characters.

Sounds *not* elementary, i. e. compound sounds, which ought surely to be expressed by a combination of the elemental or simple sounds that compose them, are represented by separate letters. Of this description are *all* the *aspirated letters*, which form so large a proportion of the Deva Nagari and other Indian alphabets. Who can say that this is not a very *unnecessary multiplication* of alphabetic characters? How vastly more rational and philosophical the simple expedient of having *one* clear *mark*, or *letter*, for the aspiration, which could be applied to *all* vowels and *all* consonants. This is the expedient, not less admirable in theory than convenient in practice, which has been resorted to in the European alphabets. And, if after this truly philosophical model the Sanskrit and other Indian alphabets were framed anew, we should at once get rid of a great number of very *superfluous* characters.

2. It follows from this that the proposed substitution is expedient, because, by rendering the Indian alphabets more perfect, and thereby getting quit of *many wholly useless letters*, the *complexity* which at present characterises these alphabets would be greatly diminished, and the *progress* of *every learner* in the *same degree* facilitated.

3. The substitution is expedient, as it would remove one grand impediment to the free reciprocation of sentiment and feeling among the millions of Hindoostan.

To illustrate this, let me revert to an example. If a book

in Latin, English, French, Spanish, and Italian were presented even to an unlearned Englishman, in the Roman character, he would readily perceive that numberless words, and roots of words, were the *same* in all; and would conclude that the study of one, two, or more of these might be a comparatively easy task, in consequence of this *palpable radical similarity.* But were the book presented in Roman, Modern Gothic, Old Gaulish Visigothic, and Lombardic characters, he could scarcely be persuaded that under forms so wholly different there could lurk any similarity at all. And the study would be regarded a forbidding, difficult, if not a hopeless one. So actually stands the case in India; the number of *dialects* is immense: and each dialect must have letters of a different figure. Let then a specimen of each be presented to an unlearned Hindoo: what must be his conclusion? What *can* it be, except that his country abounds with totally *different languages?* And, if so, the attempt to hold any communication with natives not of his own province must be abandoned as hopeless. Now, were the whole presented in *the same character,* it would be *seen* and *felt* that the natives are not divided into so many sections of foreigners to each other, that they have *all fundamentally* the *same* language, and that without much difficulty a community of interest and a beneficial reciprocation of thought might be effected to an extent at present unknown, and, from the repulsive aspect of so many written characters, deemed utterly impracticable.

4. It is expedient, as it would tend mightily to encourage the study of the English language.

In the present state of things this is a matter of paramount importance. Of all earthly boons, the bestowment on a native of a sound English education is beyond all question the highest and the noblest. It is by the quickening impulse of the knowledge to be derived through the medium of English that we are to expect the *first* awakening of the national mind from its present lethargy. Now, by the universal introduction of Roman characters, every Hindoo might become familiar with them from infancy. The study of English would no longer be looked upon as *entirely new,* nor the language *entirely foreign.* It would appear in all respects more inviting: yea, it would allure thousands to engage in it who are now scared away altogether from the task.

5. It is expedient, as regards the enriching of the Indian languages.

If there must be an infusion of a vast number of *new ideas* into the languages of the East, ere the dense *mass* of the people can be elevated in the scale of moral and intellectual being, there must be a corresponding number of *new terms* to express these. Now, while it is conceded that the Indian letters are well suited to the expression of Indian sounds and words, every Orientalist must bear me testimony in saying that they are *very ill adapted* to the expression of sounds and words in foreign languages. By the adoption, therefore, of Roman characters, the incorporation of *new terms*, implying an accession of *new ideas*, may go on indefinitely, without any difficulty, and without any confusion.

6. The substitution is expedient, as it would save much valuable time and useless trouble to hundreds, and thousands, and tens of thousands of our fellow-creatures.

It cannot be doubted that soon great numbers in every province, from the Himalaya to Cape Comorin, will be engaged in the study of English. These, of course, *must* become acquainted with the Roman character. Besides, it will always be the lot of many to study more than one of the Indian dialects. What a prodigious saving of time and trouble must it then be, to multitudes in every province of Hindoostan, to be possessed of *one common alphabet?* Our *great* Orientalists, our philological giants, I know, will convert this into a subject for derision or scorn, because *they* can master a new alphabet in a week: but I cannot help it. In spite of *their* thundering *canons*, I must be allowed to assert, without fear of contradiction, that the *majority* of mankind cannot, in the course of a week, acquire the *same facility* and *speed* in *reading* and *writing* a totally *new* set of alphabetic characters, as they enjoy in reading and writing those with which they have been long familiar. No: *such* acquisition is *generally* the result, not of five or six days' practice, but of at least as many months. Why, then, *waste* so much precious time upon *nothing?* He who in acquiring *new* languages or dialects would *voluntarily* choose a *new* set of letters for each, instead of adopting one already known, appears to me to act the part of the foolish traveller who on reaching every *new* river, instead of availing himself of the established ferry-boat that awaited his arrival, would prefer lingering on the banks in order to construct a *new* one for himself, in which to cross to the other side.

7. The substitution is expedient, as thereby a prodigious amount of expense will be saved to the community.

It is a fact, that, from the intricacy, the complexity, of most of the Indian characters, it is utterly impossible to reduce them to so small a size as the Roman may be, without rendering them altogether indistinct, or even illegible. In this way, twice the quantity of typal matter, twice the quantity of paper, and nearly twice the quantity of binding materials and labour, must be lavished for nought. Now, considering that we have to provide books for a hundred millions of people, this surely is a consideration of too grave and important a nature to be overlooked.

On the whole, I conclude from principle and not from prejudice, in favour of Mr. Trevelyan's scheme. And not until the preceding facts are proved to be untrue, and the inferences unsound, shall I cease to advocate the possibility, the practicability, and the expediency of substituting the Roman instead of the Indian Alphabets.

ALPHA.

P. S.—To render this paper complete, a representation of the Nágarí and Persian alphabets (the two principal ones used in India) in Roman characters may be given in the next number of the *Observer*.

(10.)

THE REV. A. DUFF'S PROPOSAL OF A SCHEME FOR REPRESENTING THE DEVA NA'GARI' AND PERSIAN ALPHABETS IN ROMAN CHARACTERS.

(*Extracted from the* CALCUTTA CHRISTIAN OBSERVER *for May*, 1834.)

It has been already shown *, in a *general way*, that the substitution of the Roman in place of the Indian Alphabets is as *possible* and *practicable*, as it is unquestionably *expedient*. And it now remains to ascertain and exemplify the *particular mode* in which the substitution may be best effected.

This is the more necessary at the *present* time, since different methods have been proposed by different men, eminent for their talents, and profound as Oriental scholars; and since inextricable confusion must ensue, unless those who advocate the contemplated change agree as to some fixed and uniform system of notation.

Whoever wishes for information relative to the earlier attempts by Davy, Williams and Halhed to express Indian in Roman characters, is referred to the first volume of the Asiatic Researches. In the same volume is an elaborate account of the system adopted by the celebrated Sir William Jones. The labours of Dr. Gilchrist in this field are very generally known. Foster, Carey, Shakespear, Haughton, and others have also lent their aid in solving the problem that regards the *best practical method* of adapting the Roman to the Oriental alphabets, a problem for the most successful solution of which a premium has been held out by the Asiatic Society of Paris.

All of those now named have adopted and applied, with more or less success, certain prosodial, accentual, or algebraic symbols. Recently, however, Messrs. Arnot and Forbes, in several valuable elementary treatises published in London, have suggested the adoption of "a system of writing like the Hindee-Persi-Arabic, to which several Oriental nations have

* See page 66, supra: No. IV. of the Calcutta Christian Observer: the Courier of 2nd April: the Hurkaru and India Gazette of 3rd April: and the Englishman of the 4th and 5th April.

partly contributed, by calling in the aid of two or three of the European alphabets most generally known." Hence, an Italian letter, a Spanish letter, a Persian letter, and Greek letters have been intermixed with Roman letters. This may possibly be the readiest way of conveying to self-taught Europeans some idea of the *sound* of each letter; but assuredly it is not the most comely to the sight, nor the most suitable in practice.

On the whole, after the maturest consideration of the subject, it appears beyond all dispute that Sir William Jones's system, with such alterations and modifications as experience has suggested, is not only the simplest in itself, but the most convenient in practice, as well as the most susceptible of *universal* application; and it carries with it one special recommendation, that it is already familiar to every Oriental scholar in every part of the known world. It is therefore proposed to adopt and apply this system, altered and modified to a certain extent, to all alphabets whether of Sanskrit or Persian origin.

These being the two chief sources of all the Indian alphabets, it is expedient primarily to represent them. For these being once successfully represented, all the rest will easily follow; since no other Indian alphabet contains sounds radically dissimilar, and the few anomalies that do occur, will best be explained under each of the alphabets that are only so many branches springing from the two parent stocks.

I. The letters of the Roman alphabet, which may be successfully employed for the representation of the Sanskrit and Persian alphabets, are the following:—a, b, d, e, f, g, h, i, j, k, l, m, n, o, p, q, r, s, t, u, v, w, y, z. But these, even when used singly, are employed so irregularly in English orthoëpy, that it is absolutely necessary at the outset to fix the precise sound which in the proposed scheme they are intended *invariably* to express.

Short Vowels.

a, has uniformly one sound, and that is the shut or short a; or ă, as represented by lexicographers. It occurs in such words as *America, adept, quota*, &c., and must never be confounded with the sound of a, in *mate, fate; fall, all; far, tar,* &c.

i, the short or shut sound, as in *fit, sit, pin,* &c.: never as in *fine, mite, pine,* &c.

u, the short obtuse sound: as in *bull, pull,* never short, as in *but, rut,* &c.; nor long, as in *mute, pure, secure,* &c.

Simple Consonants.

b, has its regular sound, as in *bed, bell,* &c.

d, has the soft dental sound formed with the point of the tongue, slightly pressed on the roots of the upper teeth, nearly as in *duke, due;* or still more nearly, as the soft French dental *d* in *des,* &c.

f, has its regular sound, as in *fit, fix,* &c,

g, has its regular hard sound, as in *got, go,* &c. Never soft, as in *gender, gentle,* &c.

h, has its regular sound, as in *house, horse,* &c. It is the letter that expresses the aspiration of any other.

j, has its regular sound, as in *jam, join,* &c.

k, has its regular sound, as in *keep, king,* &c.

l, has its regular sound, as in *law, land,* &c.

m, has its regular sound, as in *man, mind,* &c.

n, has its regular sound, as in *nap, nay,* &c. It is the nasal that corresponds with the dental letters.

p, has its regular sound, as in *pot, pan,* &c.

q, has nearly the same sound, as in *quack, clique, quoit,* &c. It has been happily described by Gilchrist as "our *k* articulated by raising the root of the tongue simply towards the throat, which must not be in the smallest degree ruffled. The *q* may consequently be styled a deep, but liquid lingual letter, produced by clinking the root of the tongue against the throat, so as to cause a sort of nausea. The same sound will be recognised when pouring water in a particular manner from a long-necked goblet, as the liquid decanting may represent the lower part of the tongue acting upon the throat or neck of the vessel in question, unruffled by the water gushing from it."

r, has its soft sound, as in *morn, scorn,* &c.

s, has its regular sound, as in *sin, dusk,* &c.

t, has the soft dental sound, formed with the point of the tongue, slightly pressed on the upper front teeth, nearly as in *tube, tunic,* &c. It resembles, says Dr. Carey, the Yorkshire pronunciation of *t* in *butter.* It also resembles as nearly as possible the soft French dental *t* in *tu,* &c.
v, has its regular sound, as in *vain, vale,* &c.
w, has its regular sound, as in *way, wet,* &c.
y, has its regular sound, as in *yea, yes,* &c.
z, has its regular sound, as in *zeal, zone,* &c.

The greater part of the foregoing letters may be employed *directly,* with the sounds now explained *invariably* annexed to them, to represent corresponding letters in the Sanskrit and Persian alphabets, thus:

Rom.	a	i	u	b	d	f	g	h	j	k	l
Sans.	अ	इ	उ	ब	द	—	ग	ह	ज	क	ल
Pers.	ا	اِ	اُ	ب	د	ف	گ	ه	ج	ک	ل

Rom.	m	n	p	q	r	s	t	w	v	y	z
Sans.	म	न	प	—	र	स	त	—	व	य	
Pers.	م	ن	پ	ق	ر	س	ت	و	و	ي	ز

In this clear, distinct, and satisfactory manner can all those letters that are of *most frequent* occurrence be *directly* expressed by Roman letters, unmarked by accents or points, and uncompounded.

II. We come now to a class of letters the sounds of which, not being *radically* diverse from the fundamental sounds already expressed, may be accurately represented by certain appropriate marks. In these the difference exists chiefly either in the elongation of the short vowel sounds, or in a varied pronunciation of consonant sounds. And for the sake of distinction and uniformity, it is proposed to distinguish *elongated* sounds by *accents* placed above*, and *varied* sounds, by *dots* placed underneath.

* In the case of *e* and *o*, which have not, like *a*, *i*, and *u*, any corresponding short sound among the short vowels, the accent over the letter is unnecessary, and is therefore omitted.

Long Vowels.

á, with an accent, has *invariably* the long broad sound, as in *father, ask,* &c.

e, has *invariably* the long broad sound, nearly as in *there,* or as *ei* in *neighbour,* or exactly as *ê* in the French *tempête, flêche,* &c.

í, with an accent, *invariably* as long slender *i,* in *police,* or as *ee* in *feel, sleep,* &c.

o, *invariably* long, as in *note, cold,* &c.

ú, with an accent, *invariably* the long obtuse sound, as in *rude, rule,* &c.

Consonants with diacritic marks.

ḍ, with a dot below, is the hard palatal *d,* formed by forcibly striking the tongue against the palate or roof of the mouth; nearly like *d* in *dull, ladder,* &c. The English *d* may be said to be somewhat softer than this Indian *d,* and somewhat harder than the Indian dental *d.* It, however, more nearly resembles the former than the latter. Still, as the latter occurs *ten times* more frequently than the former, it is deemed advisable to restrict the *dot* to the former; on the principle that it is expedient to employ diacritic marks as little as possible.

ḥ, with a dot below, is the common *h,* sounded more forcibly in the throat, nearly as in *hay, hot,* &c.

ṇ ṇ̈ ṇ̤, with *one, two,* or *three* dots below, are nasals corresponding respectively to the three classes of linguals, palatals, and gutturals. The latter two are not often used, unless compounded with another letter: and as that letter determines the class of the n, the dots may in such case be omitted. The reason there are so many nasals is thus distinctly explained by Haughton. "In the Déva Nágarí alphabet no change takes place in sound without a corresponding change in writing, in consequence; as the sound of the nasal entirely depends upon the consonant by which it is followed, it will for this reason depend upon the latter, what form the nasal shall assume in writing. As an example, the sound of *n* in *king* is different from the sound of *n* in *lent* (and from the sound

*G

of *n* in *launch*), and for the first the guttural ŋ̥ would be required, and for the last the lingual ṇ (and for the other the palatal n̤), if it were desired to represent these words in Déva Nágarí characters; because the *g* of *king* is guttural, and the *t* of *lent* lingual" (and the *ch* of *launch*, palatal). Hence ṇ is sounded with the point of the tongue reverted to the palate, as *n* in *lent:* n̤, "by pressing the whole breadth of the tongue into the hollow of the palate, the tip turned downwards, and by forcing the sound through the nose, with the mouth open something like *gn* in the French *digne:*" ṋ like the French *n* in *sans, bon;* or like *ng* in *ring, sing,* &c.

ṣ s̤, with *one* or *two* dots below, like *s* in *see, sin,* &c. These are only introduced to distinguish two Persian letters, the sounds of which, as used by the people of India, are in reality identical with that of the common *s*, i. e. possess the same phonic value.

ṭ, with a dot, stands exactly in the same relation to *t*, as ḍ does to *d*. It is uttered by striking the point of the tongue on the palate, nearly as in *tub, tin,* &c.

t̤, with two dots, and a slight shade of difference in the sound, is the Persian *toé*, so marked to correspond with *zoé*, of the same class of letters.

ẓ z̤ z̤̣, with *one, two,* or *three* dots below, are all of them sounded by the people of India like *z* in *zeal, zone,* &c. They are here adopted merely to distinguish three Persian letters that differ in form, but not in sound.

The following, then, are the letters that may be clearly represented by Roman characters, with diacritical marks:

Rom.	á	e	í	o	ú	ḍ	ḥ	ṇ	n̤	ṋ	ṣ	s̤	ṭ	t̤	ẓ	z̤	z̤̣
Sans.	आ	ए	ई	ओ	ऊ	ड	—	ण	ञ	ङ	—	—	ट	—	—	—	—
Pers.*	آ	اي	ي	و	و	—	ح	—	—	—	ص	ث	—	ط	ض	ظ	ذ

a, with a dot below, may represent the singular vowel-consonant ع named *ígn*, as in *sígn*. "It is," says Shakespear,

* The mode of using these will be explained more fully afterwards.

"one of the guttural letters, being formed in the lower part of the throat. Its sound has been compared to the voice of a calf calling its mother, or to that of a person making some painful exertion." "This letter," says Mr. Yates in his valuable Hindústaní Grammar, "is generally pronounced *a* or *i*, sometimes long and sometimes short." When short, it may fitly be expressed by ạ, ị. When long by ạ́, ị́, agreeably to the notation already explained. To mark the distinction of these vowels from the others, a dot is placed below them.

III. We next proceed to describe those letters, chiefly *compound*, that may most satisfactorily be represented by a *combination* of two or more Roman characters.

Anomalous Vowels and Diphthongs.

ṛi, with a dot under it, to distinguish it from the consonant *r*, is reckoned a vowel in Sanskṛit, and is pronounced, as in *ri*ll, *ri*ch, &c.

ṛí, is the same sound elongated, as in ma*ri*ne, or *ree* in *ree*d.

lṛi, is nothing but ṛi with the liquid l placed before it, and pronounced simultaneously.

lṛí, is ṛí, with the liquid l similarly placed before it.

ai, which is compounded of a and i, and is pronounced like *ai* in *ai*sle, *oi* in *oi*l, or *ie* in d*ie*, &c. — but a little broader.

au, which is compounded of a and u, and is pronounced like *ou* in *ou*r, *ow* in *ow*l. &c. — but a little broader.

To these are commonly added ं, or *ang*, a very strong nasal, as in *gang:* and ः, or *ah*, a silent *h*, generally employed as a final.

Compound Consonants.

There is a class of consonants which many have accounted simple sounds, for the expression of which there is no *single* letter in the Roman alphabet. But these have been, and may be, *adequately* represented by an appropriate *combination* of letters.

These letters are *c*, *g*, *k*, *s*, *z*, followed by *h*; not the strong aspirating *h*, but *h* soft and subservient, i. e. *h* so modifying the sounds of *c*, *g*, *k*, *s*, *z*, as to aid in producing the peculiar sound required, thus:

ch, is sounded *invariably* like *ch* in *cheat*, *church*, *China*, &c.

g̣h, or Persian gh-ígn, with a dot below it, to distinguish it from the aspirated Sanskṛit *g*, soon to be noticed. It is a peculiar guttural sound, like the Northumberland *r*, or that sound which is heard when gargling the throat with water.

ḳh, or Persian ḳhe, with a dot below it, to distinguish it from the aspirated Sanskṛit *k*. It is a guttural sound like the Greek χ as pronounced by the Scotch; or *ch* in the Scotch word *loch*; or *ch* in the German *macht*. "It is," says Gilchrist, "the rough guttural *k*, pronounced in the very act of hawking up phlegm from the throat."

sh, is sounded exactly like *sh* in *shine*, *shell*, &c.

ṣh, with a dot below it, is pronounced in the same way as *sh*; and is so marked, because it has a distinct letter in Sanskṛit, and, as a sibilant, belongs to the class of linguals, which have been similarly marked.

zh, is sounded exactly like *z* in *azure*, *s* in *pleasure*, or the French *j* in *jour*.

There is another class of consonants compounded of single letters and the aspirate, i. e. aspirated consonants. To express the aspirate, the Greeks employed a small mark like an inverted comma (‘). The Romans substituted *h*; and this letter is, for various reasons, the most convenient for the expression of the Indian aspiràtes. These, by the annexation of *h* to the single consonants, may be most significantly represented. Care must be taken, however, not to pronounce the consonants with the aspirate *as one sound*, which generally happens in the European alphabets. Each letter in the combination must have its sound audibly enunciated, though both sounds be closely united.

b'h or bh, is *b* aspirated and pronounced as in Ho*b*-*h*ouse; or, dropping the first syllable, *b*-*h*ouse.

ch'h or chh, is *ch* aspirated, as in chur*ch*-*h*ill; or, dropping the first part, *ch*-*h*ill.

ḍ'h or ḍh, is the dental *d* aspirated.
d'h or dh, is the lingual *d* aspirated, as in col*d*-*h*and, or *d*-*h*and.
g'h or ġh, is the hard *g* aspirated, as in do*g*-*h*ouse, or *g*-*h*ouse.
j'h or jh, is *j* aspirated, as soft *g* in colle*g*e-*h*all, or *g*e-*h*all.
k'h or kh, is *k* aspirated, as in mil*k*-*h*ouse, or *k*-*h*ouse.
p'h or ph, is *p* aspirated, as in u*p*-*h*ill, or *p*-*h*ill.
t'h or th, is the dental *t* aspirated.
ṭ'h or ṭh, is the lingual *t* aspirated, as in fa*t*-*h*en, or *t*-*h*en.

These illustrative words are written at length, to convey, if possible, the notion of the consonant and the aspirate's being distinctly enunciated: and they are contracted, to show that, in the enunciation of the combined letters, they must not be too much separated.

The following, therefore, are all the *combined* letters required to complete the representation of the Indian alphabets:

Compound Vowels.

Rom.	ṛi	ṛí	lṛi	lṛí	ai	au	ang	ah
Sans.	ऋ	ॠ	ऌ	ॡ	ऐ	औ	ं	ः
Pers.	—	—	—	—	ي	و	—	—

Peculiar Combinations.

Rom.	ch	gh	kh	sh	ṣh	zh
Sans.	च	—	—	श	ष	—
Pers.	چ	غ	خ	ش	—	ژ

Aspirated Consonants.

Rom.	chh	dh	ḍh	gh	jh	kh	ph	th	ṭh
Sans.	छ	ध	ढ	घ	झ	ख	फ	थ	ठ
Pers.	—	—	—	—	—	—	—	—	—

We have now completely exhausted all the letters in Sanskṛit and Persian alphabets. In the former, the compound letter क्ष is generally added; but it is exactly represented by *ksh.* Let us then collect and arrange all the foregoing letters agreeably to the Indian mode of alphabetic order.

THE DE'VA NA'GARI' ALPHABET.

Vowels.

अ a, आ or ा á; इ ि i, ई ी í; उ ु u, ऊ ू ú; ऋ ृ ṛi, ॠ ॄ ṛí; ऌ ॢ lṛi, ॡ ॣ lṛí; ए े e, ऐ ै ai; ओ ो ó, औ ौ au; ं ang, ः ah.

Consonants.

Gutturals,	क k,	ख kh;	ग g,	घ gh	ङ n.
Palatals,	च ch,	छ chh;	ज j,	झ jh;	ञ n.
Linguals,	ट ṭ,	ठ ṭh;	ड ḍ,	ढ ḍh;	ण ṇ or cerebrals.
Dentals,	त t,	थ th;	द d,	ध dh;	न n.
Labials,	प p,	फ ph;	ब b,	भ bh;	म m.
	य y,	र r;	ल l,	व v;	
	श sh,	ष ṣh;	स s,	ह h;	क्ष ksh.

Of the two last orders of letters, h ranks with the gutturals; y and ṣh with the palatals; r and ṣh with the linguals; l and s with the ḍentals; and v with the labials.

PERSIAN ALPHABET.

ا a, آ á, إ i, أ u.	ت t	چ ch
ب b	ث s̤	ح ḥ
پ p	ج j	خ kh

د	d	ط	t̤	م	m
ذ	ẕ	ظ	z̤	ن	n
ر	r	ع	a̤, á̤, i̤, í̤, &c.	و	w or v; as vowels, ú, ó, or au.
ز	z	غ	gh	ة	h
ژ	zh	ف	f	ي	y; as vowels, í, é, or ai.
س	s	ق			
ش	sh	ک	k		
ص	ṣ	گ	g		
ض	ẓ	ل	l		

Concluding Remarks.

I. In the above scheme for Nágarí consonants, the inherent vowel or short अ has been omitted. It may however be supplied by any one in reading the alphabet thus, ka, kha—ga, gha—ṉa, &c., the *a* being the obscure short *a* in *America*, or like *a* in *adrift*. It is more agreeable to the genius of the Roman alphabet to supply this vowel in writing or printing, instead of leaving it to be understood.

When no vowel is subjoined to a consonant, it is supposed to be quiescent; and the small mark (ˎ) that usually indicates a silent consonant is not subscribed, in order to preserve a uniformity between the Nágarí and Persian alphabets.

The letter क or *k* was represented by Sir William Jones by *c*, and the letter ष or *sh* by *s′*. The former has been altered as too indefinite, and the latter as not being uniform. For the sake of distinction the accentual mark (′) has been applied only to vowels and not to consonants: besides it is now universally acknowledged that *sh*, as in *short*, is the true sound.

The nasals also have been more minutely distinguished by diacritical marks.

For all languages derived from the Sanskṛit, such as the

Bengalí, Hinduí, Uriya, Marathí, the above scheme may be successfully applied.

II. The greatest difficulty in the Persian Alphabet has been the representation of the different *s*, *t*, and *zs*. The practical difficulty, however, is greater in appearance than in reality, as those letters with the diacritical marks are of unfrequent occurrence. Indeed it has been adopted as a standing rule, that these marks should be used as sparingly as possible; and, when used, should be restricted to those letters that more rarely enter into the composition of words.

To prevent misconception, it may be proper to explain here somewhat more fully the Persian system of vowels.

There are three short vowels, ـَ zabar, ـِ zér, ـُ pésh; zabar and pésh being written above, and zér below, the letter which it follows in the enunciation; thus, بَ ba, بِ bi, بُ bu.

A letter having one of these accompanying it, expressed or understood, is said to be *harkat*, or movable by that vowel; thus, in بَ ba, *b* is movable by zabar; in بِ bi, *b* is movable by zér; in بُ bu, *b* is movable by pésh. If there is no short vowel expressed or understood, the consonant is said to be *sakin*, or quiescent; thus, بر *bar*, not *bara*, *bari*, or *baru*, &c.

ا Alif, when beginning a word or syllable, is reckoned by Oriental grammarians a very slight aspirate, like *h* in *hour*. But its chief purpose is to subserve the expression of short or long vowels; thus, اَ a, اِ i, اُ u, short vowels. Again, ا with ~ above it, generally written آ, is the long vowel á. So ا, when the last letter of a word or syllable, preceded by another letter with zabar (ʼ) above it (and it is always so preceded), becomes the long vowel á, as in بَا ba, &c.

و Wao, when movable by a short vowel, or beginning a word or syllable, is a consonant like *w* in *with*, and sometimes as *v* in *void;* thus, وَ wa, &c. But و quiescent, i.e. terminating a word or syllable, when preceded by a letter movable by zabar (ʹ) forms the diphthong *au*, like *au* as pronounced by many in *caustic*, or *ou* in *loud;* thus, بَو *bau*, &c. Again, quiescent, preceded by a letter movable by pésh (ʼ) forms the long vowel *u*, like *u* in *rude*, or *oo* in *moon;* thus بُو bú, &c. This combination, however, in Persian has often the power of long ó, as *o* in *whole, more,* &c.; thus, بُو *may be* sounded *bó*, &c.

ي Ya, when movable by a short vowel, or beginning a word or syllable, is a consonant like *y* in *yet;* thus, يَ ya, &c. But يْ quiescent, when preceded by a letter movable by zabar (ʹ) forms the diphthong *ai*, like *ai* in *aisle*, or *i* in *fine*, &c.; thus, بَي *bai*, &c. Again, ي quiescent, preceded by a letter movable by zér (ͺ) forms the long vowel *í*, like *i* in *marine*, or *ee* in *feel;* thus, بِي *bi*, &c. But in Persian this combination has often the sound of long broad *e*, like the French *é* in *naïveté*, &c.*

Hence it appears that in Persian there are three short and five long vowels, and two diphthongs.

Three short, as in اَ a, اِ i, اُ u: or in بَ ba, بِ bi, بُ bu.

Five long, as in آ á, or بَا bá; بِي bí or bé; بُو bú or bó.

Two diphthongs, as in بَي bai; بَو bau.

In Roman characters three short, a, i, u: five long, á, í, é, ú, ó: two diphthongs, ai, au.

* Whoever wishes for a simple and concise view of Persian Grammar will find it in the admirable elementary works of Messrs. Arnot and Forbes of the London Oriental Institution. To be had of Messrs. Thacker and Co., Calcutta.

Hence, in reading Romanised Persian, nothing can be easier than to reverse the process, by substituting, if required, the Persian in place of the Roman letters.

The scheme now proposed will suffice for all languages which bear a close affinity to the Persian, such as the Hebrew, Arabic, Syriac, Chaldee, Samaritan, &c.

III. It would be easy to find other Roman letters which might express the sounds of the Nágarí and Persian alphabets. For instance, *a* might be short *u*, and *á* might be *au, aw, eo, o, oa,* or *ou,* as in *taught, law, George, nor, groat, thought,* &c. Instead of *i* and *í;* we might have *i, ee, ie,* &c. Instead of *u, ú;* we might have *oo, ou, eu, ew,* &c. Instead of *é, ai;* we might have *ay, ai, i, oi,* &c. Instead of *ó, ou;* we might have *oa, ow,* &c. But it is conceived impossible for any letters to represent the sounds in question more concisely or more appropriately than those which have been adopted.

If this has been fully substantiated, (and it can readily be verified by any one who will take the trouble to ponder the subject in all its bearings,) then, for the sake of that uniformity which is so truly desirable, it is to be hoped that every one will be disposed to merge private differences in one grand general plan for the securing of national benefits: it is to be hoped that one and all will be cheerfully prepared to sacrifice little partialities and peculiarities of opinion at the shrine of the PUBLIC GOOD.

P.S.—The author, in behalf of several others who with himself advocate the substitution of the Roman character, embraces this opportunity to notify that it was once their intention to make a direct personal application to Oriental scholars, generally, for their opinion as to the best practical method to be adopted in the proposed substitutionary process. On further consideration, however, it has been deemed most expedient, in order to save time and labour, and prevent unintentional partialities, to make this general appeal to all those literati who take an interest in the subject. Be it then understood, that, if any individual has any suggestions to offer, he is hereby solicited to make known the same, through the medium of the *Christian Observer*, or any other public journal. Conscious only of a sincere desire to promote the welfare of the people of India, we are open to *sound advice, from whatever quarter it may proceed.* Any *real* improvement that may be pointed out will receive speedy and due attention. *But should none be suggested which is likely to meet with general approbation, the scheme now propounded may be considered as final.*

Not to swell this paper to an inordinate length, it is proposed to insert in the next *Observer* a complete representation of all the principal alphabets in Eastern India, together with specimens of the different languages and dialects in Roman characters. In conclusion, the author has here gratefully to acknowledge the valuable assistance derived, in drawing up the preceding paper, from the suggestions of the Rev. Messrs. Yates and Pearce, gentlemen whose separate and united labours in the cause of native improvement are too well known to require any statement on his part.

ALPHA.

(11.)

THE REV. A. DUFF'S REPRESENTATION IN ROMAN CHARACTER OF THE PRINCIPAL ALPHABETS IN EASTERN INDIA, WITH NOTICES OF DIALECTIC PECULIARITIES, SPECIMENS OF THE MODE OF APPLYING THE LETTERS IN PRACTICE, AND ANSWERS TO OBJECTIONS.

(*Extracted from the* CALCUTTA CHRISTIAN OBSERVER *for June,* 1834.)

The scheme developed in the last *Observer* for representing the Deva Nágarí and Persian alphabets in Roman characters has excited a warmer interest, and secured a more general acquiescence, than could well have been anticipated. It has led in some quarters to frequent conversations and repeated discussions, and drawn forth from others various communications of a nature at once friendly and instructive. Every thing around us seems decisively to prognosticate the ultimate triumph of our designs.

When "the scheme" was put forth, observations were solicited from all whose course of study might qualify them to form a practical judgment on the subject. Nor was the solicitation fruitless. While approbation of by far the greater part has been expressed, a few, and only a very few, alterations have been proposed. These it is proper now briefly to notice. They may be divided into two classes: those that may, and those that cannot, well be adopted.

1. The latter class, or that which includes the alterations that cannot well be adopted, refers exclusively to certain letters, which, though originally identical in sound, and though still retained in the original form, yet, in consequence of the mutations to which all things human are liable, have become, in different alphabets, somewhat changed in phonic power. To exemplify what is meant, take the first letter in every Indian alphabet, the Deva Nágarí अ or short *a*. "This," says Sir William Jones, "is the simplest element of articulation, or vocal sound. The word *America* begins and ends with it. In our own anomalous language, we commonly mark this elementary sound by our *fifth* vowel (or short *u*). The Nágarí letter is acár; but it is pronounced in Bengal like our *fourth* vowel (or short *o*); and in the west of India like our *first*." In Hindústání, our short *u*, as in *up*, *sun*, &c., would exactly represent this letter; hence it is so represented by Dr. Gilchrist. Our short *u* being thus pre-occupied, the Doctor was obliged to express उ and ऊ, or our short obtuse and long obtuse *u*, as in *push*, *cube*, by the symbols *oo* and oo. Now, if we had to do *only* with Hindústání, this probably might be the most appropriate notation. But our object is totally different, we have to provide for *all* the Indian alphabets. The question is not, what will suit *best one particular* alphabet; but what, so far as we can judge, will suit *every* alphabet best, so as to secure the nearest possible approximation to a *universal conformity?* How, for instance, would Dr. Gilchrist's short *u*, as in *up*, answer in the Bengalí, where

the letter is sounded like our short *o?* How would it suit in those dialects where it is pronounced like our *a?* Would it, in these several instances, answer the purpose better than short *a*, as in *America?* Surely not. And if not, since we have to make provision for *all* the alphabets, and forestall the peculiar deviations from the parent stock in each, is it not better, more consistent, more uniform, to employ the letter which exactly represents the corresponding one in the *primitive* Indian alphabets, and mark as *anomalous*, in any particular *dialect* the *retention* of the *original letter*, while the pronunciation is more or less *varied?* In this case, most palpable it is that the *anomaly* lies not in our system of representation, but is wholly chargeable on the varying powers of the *literal form* represented. And if it be distinctly borne in mind, that *our concern is not with what may answer best in this or that language, but with what may, on the whole, answer best in all the Indian languages, sure we are that this single circumstance of paramount importance were enough to obviate every difficulty, and remove every objection that can possibly arise on the present head.*

2. The other class, or that which embraces alterations that may well be adopted, appears to be restricted to the two vowel sounds *e* and *o*, and to the nasals ṇ, ṉ̤, ṉ̣.

In no Indian language are the vowels *e* and *o short.* They retain *invariably* the *long* sound. Still, as we find the *short* and *long* sound of *a*, *i*, and *u* perpetually occurring, and as it was necessary to mark this difference, it was proposed, in accordance with established usage, to let the *simple* letters express the *short* sound, and distinguish the *long* sound by accents placed above them; thus *a*, *á*, &c. Since then an *accent* became the special symbol of an *elongated* sound, it was deemed proper, for the sake of *uniformity*, to place it over *e* and *o*, as well as over long *a*, *i*, and *u*. And it cannot for a moment be doubted that this preserves the unity and harmony of the system, by effectually excluding any thing like inconsistency or contradiction. On the other hand, it has been urged that these letters (*e* and *o*), and especially *e*, pervade the language to a greater extent than perhaps any others; and that we ourselves laid down the indisputable canon, that "it is *expedient* to employ diacritic and other marks as sparingly as possible." Influenced by these and other reasons, we have resolved to drop the accent from the long vowels *e* and *o*, assured that no mistake can arise, when we apprise the learner that these, in every Indian language and dialect, possess *invariably* the *long* sound, the former nearly like *e* in *there* or exactly like *e* in the French *tempête*, and the latter like *o* in *note*.

Again, with reference to the nasals, it has been suggested that the notation may in *practice* be simplified. Of this no doubt was ever entertained. In "the scheme" it was shown, how by a few dots these nasals might be distinguished with the utmost precision. To save repetition, let the reader consult the explanation there given. He will find that the different classes of gutturals and palatines have each a nasal *n*, marked respectively ṇ, n̤. Now it so happens that these are *never interchanged*, i. e. the ṇ belonging to the gutturals never precedes a palatal letter, the n̤ belonging to the palatals never precedes a guttural. In this case, the notation of *n* in practice may be perfectly intelligible without further precision. That is, if n without any dot be found preceding a guttural, the reader may be sure it can be none other than ṇ; if preceding a palatal, it can be none other than n̤; and if preceding s or sh, h or a semivowel, none other than ng. By attending to this plain remark we shall get quit of several dots, and so simplify the practical use of the Roman character.

Altogether, when we consider the conflicting state of opinions on this subject amongst Orientalists, we have been delightfully surprised at the average rate of unanimity that now prevails amongst those friendly to the substitution, an auspicious concord, that must proceed from the noble resolve to sacrifice selfish partialities on the altar of social well-being and national prosperity.

These preliminary remarks we shall now follow up by giving in separate tables the two parent alphabetic stocks, with the derivatives principally employed in Eastern India.

1.—*The Deva Nágarí and its branches.*

VOWELS.

Bengálí.	Deva Nágarí.	Kaithi Nágarí.	Mahráthí.	Uriya.	Burman.	Butan.	Sound in Roman character.
অ	अ	𑂃	𑘀	ଅ	အ	ཨ	*a*
আ	आ	𑂄	𑘁	ଆ	အာ	ཨཱ	*á*
ই	इ	𑂅	𑘂	ଇ	ဣ	ཨི	*i*
ঈ	ई	𑂆	𑘃	ଈ	ဤ	ཨཱི	*í*
উ	उ	𑂇	𑘄	ଉ	ဥ	ཨུ	*u*
ঊ	ऊ	𑂈	𑘅	ଊ	ဦ	ཨཱུ	*ú*
ঋ	ऋ	ऋ	𑘆	ଋ*	—	རྀ	*ṛi*
ৠ	ॠ	ॠ	𑘇	ୠ*	—	རཱྀ	*ṛí*
ঌ	ऌ	ऌ	𑘈	ଌ*	—	ལྀ	*lṛi*
ৡ	ॡ	ॡ	𑘉	—	—	ལཱྀ	*lṛí*
এ	ए	𑂉	𑘊	ଏ	ဧ	ཨེ	*e*
ঐ	ऐ	𑂊	𑘋	ଐ	အဲ	ཨཻ	*ai*
ও	ओ	𑂋	𑘌	ଓ	ဩ	ཨོ	*o*
ঔ	औ	𑂌	𑘍	ଔ	ဪ	ཨཽ	*au*
ং	ं	𑂁	𑘽	ଂ	အံ	ཨཾ	*ang*
ঃ	ः	𑂂	𑘾	ଃ	အး	ཨཿ	*ah*

* Sounded ṛu, ṛú, lṛu, in the Uriyan alphabet.

CONSONANTS.

Bengáli.	Deva Nágari.	Kaithi Nágari.	Mahráthi.	Uriya.	Burman.	Butan.	Sound in Roman character.
ক	क	𑂍	क	କ	က	ཀ	*k*
খ	ख	𑂎	ख	ଖ	ခ	ཁ	*kh*
গ	ग	𑂏	ग	ଗ	ဂ	ག	*g*
ঘ	घ	𑂐	घ	ଘ	ဃ	གྷ	*gh*
ঙ	ङ	𑂑	ङ	ଙ	င	ང	*ṅ*
চ	च	𑂒	च	ଚ	စ	ཅ*	*ch*
ছ	छ	𑂓	छ	ଛ	ဆ	ཆ*	*chh*
জ	ज	𑂔	ज	ଜ	ဇ	ཇ*	*j*
ঝ	झ	𑂕	झ	ଝ	ဈ	ཛྷ	*jh*
ঞ	ञ	𑂖	ञ	ଞ	ဉ	ཉ	*ñ*
ট	ट	𑂗	ट	ଟ	ဋ	ཊ	*ṭ*
ঠ	ठ	𑂘	ठ	ଠ	ဌ	ཋ	*ṭh*
ড	ड	𑂙	ड	ଡ	ဍ	ཌ	*ḍ*
ঢ	ढ	𑂛	ढ	ଢ	ဎ	ཌྷ	*ḍh*
ণ	ण	𑂝	ण	ଣ	ဏ	ཎ	*ṇ*
ত	त	𑂞	त	ତ	တ	ཏ	*t*
থ	थ	𑂟	थ	ଥ	ထ	ཐ	*th*
দ	द	𑂠	द	ଦ	ဒ	ད	*d*
ধ	ध	𑂡	ध	ଧ	ဓ	དྷ	*dh*
ন	न	𑂢	न	ନ	န	ན	*n*
প	प	𑂣	प	ପ	ပ	པ	*p*
ফ	फ	𑂤	फ	ଫ	ဖ	ཕ	*ph*
ব	ब	𑂥	ब	ବ	ဗ	བ	*b*
ভ	भ	𑂦	भ	ଭ	ဘ	བྷ	*bh*
ম	म	𑂧	म	ମ	မ	མ	*m*
য	य	𑂨	य	ଯ	ယ	ཡ	*y*
র	र	𑂩	र	ର	ရ	ར	*r*
ল	ल	𑂪	ल	ଲ	လ	ལ	*l*
ব	व	𑂫	व	ବ	ဝ*	ཝ	*v*
শ	श	𑂬	श	ଶ	သ*	ཤ	*sh*
ষ	ष	𑂭	ष	ଷ	—	ཥ	*ṣh*
স	स	𑂮	स	ସ	—	ས	*s*
হ	ह	𑂯	ह	ହ	ဟ	ཧ	*h*
ক্ষ	क्ष	𑂍𑂹𑂭	क्ष	କ୍ଷ	ဿ*	ཀྵ	*ksh*

* The Burman and Butan letters thus marked are pronounced anomalously.

2.—*The Arabic and its Branches.*

Hindustáni.	Persian.	Arabic.	Roman.	Hindustáni	Persian.	Arabic.	Roman.
ا آ اِ اُ	ا	ا	a, á, i, u,	ڑھ	—	—	ṛh
ب	ب	ب	b	ژ	ژ	—	zh
بھ	—	—	bh	س	س	س	s
پ	پ	—	p	ش	ش	ش	sh
پھ	—	—	ph	ص	ص	ص	s
ت	ت	ت	t	ض	ض	ض	z
تھ	—	—	th	ط	ط	ط	t
ٹ	—	—	ṭ	ظ	ظ	ظ	ẕ
ٹھ	—	—	ṭh	ع	ع	ع	ạ ạ́ ị ụ
ث	ث	ث	s	غ	غ	غ	gh
ج	ج	ج	j	ف	ف	ف	f
جھ	—	—	jh	ق	ق	ق	q
چ	چ	—	ch	ک	ک	ک	k
چھ	—	—	chh	کھ	—	—	kh
ح	ح	ح	ḥ	گ	گ	—	g
خ	خ	خ	ḳh	گھ	—	—	gh
د	د	د	d	ل	—	ل	l
دھ	—	—	dh	م	م	م	m
ڈ	—	—	ḍ	ن	ن	ن	n
ڈھ	—	—	ḍh	ں	—	—	ṉ
ذ	ذ	ذ	z̤	و	و	و	w
ر	ر	ر	r	ه	ه	ه	h
ڑ	—	—	ṛ	ي	ي	ي	y

Note.—In the above tables, all the regular letters, with their proper sound, are given. This is in accordance with our plan of reserving explanations of particular variations or anomalies for each of the alphabets separately. But ere we proceed farther, it may be interesting and useful to collect and arrange in one tabular view all the Roman characters, combinations, &c., with such points and marks as have been adopted to complete the representation of the Indian alphabets.

Out of all the Alphabets arises the following complete Roman Alphabet.

Letter.	Name.		Sound.
a	akár,	as in	*A*meric*a*.
á	ákár,	—	*a*rt.
ạ ạ́ &c.	aign,	—	j*a*m*a*.
ai	aikár,	—	*ai*sle.
au	aukár,	as ow in	c*ow*.
ang	anuswár,	as in	s*ung*.
ah	visarga,	—	*ah*.
b	ba,	—	*b*ut.
bh	bha,	—	ho*b*-*h*ouse.
ch	cha,	—	*ch*ur*ch*.
chh	chha,	—	chur*ch*-*h*ill.
d	da,	—	*d*uke.
dh	dha,	—	ma*d*-*h*ouse.
ḍ	ḍa,	—	ba*d* col*d*.
ḍh	ḍha,	—	col*d*-*h*and.
e	ekár,	—	th*e*re.
f	fa,	—	*f*it.
g	ga,	—	*g*ot.
gh	gha,	—	do*g*-*h*ouse.
gh	gha,	—	*gh*astly.
h	ha,	—	*h*ave.
ḥ	ḥa,	—	*h*ouse.
i	ikár,	—	*i*n.
í	íkar,	—	pol*i*ce.
j	ja,	—	*j*am.
jh	jha,	—	colle*g*e-*h*all.
k	ka,	—	*k*eep.
kh	kha,	—	mil*k*-*h*ouse
ḳh	ḳha,	—	lo*ch* (Scotch).
ksha	ksha,	—	bri*ck*-*sh*op
l	la,	—	*l*and.

Letter.	Name.		Sound.
lṛi	lrikár,	as in	ful*l*-*ri*ll.
lṛí	lríkar,	—	ful*l*-*ree*l.
m	ma,	—	*m*an.
n	na,	—	*n*ap.
ṇ	ṇa,	—	*n*ot.
ṉ	ṉa,	—	bo*n* (French).
o	okar,		n*o*te.
p	pa,	—	*p*an.
ph	pha,	—	u*p*-*h*ill.
q	qa,	—	cli*que*.
r	ra,	—	*r*ace.
ṟ	ṟa,	—	ete*r*nel (French).
ṟh	ṟha	—	Boe*rh*aave (Greek).
ṛi	ṛikar,	—	*ri*p.
ṛí	ṛíkar,	—	r*ee*l.
s	sa,	—	*s*in.
ṣ	ṣa,	—	*s*ahib,
s̤	s̤ ,	—	hi*ss*.
sh	sha,	—	*sh*all.
ṣh	ṣha,	—	*sh*ot.
t	ta,	—	po*t*.
th	tha,	—	po*t*-*h*ouse.
ṭ	ṭa,	—	fa*t*.
ṭh	ṭha,	—	fa*t*-*h*en.
u	ukar,	—	p*u*sh.
ú	úkar,	—	c*u*be.
v	va,	—	*v*ain.
w	wa,	—	*w*et.
y	ya,	—	*y*our.
z	za,	—	*z*eal.
ẓ	ẓa,	—	———
z̤	z̤a,	—	*z*one.
z̧	z̧a,	—	*z*ephyr.
zh	zha,	--	a*z*ure.

It has been already stated, that in the derivative alphabets certain anomalies, such as the *retention* of the *original* letter, with a *different pronunciation*, &c., have in the lapse of time slowly crept * in. This circumstance alone were

* We cannot in connexion with this subject refrain from quoting a few extracts from the truly admirable grammar of the Gaelic language by the late Rev Dr. Alexander Stewart: "In the first exhibition," says he, "of the sounds of a living language, by alphabetical characters, it is probable that the principle which regulated the system of orthography was, that every elementary sound should be represented by a corresponding character, either simple or compounded: and that the same sound should be represented by the same character. If different sounds were represented by the same letter; if the same sound were represented by different letters; if more letters were employed than were necessary to exhibit the sound; or if any sound were not represented by a corresponding character; then the written language would not be an adequate representation of the spoken. It is hardly to be supposed that, in the first rude attempt at alphabetical writing, the principle above laid down could be strictly and uniformly followed. And though it had, yet in the course of a few generations many causes would occur to bring about considerable departures from it. A gradual refinement of ear, and increasing attention to euphonia; contractions and elisions brought into vogue by the carelessness or the rapidity of colloquial speech, or by the practice of popular speakers; above all, the mixture of the speech of different nations, would introduce numberless varieties into the pronunciation. Still those who wrote the language might choose to adhere to the original orthography, for the sake of retaining the radical parts, and preserving the etymon of vocables undisguised; and for maintaining an uniformity in the mechanism of the inflections. Hence the pronunciation and the orthography would disagree in many instances, till at length it would be found expedient to alter the orthography, and to adapt it to such changes in the speech or spoken language as long use had established; in order to maintain what was most necessary of all, a due correspondence between the mode of speaking and the mode of writing the same language.

"It will probably be found on inquiry, that in all languages, when the speech has undergone material and striking changes, the written language also has varied in a considerable degree, in conformity to these changes; but that it has not scrupulously kept pace with the spoken language in every smaller variation. The written language of the Greeks suffered many changes between the time that the old Pelasgic was spoken and the days of Demosthenes. The various modes of pronunciation, used in the different districts of Greece, are marked by a diversity in the orthography of the written language. The writing of the Latin underwent considerable alterations between the era of the Decemviri and the Augustan age; corresponding, no doubt, to the changes which had taken place during that interval in speaking the Latin. English and French books printed within the last century exhibit a mode of orthography very different from what is found in books printed two or three hundred years ago. These instances show the tendency which the written language has to follow the lead of the spoken language, and to maintain a certain degree of conformity to those modes of pronunciation which are from time to time adopted by those who speak it.

"On the other hand, numberless examples might be adduced from any sufficient to expose the emptiness of the boast, that absolute *regularity* and *unchangeableness* characterise the Indian alphabets. But our object is not to recriminate: our wish is merely to point out the actual state of things, in order to facilitate the progress of the learner. With this view, we shall endeavour to mark what may be termed the *anomalies* or *peculiarities* of some of those dialects which, from their proximity to us, require *immediate* attention; it is chiefly the discrepancies found to exist between certain letters and their modern phonic power. There are two ways of marking these anomalies. Thus in Bengálí the Deva Nágarí व or *v* is retained and written ব or *v*. But, the natives almost without exception now pronounce it not *va* but *ba*, exactly the same as ব or *ba*, from which also it is not to be discriminated in shape. *Either* then we must represent this letter always by *v*, and place some mark above or below it, to denote that the current pronunciation is not *v* but *b*; *or*, we must at once represent it by *b*, the actual modern sound, and place some mark above or below it, to signify that it is the *anomalous b*, or the *b* which exactly expresses the *modern* sound of the ancient *v*. On the whole, the latter seems to be the preferable expedient. Let us then in imitation of many learned Orientalists adopt the horizontal (–), and let us define it to be the symbol that denotes *anomalies* or *peculiarities* in particular dialects. Thus, if in Bengálí we meet with the word "ḇeda" in Roman character, we shall at once conclude that this is not the regular *b*, but the anomalous *b* that expresses the current sound of the ancient *v*, and so with other letters.

living language, to prove that the written language does not adapt itself, on all occasions, and with strict uniformity, to the sounds of speech. Words are written differently which are pronounced alike. The same combination of letters, in different situations, represents different sounds. Letters are retained in writing, serving to point out the derivations of words, after they have been entirely dropped in speaking.

"From such facts as these, it appears a just conclusion, that written language generally follows the spoken language through its various revolutions, but still at a certain distance; not dropping so far behind as to lose sight of its precursor, nor following so close as to be led through all its fantastic deviations."

With this explanation, we shall proceed to delineate, as proposed, the existing anomalies in those dialects in which books are to be *immediately* prepared.

1.—*Anomalies in Bengálí.*

The letters ড *da* and ঢ *dha* are very frequently pronounced *ra* and *rha,* with the tip of the tongue reverted to the palate. To mark this deviation in Bengálí, a point is usually placed beneath the letters; thus ঢ় *rha.* Now let us retain *r,* which expresses the *sound,* and distinguish it as *anomalous* by the horizontal (–), and thus we shall obtain *r̲a* and *r̲ha.* Whenever, then, we meet with *r̲a* or *r̲ha,* we shall know that these exhibit the *anomalous* sound of ড *da* and ঢ *dha.*

The letter য *ya* is often pronounced *ja* ; and when য retains its genuine sound *ya,* it is distinguished by a dot put below it, as য় *ya.* To express its *anomalous* sound *ja,* let us adopt our fixed symbol, and write *j̲a.*

The letter ব *va,* when used *anomalously* for *b,* will be written *b̲a.*

The letter ব *va,* when following a consonant with which it is combined, has the sound of *wa:* thus in দ্বারা, through or by, ব is subjoined to দ, and the word pronounced *dwárá.* Hence, ব used anonymously for *w,* is marked *w̲.*

জ্ঞ *jna* compounded of জ *ja* and ঞ *n̤a,* the palatine nasal, sounded like *gn* in the French *digne.* It is however pronounced *gya* with a nasal sound. জ্ঞ therefore will be represented by *g̲y̲a.*

ক্ষ *k̲sha* is ক *ka* and ষ *sha,* but is always sounded *khya.* It will therefore be represented by *k̲h̲y̲a.*

ঁ, named Chandra-bindu, properly speaking is the common *n,* but in Bengálí is used as a symbol often written over vowels, to express a strong nasal sound, like *n* in the French *bon,* or *ng* in *ring,* as in বাঁশ, which is pronounced *bángs,* a bamboo. We must therefore represent it by *an̲.*

In Hindustání, it is written as a component part of the word.

Table of Anomalies.

Letters.	Proper sound.	Anomalous sound.
ড	ḍa	*ṛa*
ঢ	ḍha	*ṛha*
ব	va	*b̲a*
—	—	*w̲a*
জ্ঞ	jṇa	*g̲y̲a*
ক্ষ	ksha	*k̲h̲y̲a*
ং	an	*an̲*

The first letter, অ *a*, is generally corrupted by the people of Bengal into an obscure sound like *short o* in *dot, cot,* &c. This must be remembered by all who read the Bengálí Romanised.

2. — *Anomalies in Hindúí.*

The ड *ḍ* and ढ *ḍha* are often pronounced *ra* and *rha*, as in Bengálí, by reverting the tip of the tongue to the palate. ड and ढ, therefore, are represented by *ṛa* and *ṛha.*

ष *sha* is commonly sounded as *kha.* It is, in this case, expressed by *k̲ha.*

क्ष *ksha* is sounded like *chha,* and is expressed by *c̲h̲ha.*

Table of Anomalies.

Letters.	Proper sound.	Anomalous sound.
ड	ḍa	*ṛa*
ढ	ḍha.	*ṛha*
ष	sḥa	*k̲ha*
क्ष	ksha	*c̲h̲ha*

3. — *Anomalies in Hindustání, &c.*

The letters ڈ *ḍa* and ڈھ *ḍha* are often sounded *r̲a* and *r̲ha,* and must be expressed as before, *r̲a, r̲ha.*

Anomalous sounds of various letters in the other languages might here be pointed out, such as ث, which in Arabic is often sounded *th,* &c., with more important variations in Butan, Burman, &c.; but we purposely omit them at present, because not *immediately* required, and because it is our intention to prefix to every book that may be prepared in any language or dialect a table of regular and anomalous sounds in the alphabet of the particular language or dialect; which tabular representation may form the key to the easy and infallible deciphering of the contents of the work. And the specimens now given in Bengálí, Hindúí, and Hindustání may serve as illustrations of the facility with which not only ordinary, but extraordinary, sounds may be represented in Roman character.

Having thus unfolded the common and anomalous sounds in the three Indian alphabets that more *immediately* concern us, we now present a few specimens in the Romanised form:—

BENGA'LI'.

PARABLE OF THE PRODIGAL SON.

In Bengálí character.

Luke xv. 11—24.

১১ এক ব্যক্তির দুই পুত্র ছিল; তাহার কনিষ্ঠ পুত্র পিতাকে
১২ কহিল, হে পিতঃ, তোমার বিষয়ের যে অংশ পাইব তাহা
১৩ বিভাগ করিয়া দেও। তাহাতে পিতা নিজ সম্পত্তি ভাগ করিয়া
তাহাকে দিলে পর সেই পুত্র সমস্ত ধন একত্র লইয়া দূর দেশে

১৪ প্রস্থান করিয়া দুষ্টাচরণেতে সমস্ত সংস্থান উড়াইয়া দিল। পরে
সে দেশে মহা দুর্ভিক্ষ উপস্থিত হইল, এবং তাহার সকল ধন
১৫ ব্যয় হইলে তাহার দৈন্য দশা ঘটিতে লাগিল। পরে তদ্দেশীয়
এক গৃহস্থের আশ্রিত হইলে, সেই ব্যক্তি শূকরপাল চরাইতে
১৬ তাহাকে মাঠে পাঠাইয়া দিত; কিন্তু তাহাকে কেহ কিছু আ-
হার না দেওয়াতে সে শূকরের খাদ্যখোশাপ্রভৃতিদ্বারা উদর পূর্ণ
১৭ করিতে বাঞ্ছা করিত। অবশেষে সে মনে২ চেতনা পাইয়া
কহিল, হায় আমার পিতার নিকটে কত২ বেতনগ্রাহিদাস
যথেষ্ট আহার পাইতেছে, কিন্তু আমি ক্ষুধায় মরিতেছি।
১৮ অতএব এখন উঠিয়া পিতার নিকটে গিয়া এই কথা বলিব,
হে পিতঃ, ঈশ্বরের বিরুদ্ধে এবং তোমার নিকটে পাপ করি
য়াছি, একারণ তোমার পুত্র বলিয়া বিখ্যাত হইবার যোগ্য
১৯ নহি; আমাকে আপনার এক বেতনগ্রাহি দাস করিয়া রাখুন।
২০ ইহা ভাবিয়া সে গাত্রোত্থান করিয়া পিতার নিকটে গমন
করিল; তাহাতে তাহার পিতা দূরহইতে তাহাকে দেখিয়া
ধাবমান হইয়া তাহার গলা ধরিয়া তাহাকে চুম্বন করিল।
২১ তখন পুত্র তাহাকে কহিল, হে পিতঃ ঈশ্বরের বিরুদ্ধে এবং
তোমার নিকটে পাপ করিয়াছি, অতএব এখন তোমার পুত্র
২২ বলিয়া বিখ্যাত হইবার যোগ্য নহি। কিন্তু তাহার পিতা
নিজদাসদিগকে আজ্ঞা দিয়া কহিল, সর্ব্বোত্তম বস্ত্র আনিয়া
ইহাকে পরাও, এবং ইহার অঙ্গুলীতে অঙ্গুরীয় দেও, এবং
২৩ ইহার পায়েতে পাদুকা দেও, আর হৃষ্ট পুষ্ট বাছুর আনিয়া
২৪ মার, তাহা ভোজন করিয়া আমরা আনন্দ করি। যে হেতুক এই
যে আমার পুত্র সে মৃত হইয়া এখন সজীব হইয়াছে, ইহাকে
হারাইয়া পুনশ্চ পাইয়াছি; তাহাতে তাহারা আনন্দ করিতে
লাগিল ॥

The above, in Roman character.

11 Ek byaktir dui putra chhila;

12 Táhár kanishṭha putra pitáke kahila, He pitah, tomár b̲ishayer je ansha páiba táhá b̲ibhág kariyá deo.

13 Táháte pitá nij sampatti bhág kariyá táháke dile par, sei putra samasta dhan ekatra laiyá dúr deshe prasthán kariyá dushṭácharaṇete samasta sansthán uṛáiyá dila.

14 Pare se deshe mahá durbhikhya upasthit ha-i-la, ebang táhár sakal dhan byay ha-i-le táhár dainya dashá ghaṭite lágila.

15 Pare taddeshíya ek gṛihashṭher áshrita ha-i-le, sei byakti shúkarpál charáite táhāke máṭhe paṭháiyá dita;

16 Kintu táháke keha kichhu áhár na dewáte se shúkarer khádya khoshá prabhṛiti dw̲ārá udar púrṇa karite bánchhá karita.

17 Abasheṣhe se mane mane chetaná pá-iyá kahila, Háy ámár pitár nikaṭe kata kata betangráhi dás jatheṣhṭa áhár pá-itechhe, kintu ámi k̲hudháy maritechhi.

18 Ata-eb ekhan uṭhiyá pitár nikaṭe giyá ei kathá baliba, He pitah, I′shw̲arer b̲iruddhe ebang tomar nikaṭe páp kariyáchhi, e káraṇ tomár putra baliyá b̲ikhyáta haibár jogya nahi.

19 A′máke ápnár ek betangráhi dás kariyá rákhun.

20 Ihá bhábiyá se gátrotthán kariyá pitár nikaṭe gaman karila; táháte táhár pitá dúrhaite táháke dekhiyá dhábamán haiyá táhár galá dhariyá táháke chumban karila.

21 Takhan putra táháke kahila, He pitah, I′shw̲arer b̲iruddhe ebang tomár nikaṭe pap kariyáchhi, ata-eb ekhan tomár putra baliyá b̲ikhyáta haibár jogya nahi.

22 Kintu táhár pitá nij dásdigke ágyá diyá kahila, Sarbottam bastra ániyá iháke paráo, ebang ihár angulete anguríya deo, ebang ihár páyete páduká deo.

23 A′r hṛishṭa pushṭa báchhur ániyá mára, táhá bhojan kariyá ámrá ánanda kari.

24 Je hetuk ei je ámár putra se mṛita ha-iyá ekhan sajíb ha-iyáchhe, iháke há-rá-i-yá punascha pá-iyáchhi; táháte táhárá ánanda karite lágila.

HINDUI.

PARABLE OF THE PRODIGAL SON.

In Nágarí character.

Luke xv. 11—24.

११ किसी मनुष्यके दो पुत्र थे। उनमेंसे छुटकेने पिता-
१२ से कहा कि हे पिता संपत्तिमेंसे जो मेरा भाग होवे
१३ दीजिये तब उसने उन्हें उपजीवन बांट दिया। और
बहुत दिन न बीतने पाये छुटका पुत्र सबकुछ एकठा
करके परदेशको चल निकला और वहां कुकर्म्ममें
१४ अपनी समस्त संपत्ति नष्ट की। और जब वुह सब-
कुछ उठाचुका उस देशमें बडा अकाल पडा और
१५ वुह दरिद्र होने लगा। तब वुह जाके उस देशके
एक प्रजाका सेवक बना और उसने उसे अपने खेतों-
१६ में भेजा कि सूअरोंको चरावे। और वुह लालसा
रखता था कि उन छिलकोंसे जो सूअर खाते थे
१७ अपना पेट भरे और कोई उसे न देता था। और
जब वुह अपने चेतमें आया उसने कहा कि मेरे पि-
ताके कितने बनिहार हैं जिनकी रोटी बचरहती है
१८ और मैं भुखसे मरताहों। मैं उठूंगा और अपने

पिता पास जाऊंगा और उसे कहूंगा कि हे पिता
१९ मैं स्वर्गके और तेरे आगे अपराधी हूं। और अब
मैं योग्य नही कि तेरा पुत्र कहाऊं मुझे अपने बनि-
२० हारोंमेंसे एकके समान बनाइये। तब वुह उठके अप-
ने पिता पास आया परंतु जब वुह दूरही था उसके
पिताने उसको देखा और दयाल हुआ और दौडा
२१ और उसके गलेमें गिरके उसे चुमने लगा। और
पुत्रने उसको कहा कि हे पिता मैंने स्वर्गका और
तेरा अपराध कियां है और अब इस योग्य नही
२२ कि तेरा पुत्र कहाऊं। तब पिताने अपने सेवकोंको
कहा कि अच्छेसे अच्छे वस्त्र लाओ और इसको प-
हिनाओ और उसके हाथमें अंगूठी और पाओंमें
२३ जूती पहिनाओ। और वुह मोटा बछडा इधर ला-
ओ और मारो कि हम खावें और आनंद करें।
२४ क्यूंकि मेरा यिह पुत्र मर गया था और फिर जी-
ता है वुह खोगया था और मिल गया है। तब वे
आनंद करने लगे॥

The above, in Roman character.

11 Kisí manuk̲hyake do putra the ;

12 Un-men̲-se chhuṭkene pitáse kahá, ki he pitá, sampatti-men̲se jo merá bhág howe, díjiye ; tab usne unhen̲ upajívan ban̲ṭ diyá.

13 Aur bahut din na bítne paye, chhuṭká puṭra sab kuchh ekṭhá karke, pardeshko chal niklá, aur wahán̲ kukarmamen̲ apní samasta sampatti nashta kí.

14 Aur jab wuh sab kuchh uṭhá chuká, us deshmeṉ baṛá akál
paṛá; aur wuh daridra hone lagá.
15 Tab wuh jáke, us desh ké ek prajáká sebak baná; auṛ
usne use apne kheton̠ men̠ bhejá ki sú-aron̠ ko charáwe.
16 Aur wuh lálasá rakhtá thá ki un chhilkonse jo sú-ar kháte
the apná pet bhare; aur koí use na detá thá.
17 Aur jab wuh apne chetmen̠ áyá, usne kahá, ki mere
pitáke kitne banihár hain̠ jinkí roṭi bach rahtí hai, aur
main̠ bhúkhse martá hon̠.
18 Main̠ uṭhún̠ga aur apné pitá pás jáúnga, aur use kahúnga,
ki he pitá, main̠ swargke aur tere áge aparádhi hún̠.
19 Aur ab main̠ jogya nahí ki terá putra kaháún; mujhe
apne banihárон̠ men̠-se ek ke samán banáiye.
20 Tab wuh uṭhke apne pitá pás áyá; parantu jab wuh
dúrhí thá, uske pitáne usko dekhá, aur dayál húá, aur
dauṛá, aur uske galemen̠ girke, use chumne lagá.
21 Aur putra ne usko kahá, ki he pitá, main̠ ne swargká
aur terá aparádh kiyá hai, aur ab is jogya nahín̠ ki terá
putra kaháún̠.
22 Tab pitáne apne sebakon̠ ko kahá, ki achchhese achchhe
bastra láo, aur isko pahináo; aur uske haṭh men̠ augúṭhí,
aur páon̠ men̠ jútí pahináo.
23 Aur wuh motá bachhṛá idhar láo, aur máro; ki ham
kháwen̠ aur ánand karen̠:
24 Kyunki merá yih putra margayá thá, aur phir jítá hai;
wuh kho gayá thá, aur mil gayá hai; tab we ánand karne
lage.

HINDU'STA'NI'.

PARABLE OF THE PRODIGAL SON.

In Persian character.

Luke xv. 11—24.

۱۱ ایک شخص کے دو بیٹے تھے ۞
۱۲ اُن مین سے چھوٹکے نے باپسے کہا کہ ای باپ مالسے
جو میرا حصّہ ہو مُجھے دیجیے تب آسنے بقدر معاش
اُنھین بانٹ دیا ۞
۱۳ اور بہت روز نہ گزرے تھے کہ چھوٹکے بیٹےنے سب
کچھ جمع کرکے ایک ملک بعیدکا سفر کیا وہاں بد
معاشیمیں اپنا مال برباد کر دیا ۞
۱۴ اور جب وہ سب کچھ خرچ کر چُکا اُس سرزمین میں
سخت کال پڑا اور وہ بےمایہ ہو چلا ۞
۱۵ تب وہ جاکے اُس ملک کے ایک متوطن کا نوکر بنا
اُسنے اُسے اپنے کھیتوں پر بھیجا کہ سور چرایا کرے ۞
۱۶ اور اُسے آرزو تھی کہ اُن چھلکوں سے جو سور کھاتے تھے
اپنا پیٹ بھرے سو بھی کسینے اُسے نہ دیے ۞
۱۷ اور جب وہ اپنے ہوشمیں آیا تو کہا کہ میرے باپ
کے کتنے ہی مزور ہین جنھیں روٹیاں وافر ہیں اور میں
بھوکھسے مرتا ہوں ۞

۱۸ میں اُٹھکر اپنے باپ پاس جاونگا اور اُسے کہونگا کہ ای
باپ میں آسمن‌کا اور تیرا گنہگار هوں ۞

۱۹ اور اب اس لایق نہیں کہ تیرا بیتا کہلاوں مُجھے اپنے
مزوروں میں سے ایک کے ماند بنایے ۞

۲۰ تب وہ اُتھکر اپنے باپ پاس آیا اور وہ هنوز دور تھا کہ
اُسکے باپ‌نے اُسے دیکھا اور رحم کیا اور دورکے اُسکے
گردن پر جا لپتا اور اُسکے مچھیاں لیں ۞

۲۱ بیقےنے اُسے کہا کہ ای باپ میں نے آسمان‌کا اور تیرا
گناہ کیا هی اس لایق نہیں کہ تیرا بیتا کہلاوں ۞

۲۲ تب باپ‌نے اپنے نوکروں‌کو کہا اچھی سے اچھی
پوشاک لاو اور اسے ملبس کرو اور اُسکے هاتھمیں انگوتھی
اور پاوں میں جوتی پہناو ۞

۲۳ اور وہ پالا هوا بچھڑا لاکے ذبح کرو کہ هم کھاویں اور آنند
کریں ۞

۲۴ کیونکہ میرا یہ بیتا مر گیا تھا اب زندہ هوا کھویا گیا
تھا سو ملا تب وے عیش کرنے لگے ۞

The above, in Roman character.

11 Ek shakhs ke do beṭe the;

12 Un-meṉ-se chhuṭke ne bápse kahá, kih ái báp, málse jò merá ḥiṣṣah ho, mujhe dijie; tab usne baqadari maạ́sh unheṉ báṉṭ diyá.

13 Aur bahut roz nah guzre the, kih chhuṭke beṭene sab kuchh jamạ karke, ek mulk bạídka safar kiyá, waháṉ bad maạ́shímeṉ apná mál barbád kar diyá.

14 Aur jab wuh sab kuchh kharch kar chuká, us sar-zamín meṉ saḳht kál paṛá, aur wuh bemáyah ho chalá.

15 Tab wuh jáke us mulk ke ek mutawaṭṭin ká naukar baná; usne use apne khetoṉ pur bhejá kih sú-ar charáyá kare.

16 Aur use árzu thí kih un chhilkoṉ se jo sú-ar kháte the apná peṭ bhare; so bhí kisíne use nah diye.

17 Aur jab wuh apne hoshmeṉ áyá to kahá, kih mere báp ke kitne hí mazúr haíṉ jinheṉ roṭíáṉ wáfir haiṉ, aur maiṉ bhúkhse martá húṉ.

18 Maiṉ uṭhkar apne báp pás jáúngá, aur use kahúngá, Kih ái báp maiṉ ásmánká aur terá gunah-gár húṉ.

19 Aur ab is lá-iq nahíṉ kih terá beṭá kahláúṉ; mujhe apne mazúroṉ meṉ se ek ke mánind banáiye.

20 Tab wuh uṭhkar apne báp pás áyá. Aur wuh hanọz dúr thá, kih uske bapne use dekhá aur raḥm kiyá, aur ḍaurke uske gardan par já liptá, aur uskí machhiyáṉ líṉ.

21 Betene use kahá, Kih ái báp, maiṉ ne ásmánká aur terá gunah kiyá hai, is láyiq nahiṉ kih terá beṭá kahláúṉ.

22 Tab bápne apne naukaroṉko kahá, achchhí se achchhí poshák lau, aur ise mulabbas karo, aur uske háthmeṉ angúṭhí, aur páoṉ men jútí pahnao.

23 Aur wuh pálá húá bachhhṛá láke, zabaḥ karo kih ham khá-weṉ aur ánand kareṉ;

24 Kyúnkih merá yih beṭá mar gayá thạ́, ab zindah húá; khoyá gayá thá, so milá: Tab we ạish karne lage.

Answers to Objections.

Having thus illustrated the *particular mode* in which the Roman alphabet may be substituted in place of the principal alphabets in Gangetic India, it seems desirable, though not necessary, to take a brief review of objections that have been advanced against the general substitutionary scheme. *Not necessary*, because many of them have been already anticipated and answered, and to the answer no reply has yet appeared, and no *new* ones have been adduced of a nature sufficiently momentous to counterbalance even *one* of the manifold advantages previously detailed. But *desirable*, inasmuch as total silence may be misconstrued by some into total incompetency to meet the objector on his own chosen field.

The only objections which have appeared in a tangible form, so far as we know, are those brought forward by a correspondent of the Gyánánweshan; and, as the author has written in a style eminently characterised by freedom from controversial virulence or offensive personality, he is justly entitled to the most candid hearing. His remarks, therefore, shall be noticed *seriatim*, together with a few others; and in the thoughtful editor of the Gyánánweshan himself, we doubt not, will be found a most powerful ally.

1. It is alleged, that "the whole native population of India will disapprove of the measure."

This, in fact, seems to be the *gravamen* of all those charges to which our opponents generally appeal. But to what does it amount? To a baseless assumption. No: says the objector, it is not a baseless assumption. But how can this *second* baseless assertion support the *first* baseless assertion? We may assert that sugar is bitter, that fire is cold, that the sun is black; but what is the use of assertion without proof? * Has the objector proposed to offer the shadow of a

* We can hardly suppose that the objector seriously meant for proof what he states respecting the fabulous origin of the Indian characters. "They" (the Hindus), says he, "will think, nay feel, it sacrilegious to abandon their native characters, which they suppose to have been invented by God," &c. Now, it is *not true* that the Indian characters *generally* are believed to be "invented by God." The *only* character, in regard to

proof? Not he: a bare, naked, unsubstantiated assertion is all that he favours us with. But this the author must be aware cannot satisfy an ingenuous mind. We feel impelled to push the matter, and ask, *Where* is the proof of so sweeping an assertion to be found? From what *data* can any living creature, with the insignia of truth before his eyes, make a declaration that is *universal*,—without limit, and without qualification? How, where, or when, have "the whole population of India" expressed such decided disapprobation? In what mode have their suffrages been obtained? What meetings, public or private, have been held to discuss this national question? What journals or pamphlets have been made the organs of announcing the unanimous verdict? But really thus to press for proof of that which admits of none may seem like forcing a man to make bricks without straw. Suppose we allow that there *may be* this universal hostility, we must still be permitted to ask, How, or by what means, has it been ascertained actually to exist? Is not the *utmost* that can be said with any semblance of truth simply this,—that *several* natives have manifested dissatisfaction at the measure? And how *can* this amount to a proof, that *all* the natives of Hindustán have done, or will do so? We may *assert* that the whole of the interior of the Andes is composed

which this superstitious belief prevails, is the Deva Nágarí. And that the Hindus have not thought it "sacrilegious" to depart from a form supposed to be communicated by the gods, is *demonstrated* beyond all possibility of doubt, by the *notorious fact, that the natives of every province have actually departed from that form—have actually invented, substituted, and employed a new and widely different form of their own:*—hence the Bengálí, the Uriya character, &c. &c. Besides, have not multitudes of Hindus actually adopted the Persian character to express Indian words, i. e. a foreign character—the character of their hated Mussulman conquerors? Farther still, though the Sanskrit is believed to be the language, even as the Deva Nágarí is thought to be the character, of the gods, strange to say, the natives generally will not read the divine language, if written or printed in the divine character. They prefer writing and reading the Sanskrit in the common character that is employed in the province to which they belong. Thus, in Bengal, the natives will not, unless constrained, even learn the Deva Nágarí; neither will they purchase Sanskrit works printed in that character. They write Sanskrit in the Bengálí character; and Sanskrit works printed in it are eagerly sought after, and obtain a speedy and extensive circulation. After hearing all this, who can any more give heed to the absurd and foolish fable, respecting "the sacrilegiousness" of departing from the alphabetic character of the gods?

of pure gold. When asked for proof, we may reply, In *some* mines gold has been discovered. Indeed, retorts our opponent, suppose *I* admit that your *universal* assertion *may be* true, how does its truth appear from the *limited* evidence adduced? *Because* gold has been found to exist in *some* mines, *therefore*, it exists to the extent of composing the *whole* of the interior of this vast mountain range! If *such* reasoning prove anything at all, it is this, that sound reason has nothing to do with it.

But we not only deny the *absence* of all evidence; we negative the assertion altogether. In regard to 999 out of a 1000, is there a *single* circumstance of a *positive* nature, beyond vague analogy and conjecture, to show that they are either favourable or unfavourable? If not; then, as to the *remaining fraction*, if it be said that some oppose our scheme, we assert, without fear of contradiction, from our own individual experience, *that some do not oppose it, yea, that many highly approve of it.*

After all, supposing what it is utterly impossible to grant, yet, for argument's sake, supposing that it was proved that "the whole population of India" were opposed to the change, what inference should we draw? — That *because* there is "a national prejudice" against it, *therefore*, it should not be attempted! He who would argue thus must surely have mistaken the age in which he lives. He must have been dreaming of the times when interested men lazily fattened on ignorance and prejudice, and dreaded all change, as they would the hurricane or the pestilence. And if this masterpiece of selfish reasoning, by which the struggle has been maintained to preserve the accumulated prejudices, corruptions, and abuses of ages, and have them consolidated into one imperishable mass of deformity, is to be still echoed and re-echoed in our hearing, the only reply which we can deign to make is, that we are drawing towards the middle of the 19th century, and that such time-serving arguments are fit only to be tossed, like the ravings of the Sibylline oracle, to the four winds of heaven. The grand question with us is: May the change be pronounced a good one,— one exuberant with blessings to the deluded people of India? If so, regardless of abuse, and fearless of difficulty, let us arouse our inmost energies to enforce it on the attention of all around us, and so labour to banish venerated follies, and extinguish for ever "national prejudices."

2. It is said, that as the system "can be adopted (only) on a limited scale at first," those who learn the Roman characters must acquire a knowledge of the native alphabets too, in order to communicate with their countrymen; hence, it is added, "much time will be lost for nothing."

Admitting these premises, we must flatly deny the conclusion. Much time will *not* be lost for nothing. Almost all those who *at first* learn the new system are the boys and young men already engaged, or about to engage, in the study of the English language; and most palpable it is that these must learn the Roman alphabet at any rate; so that to them there can be *no additional* loss of time. Now those who study English will be daily increasing in number and respectability; and these assuredly are the individuals who will give the *tone* to Hindu society; and, through their influence and example, hundreds and thousands will gradually become acquainted with the Roman character, who have not studied, nor intend to study, the English language; and the necessity for communicating in the native character will be proportionately diminishing. In this way, a knowledge of the system will necessarily overspread every corner of the land, till the number that has mastered the new character will equal that which has not, and ultimately become preponderant: then will the necessity for acquiring the native character wholly vanish.

But let us freely and frankly admit that those who live during the *transition process* must labour under disadvantages from which their descendants will be exempt; yea, more, let us suppose the disadvantages to be vastly greater than they ever can be; and what of all this? *Because* the securing of certain lasting benefits must be attended with temporary disadvantages, shall we *therefore* sit down in ignoble repose, and make no attempt to secure them at all? To compare *great* things with *small*, what should *we* have been now, had *our* forefathers acted in this despicable *spirit?*

What perils by land and by water, what ceaseless anxieties, what painful watchings by night and by day, what cruel persecutions, did they not endure? And for whom did they endure them? Chiefly for us. Boldly did they encounter a thousand difficulties and dangers, which, when overcome, insured to us the charter of numberless inestimable privileges. And is not the circumstance that they submitted to such sacrifices, in order to bequeath so rich and noble a legacy to their children, part of their chiefest glory? Is it not this that encircles their brows with the halo of an earthly immortality? Now, in a cause far inferior it may be, and encompassed with far fewer difficulties, may we not be permitted to emulate so splendid an example? Though destined, we fear, to follow these at an immeasurable distance, still we should not hesitate thus to address the *present* generation of Hindus:—A change has been proposed which promises to secure for you, and especially those that follow after you, unspeakable benefits; but, like every other ameliorating change, it cannot be effected without subjecting you to certain temporary inconveniences. One monitor has arisen who suggests, and by inference seems to exhort you, not to adventure on the change, because of the great personal trouble with which it may be attended; will you listen to the suggestion, will you brook the exhortation? Long have the Hindus been charged with selfishness and cowardice: will you still perpetuate the grounds of this charge? Rather, will you not arise, and demonstrate to your accusers that you can acquit yourselves like men? Will you not arise and disclaim the imputed baseness of not adopting what is beneficial, merely because it may occasion some additional trouble? Will you not arise, and prove that you are capable of forming disinterested resolutions, and achieving generous deeds—deeds of unfading renown? If the great change now proposed cost *you* some trouble, and subject *you* to the ordeal of opposition and contumely, will it not confer blessings that cannot be numbered on millions of your countrymen, down to latest posterity? And in viewing this magnificent prospect, is there not to you a large and ample reward? Is not the very thought enough to inspire your bosoms with the fire of patriotism, stronger and purer far than the glow of heroic chivalry? And as future ages reap the golden fruits of your labour, will they not look back with exulting joy to the present era; and will not your memories be enshrined, not in "tablets of marble or of brass," but in the far more enduring tablets of the hearts of a grateful and enlightened people?

3. It is asked, "What guarantee have we for the permanency of the system to be introduced? It may happen that a few years hence, an individual holding an entire sway over the Education Committee will dislike the measure, and re-establish the native characters."

Much more importance is here attached to the Public Instruction Committee than it possesses or deserves. Its influence at best can only extend a certain length. But let that pass. Times are now changed. Formerly the Committee acted on the vilest close-borough system. Its proceedings were about as well known as those of the court of the king of Timbuctoo in Central Africa. *Hence* the silence and *apparent* acquiescence of the Indian public. But, once exposed to view, these proceedings have called forth a cry of indignation throughout the land. And if the veriest despot that ever tyrannised over it with his iron sceptre were once more to attempt to usurp supreme authority, he would be hurled from his throne by the shout of public opinion. If the projected plan succeed *now*, i. e. if a sufficient number of Europeans resolve to support it, backed by the most influential part of the press; if it be, on rational grounds, embraced by numbers of intelligent natives; if it take firm root in some of the most popular seminaries in the country, — we have every possible guarantee, of which such a case can admit, that its demolition is beyond the reach of any future Committee, public or private. In the event of general success, no Committee would dare to interpose its veto; or, if it did, its efforts would prove abortive, and its appeals would be drowned amid the expostulations of an incensed community.

If the measure should be approved of by the present enlightened Committee, and its approbation confirmed by a Government pledge not to sanction any future radical innovation or subversion of it; all good and well. But we repeat it, that the cause is independent of such approbation or pledges. For, if it be as beneficial to India as we believe it to be, it will ultimately succeed by the inherent, irresistible force of those advantages which it so liberally offers.

4. It is supposed to be impossible to establish "one fixed and uniform mode of representing the Indian alphabets in the Roman characters; because, "there are now several systems, and some stick to this, and some to that, and so on."

This we verily believe to be a most groundless assertion. It involves a most dishonourable insinuation. It is built on the hypothesis that numbers of upright men will prefer their own little peculiarities to the securing of national benefits. It supposes, therefore, a compound of pride, selfishness and infallibility, to the possession of which few, we trust, would have the ambition to aspire. It is, in fact, a libel on the good sense and fair character of many who are not less distinguished as Oriental scholars than as the best friends of the species. The authors of four different systems have been named, viz. Sir William Jones, Dr. Gilchrist, Dr. Carey, and Mr. Yates. The first of these has long since paid the debt of nature; the second is in Europe, far removed from the arena of contest; the third, through the gradual decay of nature, is fast hastening to the close of a glorious career of benevolence; and the fourth, with the genuine feelings of a philanthropist, has voluntarily and cheerfully signified his purpose of abandoning anything peculiar in his own system, for the sake of the public good, and the establishment of necessary fixedness and uniformity. A fixed and uniform scheme has, accordingly, been propounded, and it is with no ordinary satisfaction that we refer to the fact that all who are favourable to the substitution have announced their determination to adhere to it; and those who are not favourable are not likely soon to trouble us with conflicting representations of the Indian in Roman characters. *That, therefore, which has been pronounced impossible, has already been accomplished.*

But, continues our indefatigable objector, "supposing a new system to be established by common consent, a few years after some learned persons may find fault with it and make several alterations in it. In this manner, innumerable difficulties will be thrown in the way of the learner."

There is nothing *perfect* under the sun : and if, in the time to come, some slight alterations should be proposed and adopted by common consent, such alterations can no more interfere with the general system, or embarrass the mind of the learner, than the substitution of *i* for *e* in *inquirer*, or of *o* for *ou* in *labor*, &c., can be said to throw "innumerable difficulties in the way of the learner" of English orthography.

5. It is urged that, "in case of the substitution of the Roman characters, there must be two sorts of letters, one for printing and the other for writing, and that this is a great inconvenience."

If this be an "inconvenience" in a certain sense, it is one that repays itself with compound interest. What is the perfection of a *printed* character? Is it not a vivid obtrusive *legibility*; such a legibility that an experienced eye could devour, as it were, at a *single glance*, the contents of a *whole page?* In this respect, the Roman character, as exhibited in the most improved modern type, is unimitated and inimitable.

And no doubt much of this *perfect legibility* arises from the use of *capitals*. This topic has been thus noticed by the intelligent editor of the *Enquirer:* "We are still thinking of the new scheme to represent the native sounds by the Roman alphabet. One very great advantage will be gained from the capital and small letters with which the latter abounds. The reading of Sanskrit, Bengálí, Persian, &c., would not receive an inconsiderable facility if all proper names were to begin with capital initials. This would contribute to render the reading of the native languages much easier than it at present is; and of course this circumstance is, in proportion to the advantage, favourable to the new plan." This is a sound practical observation. Let the reader open the first Oriental work that comes in his way, and he will perceive its appositeness. From the first page to the last it will be found to exhibit one continued sheet of homogeneous uniformity. Without being over-fanciful we may compare its internal aspect to that of the plains of

Bengal. Here are no undulations of soil, no elevations, no "crags, knolls, or mounds," to diversify the scene, to serve as boundaries to the lords of the soil, or protrude as landmarks to aid the traveller in acquiring a topographical knowledge of the country. Go where you may, it is one wearisome unvaried sameness, one interminable interchange of flat paddy fields and close dingy jungle. Similar is the appearance of an Oriental work. It looks like one dull monotonous mass, without beginning, middle, or end. There is nothing *prominent*, to point out the commencement of new sentences or paragraphs; nothing *prominent* to distinguish the proper names of persons, places, objects, or events. Wearied and unaided, the reader travels onward; and if he wish to refer to some particular passage, or the account of some particular person, place, &c., he is left in his search without a clew. In a work printed in Roman characters, he would, by the aid of the capitals, *at à single glance* discover what he wanted: in a work printed in Oriental characters, he must patiently waste his precious time in plodding through almost every line of every page. Indeed so great is the inconvenience, that it has been sorely *felt;* and various have been the attempts by means of *asterisks*, &c., to apply a remedy. But, as yet, every attempt has only turned out a ludicrous failure. Have we not then a right to demand of our mighty Philologists, what expedient *their* imagination, expanded as it must be by its familiarity with the boundless flights of Oriental fancy, can now suggest, which may offer a *tithe* of the advantages conferred by Roman capitals?

Still farther, by the beautifully simple device of "Italics," an emphatic word or phrase is made to strike the eye, and thereby reach the understanding or the heart, with an ease and rapidity that almost surpass conception, and set description at defiance. In this particular, we should like to know what imaginable contrivance, equally *simple* and *perfect*, could be devised for any one of the Indian alphabets? and yet, in reading, how can the importance of such an admirable contrivance be too much exaggerated? *

* That no one may think this over-stated, let the following quotation from Murray's large grammar be duly weighed: "On the right management of the emphasis depends the life of pronunciation. If no emphasis

Again, what is the *perfection* of a *written* character? Is it not *facility of formation* combined with *distinctness?* In this respect the Roman character is unimitated and inimitable. The form of the *written* letters is not so different from that of the *printed,* as to demand much additional time in mastering it, and that little time is *more* than compensated for by the almost incredible *speed* with which it can be employed in practice.

There are, besides, other *peculiar* advantages. Men may contrive to disguise the fact as they may, nevertheless it is not the less certain, that, though *nominally* or *theoretically* the *printed* and *written* Oriental character is the *same, practically* there is a difference as wide as, and often wider than, between the printed and written Roman character. The truth is, that that form which answers best in print is far too stiff, angular, or rounded, to suit the *speed* that is so very *desirable* in *writing.* Hence it happens that a Hindu or Mussulman, when he writes his own alphabetic character with any degree of quickness, almost invariably finds himself constrained to depart from the precision and regularity of the printed form, yea, to depart so far from it, that his writing is often illegible to all but himself, and not unfrequently even to himself. More than this: as there is no acknowledged standard of written character, one man departs from the printed standard

be placed on any words, not only will discourse be rendered heavy and lifeless, but the meaning often left ambiguous. If the emphasis be placed wrong, we shall pervert and confound the meaning wholly. To give a common instance, such a simple question as this, 'Do you ride to town to-day?' is capable of no fewer than four different acceptations, according as the emphasis is differently placed on the words. If it be pronounced thus: 'Do *you* ride to town to-day,' the answer may naturally be, 'No, we send a servant in our stead.' If thus: 'Do you *ride* to town to-day?' Answer, 'No, we intend to walk.' 'Do you ride *to town* to-day?' 'No, we ride into the country.' 'Do you ride to town *to-day?*' 'No, but we shall go to-morrow.'" Now if so much of the meaning and force, and often so much of the beauty and propriety, of an expression depend on the emphatic word, is it not of the highest importance that it should be distinctly marked? From the example now given may not the most obtuse understanding perceive with what matchless ease, simplicity, and effect this can be done by means of italic letters? and may we not challenge all the Orientalists in the world to concoct, if they can, an expedient which, with the *same* ease, simplicity, and effect, can single out an emphatic term or expression in any of the Indian languages, if written or printed in the Indian characters?

in one way, and another in another. Hence necessarily arises a grotesque medley of characters, a "rudis indigestaque moles" of varying forms. Each man, in fact, may have his own system of written character, and there may be as many systems as there are writers. How inextricable then must be the resulting confusion!

Compared with this unavoidable chaos, how orderly and complete is the Anglo-Roman system! Here all is regularity and harmony. There is one universally acknowledged standard of written, as well as of printed, character, — even that which unites, in the highest possible degree, quickness in forming and distinctness when formed. And this standard being established by common consent, the deviations of particular individuals therefrom being only variations more or less minute from what is fixed and uniform, they never do, they never can, lose their similitude or identity with the original. One man can never fail to understand his own writing: and all men must be able to decipher the writing of all men. So far, therefore, from the *distinct written form* being an "inconvenience" in practice, it must be hailed as one of the greatest and happiest "conveniences" which the wit of man ever suggested, or his ingenuity contrived.

6. It is asserted that "all the useful books, that have been and will be published in the native characters before such a change takes place, must be reprinted in the Roman;" and then follows the wondering exclamation, "What an immense expense will be incurred in the reprinting of such works as Babu Rámcomal Sen's English and Bengálí Dictionary, Dr. Carey's quarto Dictionary of the Bengálí and English!" &c.

Surely there is an utter fallacy or oversight in this objection. How stands the case? Is the printing of *one* edition of a book like the opening of a perennial spring, which, when it once begins to flow, will continue to pour forth its exhaustless waters *for ever?* If it is, we grant that the printing of another edition in the same or in a different character may be said to incur an *extra* expense, large or small, according to the size of the work. But it is not so: one edition, consisting as it does of a limited number of copies, is obviously exhaustible, and when all the copies are sold it is of course exhausted. What then must be done? What else can be done, but to print a *new* edition, in order to meet the growing wants of a rising community? And if a *new* edition of a good book *must* be called for in the natural order of events, *may* it not be printed in one alphabetic character as well as another, without incurring an "immense" additional expense, or any additional expense at all? *May* not even the expense of such a reprint be vastly less than that of the original edition?

But it is added that the Indian letters, in consequence of the inherent vowel and particular combinations, may be compressed into as small a space as the Roman. It is needless to argue this point abstractly. It resolves itself into a simple matter of fact; and the best answer that can be given is, to advise the reader to look back, and, inspecting the specimens supplied in this article, let the testimony of the visual organs decide the question in debate.

7. It is objected that, by the proposed substitution, we deprive the present generation of the means of mental and moral improvement.

This is founded on a total misconception of our design. It is not in our power, nor, if it were, would we ever propose, to suppress all the existing publications, and supply no more in the same form. We know that there are hundreds and thousands of adults acquainted with the native character, who can never be expected to learn any other. And *suddenly* to deprive them of works which they can peruse, and the perusal of which is calculated to elevate and purify their minds, were either a species of inquisitorial cruelty or a sort of wicked madness. Enthusiastic and visionary as we are reputed to be, we have not yet suspended the functions of sober reason. Our object is, by all lawful means, to disseminate the knowledge of a system which we verily believe to be fraught with blessings innumerable to this benighted land. With this view, books in every department of religion, literature, and science will be immediately prepared and published on the improved plan. The mode of reading these with intelligence will be taught to those over whom our influence extends, and every reasonable encouragement will be held out to all who desire to propagate the knowledge of it. By these means the superiority of the reformed system will be *gradually* perceived, and its advantages duly appreciated; till at length it may be divulged to the extent of absorbing all the prevailing systems. In other words, the native alphabets retiring before the Roman, and being naturally displaced by its incumbent and increasing weight, will eventually, without violence or alarm, disappear from off the land.

But, during the *intermediate process*, books will be supplied to the adherents of the old systems that are to sink fast into decrepitude and final annihilation. That is, for a season there will be two contiguous and contemporaneous streams, the old and the new; the former decreasing, and the latter increasing, in volume; the one contracting itself within narrower bounds, and the other enlarging its borders; till at last *both* channels become *one*, on whose broad and expanded bosom shall flow the fresh waters that are to scatter fertility and abundance over a dry and parched land. Or, to drop the metaphor, we shall, for some time to come, have to furnish two sets of books, the one in the native, and the other in the Roman character. With the former we shall supply chiefly the aged; with the latter, chiefly the young, especially those who learn English. Let then the School-Book Society, the Bible Society, the Tract Society, &c., provide themselves with books of the two kinds now mentioned, wherewith to supply these two classes of readers; and, as the *new* order of things gains ground, the copies in Roman character will abound more and more, till they gradually supersede those printed in the native form. And when great numbers of the reading population come to understand and prefer the new arrangement, then may the Sumachar Durpun, and other journals especially designed for natives exchange their Indian for the Roman garb; and then may we witness the sublime spectacle of all books, pamphlets, magazines, and journals unitedly pouring forth floods of knowledge, through one consistent and harmonious medium, over every region of the largest and fairest empire under the sun! *

* That cavillers may no longer taunt us with the sneering question:—"Having now settled your alphabetic scheme, what use are ye going to

The foregoing are all the objections which we have seen advanced; and whether in themselves, and especially in contradistinction to the manifold advantages pointed out in a former paper, they can be allowed to possess "the weight of a feather," we leave to the candid reader to judge. Some, as fully anticipated, have again sounded the tocsin of "the letters, the letters, what is the learning of letters? A trifle, a trifle, a mere trifle." Reasons which have *not* yet been

make of it?" it may be stated, that we have ***already begun*** to apply it to its legitimate purpose. The following works are ***now*** in preparation, and some of them ***already passing through the press;*** viz.

1. The New Testament, English and Bengálí. The Bengálí version, in Roman character: to be published in single Gospels.
2. The New Testament, English and Hindustáni. Do. Do.
3. Woollaston's Grammar, Bengálí and Hindustáni.
4. Moral Precepts, English and Hindustáni verse.
5. Scientific Dialogues, &c. &c.
6. The Elementary English works, or Primers, prepared for the General Assembly's Institution, Calcutta, viz.

No. I. Instructor, interlinear Bengálí version, in Bengálí character, to be afterwards followed by the Roman.

No. II. Do. literal version in Bengálí character, and free version in Roman.

No. III. Do entirely in Roman character.

We trust it will now be seen that we are in right earnest, and that our scheme is not to evaporate in mere words. And as our earnest desire is to give offence to none, but do good to all, we sincerely hope that many who are now lukewarm, or even decidedly opposed to us, may yet be conciliated, and become our staunchest friends and supporters.

Since we wish, with the least possible delay, to translate Primers, Grammars, Histories, &c., into every language and dialect in the presidency of Bengal, we would respectfully solicit the assistance of such European and native gentlemen as are competent to the task of translation. If any one who is qualified will kindly undertake to translate one or more works into the language or dialect with which he is acquainted, he will be immediately supplied with a copy on application. When completed, the work will be printed free of expense to him, and he will be furnished ***gratis*** with a large number of copies for distribution. Already have some gentlemen promptly volunteered their valuable services; and others, who cannot lend their aid in translation, have decisively expressed their good will, by forwarding liberal donations to defray part of the expense that must, in the first instance, be necessarily incurred.

Besides providing translations of useful works, and printing these in Roman character, it is our intention, if supported by an enlightened public, to select every Oriental book that is worth anything, and turn it into the new orthography, i. e. Romanise it. In this way we may expect that the good, or at least the harmless, will help to swell the accumulating body of sound literature; while the bad and worthless will be abandoned to neglect, and left to perish as they deserve.

The entire series of native works and translations, we may designate "***The Romanised Series of Oriental Literature.***"

controverted were formerly given for dissenting *in toto* from the burden of this song. And if farther confirmation be required, it may now be furnished. Some years ago, when controversy ran high respecting the merits of Dr. Gilchrist's philological labours, these found an advocate in the Edinburgh Review. The Quarterly, on the other hand, with its tremulous dread of all change, treated the learned Orientalist with lofty disdain. But in spite of the most deadly hostility, the current of change has set in, and who can now arrest its progress? Even the Quarterly, which still doggedly clings to many antiquated errors, has in some things changed. On the present question even it has let in some gleams of light. In the last No., or the No. for October, there is an able Review of Grimm's New German Grammar. In his elaborate introduction, this author, in the genuine German style, has a lengthy dissertation on the origin and descent of the ancient European languages, the Gothic, the German, the Saxon, the Celtic, the Sclavonic, &c. Now mark the Reviewer's words:—

"The first 600 pages of the book are taken up with a minute examination of the letters in each of the dialects which come under consideration, *and here we must commend the example Grimm has shown in abolishing the use of the Gothic characters.* There is no more reason for our employing them, than for our using the Roman capitals in printing Latin; the common type was equally unknown to both nations, and the use of the uncouth Gothic letters, both increases the difficulty to the reader, and adds to the expense of printing, without affording any countervailing advantage. *Indeed, the example might be extended even to the Oriental languages with very great benefit; if, for instance, the Sanskrit were printed in European characters, we are convinced that a large class of persons would acquire at least its rudiments, who are now deterred from similar studies by the formidable difficulty of a new character looking them in the face at the very outset.*"

With such a respectable authority as this on our side, we can afford to allow objectors to regale themselves undisturbed with the music of their own favourite fancies.

Having now developed our plan, our *expository* task is ended. Henceforward "action" shall be our watchword. We have a field before us wider and nobler far than any which aroused the ambition of the Eternal City in the meridian of her glory: but, oh, how vastly different our object in entering it! Where *she* would have marched at the head of conquering legions, satisfied when terror established the invincibility of her arms, *we* go forth with the messengers of peace, the heralds of true wisdom, satisfied only when happiness, harmony, and love shall proclaim the invincible kindness of Truth. And those treasures of knowledge which surpass a thousandfold what Rome in her proudest days ever possessed, we shall disperse through the medium of *forms* which her inventive genius has supplied. And thus, along distant streams and fertile valleys, never visited by the Imperial Eagle, shall the name of "Roman" flourish in connexion with the mental emancipation of millions, when all other stately monuments that recall the remembrance of Roman greatness shall have crumbled into dust.

ALPHA.

P.S.—It has been already stated, that during the last month several friendly communications have been received respecting the substitution of the Roman in place of the Indian alphabets, and our "scheme" for accomplishing that end. Amongst these is one from a gentleman in the Upper Provinces, well acquainted with the Oriental languages, and successfully engaged in the instruction of native youth, on which accounts we deem his remarks particularly entitled to attention. Besides this, his letter briefly alludes to certain advantages attending the proposed substitution that wholly escaped our notice; we have, therefore, much satisfaction in making from it the following weighty extract. After various introductory remarks, the author thus proceeds:—

"I entirely agree with you, not because the idea is yours, but because the measure is fraught with incalculable advantages to India. It is, I really and truly believe, the most effectual mode of *any*, of diffusing knowledge, *both* Asiatic and European, among the people at large. The grand barrier to improvement in this country has been the want of *printing*, or the being obliged to impart knowledge through the slow, limited, difficult process of manuscripts. It is a most expensive and Herculean labour, to *print* in the Arabic, or Persian, or Deva Nágarí character. It would be quite as easy as printing any English work, to print books and newspapers, &c., in Roman characters, though the language be different. The benefits of *printing* their *own* books in this way would be a thousandfold, but the benefits of printing in the Urdu dialect, and Roman characters, the substance of our literature, are quite incalculable. Nothing could impart a greater impulse to civilisation. Every gentleman almost might then publish translations; for there are but few indeed who cannot explain in *Urdu* their thoughts, or the substance of any written work. Epistolary correspondence between Europeans and natives (now next to impossible, owing to the necessity of employing a third person as the medium of communication) would become as common as correspondence is between two Europeans or two natives in their respective tongues. A judge might then read all the proceedings *himself*, and write his orders *himself*. Public functionaries would then perform, singly and unaided, twice the work which they now cannot perform without the assistance of three or four natives. It would lead to the adoption of thousands of European *words* in the Urdu books and compositions, and thus the native literature would be enriched most rapidly: but there is no end to the advantages I anticipate from this most ingenious plan." &c. &c.

(12.)

ADDRESS TO THE PEOPLE OF HINDÚSTÁN.

By a True Friend to the Natives.

All who read newspapers, those winged messengers of intelligence, now know that a proposal has lately been made to write Sanskṛit, Persian, Bangálí, and other Indian languages in the letters of the English alphabet. But many do not exactly understand the *nature* and *object* of the proposal. These, therefore, it is proper briefly to explain, and let the wise and intelligent among the natives of India lend an attentive ear.

First. The *nature* of the proposal is simply this: That in writing and printing words, sentences, or books, in Sanskṛit, Persian, Bangálí, &c., English characters should be used for *all,* instead of Deva-Nágarí, Persian, or Bangálí characters. Thus, instead of using the word किसी in Nágarí characters, we might write kisí in English characters: instead of باپسے in Persian, bápse in English characters: instead of পিতাকে in Bangálí, pitáke in English characters: and so, in like manner, might we write *all* other words in *every* Indian language in English characters. In this way, *one* alphabet, i.e. *the English,* might answer the purpose of *all the Indian alphabets.*

Now, why should this proposal appear *strange* to the natives of India? Have not they themselves long been accustomed to write the words of one language in letters belonging to another? Is not this fact known to all except Harís, Majurs, Dhángars, &c., who are so miserably ignorant that they know nothing? For example: has not the Persian character been often practically used in representing Indian words, particularly in the Upper and Western Provinces? And on the other hand, has not the Nágarí character been employed in expressing Persian and Arabic terms? The Urdu, which is a compound of Persian and Indian words, has been represented indifferently by Persian or Nágarí letters. And if so, why not this, and other Indian languages, by the English? Besides, do not Bráhman Pundits, the Kúlin editor of the Chundrikā, the Mahá Rája Kálíkṛishan Báhádur, and all other learned and respectable natives, write Sanskṛit words and slokes in Bangálí characters? And if so, why might they not write Sanskṛit slokes in English characters? the characters of the language of the rulers of this land, a language which is dignified also by possessing boundless treasures of knowledge to make men good and wise, great and powerful?

To show how easily this might be done, we here present one or two specimens:—

SANSKRIT SLOKES.

In Deva-Nágarí Characters.

अनेकसंशयोच्छेदि परोक्षार्थस्य दर्शकं ।
सर्व्वस्य लोचनं शास्त्रं यस्य नास्त्यन्ध एव सः ॥

In Bangálí.

অনেকসংশয়োচ্ছেদি পরোক্ষার্থস্য দর্শকং ।
সর্ব্বস্য লোচনং শাস্ত্রং যস্য নাস্ত্যন্ধ এব সঃ ॥

In Roman.

Aneka-sanshayochchhedi parokshárthasya darshakang
Sarvasya lochanang shástrang yasya nástyandha eva sah.

Meaning.

He who is not possessed of learning, which dispels many doubts, points out hidden things, and is the organ of sight to all, is even as a blind man.

STANZA.

Arabic.

اِصْنَعْ بِنَا مَا اَنْتَ لَهُ اَهْلُهُ
وَ لَا تَفْعَلْ بِنَا مَا نَحْنُ لَهُ اَهْلُهُ

Persian.

اصنع بنا ما انت له اهله
و لا تفعل بنا ما نحن له اهله

Iṣna biná má anta lahu ahluhu,
Wa lá tafal biná má naḥnu lahu ahluhu.

Meaning.

Do Thou unto us what is worthy of Thyself; but do not to us what we deserve.

Second. The *object* of the proposal may be briefly stated to be *the benefit of the people.*

Some through ignorance, and others from sinister motives, have declared that the object is to perplex and injure the natives by destroying their vernacular languages. Now the opposite of this is the *true* statement. *One grand object is to benefit the people by preserving, enriching, and facilitating the study of the native languages.* Instead of perplexing people's minds, the proposal of substituting *one* in place of a *multiplicity* of different alphabets, is the only sure way of delivering them out of all perplexity.

If a Hindu* has several *khejur* † trees in his garden, and if his neighbour proposes to cut them down and plant a *ním* ‡

* Wherever Hindu occurs in these remarks, it denotes a native of Hindustán, whether Hindus or Mussalmáns.

† A tree that produces an inferior sort of fruit.

‡ A tree whose fruit cannot be eaten.

tree in their place,— this proposal must be injurious. But if his neighbour proposes to cut down the *khejur* trees, and plant a very large *mango* tree, which will every year be covered with the finest fruit, in their place,—would this proposal be injurious? No, all will unanimously reply, it would not be attended with injury, but real benefit. Precisely similar is the case in regard to the present proposal. It is not intended to supplant the native alphabets by the introduction of another of inferior value, for that would not be good; but it is proposed to supplant these alphabets by the introduction of one that shall secure *numberless advantages*, which all the rest combined do *not* possess,—and must not this be pronounced good? Surely it must. And in order that no one may any longer impose upon you in this matter, some of the benefits of the proposal will now be stated. We speak to the wise and intelligent among the Hindus. Let the wise and intelligent judge.

1. In most of the Indian alphabets, there are about fifty letters, with innumerable compounds, which greatly perplex and retard learners. Now all these can be perfectly represented by 24 simple English letters, with the occasional use of these three simple marks, (′) (.) (-). This, it is plain, must make the progress of every learner more easy and rapid.

2. All who wish to be useful in business, renowned for learning, or exalted to high situations and responsible offices, must learn the English language. If then, all learn to read and write the English alphabet from the time of infancy, when learning their own mother tongue, much valuable time and much useless trouble must be saved in acquiring a knowledge of the English language.

3. Besides learning English, great numbers of Hindus are obliged to learn several Indian languages. But it is well known that much valuable time is consumed by the majority of mankind in learning the *new* characters of any language. And a vast deal of time is spent in acquiring the *same facility* and *speed* in reading and writing these characters, as is enjoyed in reading and writing those with which they are long familiar. Now whole months or even whole years of un-

profitable labour may be saved by the universal introduction of the English characters.

4. The Sanskṛit is the common root of all the Indian dialects. But at present each dialect has letters of a different figure; and this leads the Hindus of one province to suppose that the Hindus of another province speak a totally different language. Consequently, they are apt to regard each other as strangers and foreigners. Now, if all the Indian dialects were presented in the *same English character*, it would be *seen* and *felt* that the natives are not divided into so many sections of foreigners to each other; that they have *all fundamentally* the *same* language; and that, without much difficulty, a community of interest and a beneficial reciprocation of thought might be effected to an extent at present unknown, and from the repulsive aspect of so many written characters deemed utterly impracticable.

5. It follows from this statement, that as almost all Indian dialects are derived from the Sanskṛit, when a native thoroughly masters one dialect, he is already acquainted with the meaning of numberless words in every other. If all were, therefore, represented in the same English character, instead of learning one, or two, or three languages, as at present, a Pandit, Shástrí, or Munshí might in the course of his lifetime master *all* the languages of Hindustán. Surely, that proposal which would lead to the accumulation of so much learning in the mind of one person must be superexcellent.

6. By the admirable contrivance of Capital and Italic letters in the English alphabet, the facility of reading with propriety, and referring to names and particular passages, is mightily increased; but, from the nature and shape of the Indian letters, this contrivance cannot be imitated. If then English letters be substituted in their place, the thousands and the tens of thousands of Hindu youth may have the unspeakable benefit of this simple and beautiful contrivance in learning to read and write their own vernacular languages. Stops in all their several gradations, marks of interrogation and admiration, inverted commas, and other aids to the correct reading and understanding of books and manuscripts, which the native literature at present either does not possess at all,

or possesses in a very imperfect degree, will be at the same time introduced; and this, it must be acknowledged, will save time, increase knowledge, and lead to the native languages becoming fixed and cultivated much sooner than it would be possible for them to become without such helps.

7. It is a fact that, from the intricacy, the complexity, of most of the Indian characters, it is utterly impossible to reduce them to so small a size as the Roman may be, without rendering them altogether indistinct, or even illegible. In this way, twice the quantity of paper, and nearly twice the quantity of binding materials and labour, must be lavished for nought. In other words, books printed in the Indian characters will cost *nearly double* what the same books would cost if printed in the English characters. And must not Hindu parents rejoice at the success of a plan that promises to save *half* the amount which they would otherwise have to pay for books in the education of their children? And must not the proposal that would save *so many rupees to every Hindu parent annually* be one of the *best* ever announced in this land?

8. As the multiplicity of different characters creates numberless difficulties in the way of studying the native languages, the mines of learning which those are said to possess remain unexplored from age to age. Consequently, the treasures of knowledge contained in them continue hidden and concealed, not only from Europeans, but from natives themselves. No native, not even a Bhaṭṭáchárjya, though so learned as to deserve the epithet of Mahá-mahopádhyá, can ever expect to know a tenth part of the lucubrations of his ancestors, so long as there is such a variety of written characters. And if even a Hindu Pandit cannot know a tenth part of the strange and rare histories, philologies, rhetorics, logics, metaphysics, astronomies, geographies, and theologies, which have been accumulated by the sages of Hindustán, will not unlearned natives and the Pandits of other countries begin to suspect that there are no such stores in existence? How then can such suspicions be removed? How can it be shown to all people, in every land, that the Hindus possess such wonderful piles of written shasters, which at present lie concealed from

view, behind thick jungles of new and strangely varied characters? What plan can be imagined half so well adapted to this purpose as that now proposed, viz. to transcribe the whole of their writings, if the Hindus so wish it, into *one* uniform character that is *already universally known*—known by all the civilised and learned in Europe, Asia, Africa, and America?

If they were to do this, the Hindus would only be following the example of the English themselves. Formerly the English language was written in various peculiar characters, which were known by the names of Saxon, German text, &c., but by degrees all these were discarded, and the Roman character (which is the one at present used in writing English) was adopted in place of them all. Now do you suppose that the existing English literature was obscured by this change? On the contrary, as the language now became transferred into a character which was universally current throughout the civilised world, the general knowledge of it was greatly promoted; and to this day, when it is desired to bring into notice books or manuscripts in any of the old characters, they are as a matter of course turned into the Roman characters, and they then become at once accessible to the whole world. If, therefore, anybody should hereafter object to the plan of changing the character, let this be your answer, *that the most civilised and prosperous nations in the world have already tried it, and that the experiment has been attended with complete success.* What ground of confidence as to what is good can we have so sure as the experience of the wise?

Instead, therefore, of obscuring the Hindu literature, and tarnishing the merits of Hindu authors, as some ignorantly suppose, this plan is the best possible for bringing the whole range of Hindu literature to light, and loading the Hindu authors with such honours as they deserve. The change of characters produces no change in words, dates, or names. All the words of the Indian languages, all historical dates, and all proper names of persons, places, and events, remain unchanged, and so far as this plan is concerned, unchangeable. If, then, the Hindus really wish that they should no longer be accounted ignorant or barbarous, if they really wish that all nations on earth should know what prodigious masses of singular writings they possess, they ought immediately to combine in one grand association, and resolve to write, print, and publish all their books in English characters. If they do this, the whole civilised world may know the extent of their merits.

That no one may presume to doubt the truth of this representation, we refer to the No. of the Quarterly Review published in London, in the month of October, last year. This work, as many of the learned Hindus already know, is one of the highest literary authorities, not only in Europe, but in the whole world. Now hear what the Quarterly Review says. "If the Sanskṛit were printed in European (meaning Roman or English) characters, we are convinced that a large class of persons would acquire at least its rudiments, who are now deterred from similar studies by the formidable appearance of a new character looking them in the face at the very outset." Here then is a glorious field of ambition open to the wise and learned among the Hindus. If they transcribe all their works in English characters, their literature, science, and religion will be known throughout Europe, and every country of the civilised world.

Who then is so blind, as not to discern the marvellous excellencies of the plan now proposed?

The foregoing are *some* of the manifold advantages which would attend the substitution of the English in place of the Indian alphabets. They may be thus briefly summed up:—

1. The substitution of the English alphabet would facilitate the progress of a Hindu in learning his own vernacular language.

2. It would facilitate his progress in learning the English language.

3. It would facilitate his progress in learning several other languages, necessary to the carrying on of business.

4. It would break down the barriers that at present separate the Hindus from one another, and lead to free communication, and a beneficial interchange of sentiment throughout the land.

5. It would enable Hindus of ordinary ability and per-

severance to master almost all the languages of India, and so put it in their power to benefit its countless tribes and families.

6. It would greatly assist young and old in reading, writing, &c., any language, with precision and propriety.

7. It would save a great deal of money, to every Hindu parent, by greatly diminishing the price of books.

8. It would bring to light the entire mass of Hindu literature, science, and theology, and make the claims of Hindu authors known to all the learned in the four quarters of the world.

More advantages might easily be enumerated; but are not these amply sufficient to prove the excellency of the present proposal? Are not these more than sufficient to demonstrate that it is fraught with the richest blessings to the people of Hindustán? And if so, however unintentionally, are not those the enemies of the people who object to and oppose it? And are not those the best friends of the people, who are its most strenuous advocates?

We speak unto you as unto wise; judge ye.

A TRUE FRIEND TO THE NATIVES.

(13.)

MR. H. T. PRINSEP'S PAPER ON THE ADAPTATION OF THE ROMAN ALPHABET TO THE ORTHOGRAPHY OF ORIENTAL LANGUAGES, AND THE SUPERIORITY OF DR. GILCHRIST'S SYSTEM.

(*Extracted from the* JOURNAL OF THE ASIATIC SOCIETY *for June*, 1834.)

All who have devoted themselves to the acquirement of any of the languages of India must have experienced, in the irreconcilable difference of the alphabets of the East and West, a stumbling-block in the porch of their studies, and a source of constant doubt and difficulty whenever the occasion has arisen for expressing in the letters of their mother tongue sounds and vocables belonging to any of those languages. It is the scholar's object to write the words so that they shall be read with a correct pronunciation by the uninitiated, and at the same time show the true spelling of the original. He seeks therefore the letters of known pronunciation that come nearest, not only to the sounds he desires to represent, but likewise to the letters used in the language from which the word is taken. Unfortunately it is not always easy to find letters that will answer this double purpose, and the difficulty is much increased by the circumstance, that all the vowels and several of the consonants in use have more than one sound in the same language of Europe, and some of them half a dozen sounds at least, if the varieties of all the countries which use the Roman alphabet are taken into account. What then was to be done when India fell into European hands, and the necessity arose for continually writing Indian words in books and public correspondence? Every one at first of course had to decide for himself, and unfortunately they who commenced the work of writing Asiatic names in the alphabets of Europe were not scholars. At present we shall confine ourselves to the proceedings of our own countrymen in this respect, putting out of view all reference to the modes of writing adopted in France and Germany and elsewhere, and those in particular which have been adopted recently, in consequence of the efforts making by the literati of Europe to bring into vogue the Sanskrit language and its literature, at the very time that the half-informed of our countrymen are seeking to discredit both here.

It would appear that they who first had occasion to write in English the names or words of the East, bethought themselves of the sounds in that language which came nearest to those they desired to represent, and spelled the words accordingly: thus *sipahee* was very generally spelt *seapoy*, doubtless from the similarity of its sound to the well-known word *teapoy*, and in the jargon of the day, *Surajood-doula* was corrupted into *Sir Roger Dowler*, and *Allahabad* became known as the *Isle of Bats*. Many absurdities of this description might be pointed out were it our object to seek them: even Governor Holwell, though himself a Bengalee scholar, has in his printed tracts, *Morattors—Shaw Zadda—Genana*

Patsha—Shaw Allum—Phirmaund—Metre (for *Mitur*), &c. &c. He had also *Sou Raja Dowla,* which is nearly as ridiculous as the English knighthood of that Nuwab.

This method of writing from the ear did very well so long as it was the half-informed addressing the absolutely ignorant. The transmutations were precisely of the same description as those of which we find examples, not only in the Greek and Roman methods of writing Teutonic and Asiatic names, but in the Leghorn and Cales of the old English writers of the past century, the Naples and Venice of the present day, and the Ecosse and Galles and Espagne, into which the less pronounceable native names of those countries have been softened in France.

But as the knowledge of the languages of the East extended, and they who had to write became themselves well acquainted with the true pronunciation and orthography of the words and names they were using, and felt likewise that they were addressing others as well informed upon the subject as themselves, they began to seek the means of spelling true, that is, of using in English corresponding letters for those used in the language from which the word or name might be taken. The Persian and Arabic are languages that have long been known in Europe, and the force and power of each of the letters of those alphabets have accordingly been attempted to be expressed in various ways, according to the native country of the interpreter; but the first we believe who accurately gave to the public the Nagree, Devanagree, and Bengalee alphabets was Mr. HALHED in the Preface to his version of the Code of Hindoo Law, compiled under the orders of Warren Hastings in 1775. His consonants correspond very nearly with those of Sir William Jones's alphabet, except that he makes no distinction between the hard and soft *d*, *t*, *dh*, and *th*. The short vowel अ he writes with a short *e*, the letter इ with a double *ĕe*, bearing similarly the short mark: ए, is expressed by *ăe*; ऐ he writes *ī* and औ *ōu*. Every vowel according to this system had its long or short mark above it, which was very inconvenient either for printing or writing.

When the Asiatic Society was established, Sir WILLIAM JONES saw the necessity of introducing a consistent mode of writing all Indian words. Not satisfied with the system of Mr. Halhed, he devised the alphabet that bears his name, and is still used by that learned body in its Proceedings; but neither the influence nor the reputation of this great linguist was sufficient to procure for his alphabet the general adoption so desirable, and indeed so essential, to the purpose he had in view. It continued as a sort of Devanagree for the learned *par excellence;* a style of writing to be reverenced and respected, but not imitated. In spite of every endeavour to recommend the Society's alphabet for universal use, the business of the country continued to be conducted either in the jargon spelling first adopted from similarity of sound, or with the *ad libitum* improvements of those who, knowing the correct spelling of the original, adopted the letters they thought best calculated to express the true sound of the words properly pronounced. It is now near fifty years since the attempt was first made to introduce this obvious benefit of a consistent and correct alphabet, and yet Sir William Jones's mode of writing has gained no ground in India, whatever may have been its fate elsewhere. What can have been the reason for this? Does not the fact itself afford irrefragable evidence that there must be some inherent defect in the system that induced its rejection, and led to others being preferred. There it was, recommended by the Asiatic Society, composed of the principal civil servants, and of all in the military, clerical, and medical professions, who were entitled by knowledge of the subject, or by situation, to take the lead in such a matter. There was this Society, periodically putting forth its volumes, and all its principal members publishing their works according to the orthography of the illustrious founder; yet no one out of the pale, and not all of those within it, could be brought to spell names, in their correspondence, as the Society spelt them. For fifty years this tree of Sir William Jones's planting has been stationary, or has grown like the aloe, repulsive and disagreeable, living still but putting forth no branches and yielding no fruit. Who after this can say that there must not be something in this system repugnant to the ideas and preconceived notions of those whose language is English? The powers and pronunciations given to the different letters are manifestly not such as have been recognised and adopted as just and appropriate by those who read and write that language. Another system has gained ground in its stead, and to its prejudice, and this in spite of the great names of Jones and Colebrooke and Wilson, whose adherence to the antiquated style has prevented its sinking into absolute disuse and oblivion. Let us inquire then what is this other system, and what the claims it possesses to the preference of the unlearned.

Towards the close of Lord Cornwallis's government, Dr. JOHN BORTHWICK GILCHRIST produced his Dictionary and Grammar of the Hindoostanee language, and, as matter of necessity, prefaced both by explaining the force of all the letters in use in the language, and the corresponding vowels and consonants of the Roman alphabet by which he proposed to express them. The difference between his system and that of Sir William Jones lies entirely in the vowels: the short unexpressed letter अ which Mr. Halhed wrote *ĕ* was written *a* by Sir William Jones and *u* by Dr. Gilchrist; the *ĕe* and *e̅e̅* of Halhed, *i ì* of Sir W. Jones, were rendered *i* and *ee* by Gilchrist; the *ŏo* *o̅o̅* of Halhed, *u ū* of Jones, were expressed by *oo;* and the *ī ai* of the two former systems by *y,* corrected but not improved to *ue;* and, lastly, the *ŏu* of Halhed and *au* of Jones by *ou* corrected to *uo.*

The more taking and popular part of this system lies evidently in the use of the short *u* instead of *a,* for the silent unexpressed inherent letter of the languages of India: people could not be brought to write *bat* for the sound of *but, tab* for *tub,* and *patee* for *putee.* Having the choice, therefore, they discarded the letter which never in any of the words of any of the languages within their knowledge had the sound it was proposed to give to it. The adoption of *oo,* instead of Sir W. Jones's *u,* followed as a necessary consequence of the appropriation of *u* to the short sound; and *au* for the sound of *ow* in how was so unnatural, that it was gladly discarded for *ou.*

It does not appear that the Government took any part, until very recently, in promoting the use of one or other of these systems: they had each therefore a fair field and no favour for thirty years at least. During the whole of that period the knowledge of the languages was extending, and the old jargon was disappearing from all the public departments, finding only a sanctuary and stronghold that bade defiance to all reform within the precincts of the Supreme Court. The issue was in a decided leaning from the first to the system of Gilchrist. This has now been that of all official correspondence for fifteen or twenty years at least, whereas it will not be found that the orthography of Sir William Jones has taken root in any single department, pertinaciously as certain learned individuals of high authority have adhered to it.

In 1822, the design was conceived of forming an accurate record in the English language and character of all the land tenures of the country. It was felt to be necessary to determine upon some alphabet or system for the conversion of names correctly, prior to the formation of these registers, and then first did the Government officers indicate any system under authority for preference. The merits of each method were fully weighed and considered, prior to the determination, and the scheme of Gilchrist was adopted, simplified by the rejection of some of his quaint methods of expressing the nicer distinctions of sound. This alphabet was circulated, and great progress was made all over the country in producing registers in which the names of persons and places and properties were so written, that no one could hereafter find difficulty in writing them back into any given character upon bare inspection.

Contemporaneously with this measure, and as part of the same scheme, revenue surveys were put in hand, and maps on a large scale were constructed, in which the name of every place or object was accurately entered according to the same system. Up to this time no attempt had ever been made to make this grand improvement in the geography of India. The maps of Bengal were copied to the letter from the surveys of Rennell made in the era of jargon, and though better spelt than most of the documents of that period, yet still partaking largely of the miscellaneous mode of writing so liable to mislead. All the surveyors subsequently employed had been left to pick up the names of places by the ear, and it had never been made an instruction to them to ascertain how they were written in any dialect or language of India, and to transfer them according to system into their maps. The surveyors too, unfortunately, were very seldom scholars. In order to show the consequences of this neglect, and to expose at once the absurdity of trusting to the ear in a matter of this kind, an extract is annexed* from a map of the Dooab, compiled not ten years ago, and now in our possession: it bears the official signature of the surveyor-general of the day, and professes to be from the best materials then in the archives of that department. In this extract it will be seen that the well known road from Cawnpoor (Kanhpoor) to Ukburpoor is laid down double, being taken apparently from two routes made with compasses or theodolites varying in a small degree, so as to give a different direction; and the copyists of the surveyor-general's department have not discovered that the routes are the same, *because all the names are spelled differently.* There are regularly—

Kuttra,	Gittera,
Chichehree,	Chichindy,
Bhysour,	Bhysawn, Bheisawn, (Bhenour ?)
Fattip^{r}.	Futtehp^{r}.
Reneea,	Runneah,
Oomrun,	Oomeron,

with sundry other names, till one road comes to Akberpoor and the other to Akbarpoor, the relative distances of all these places being the same. Like absurdities might be shown in many maps similarly constructed from materials in which the names have been set down by the ear, without the observance of any system of spelling. It is no fault of the map-compiler, if he has not recognised Chicheree to be the same place as

* See Plate.

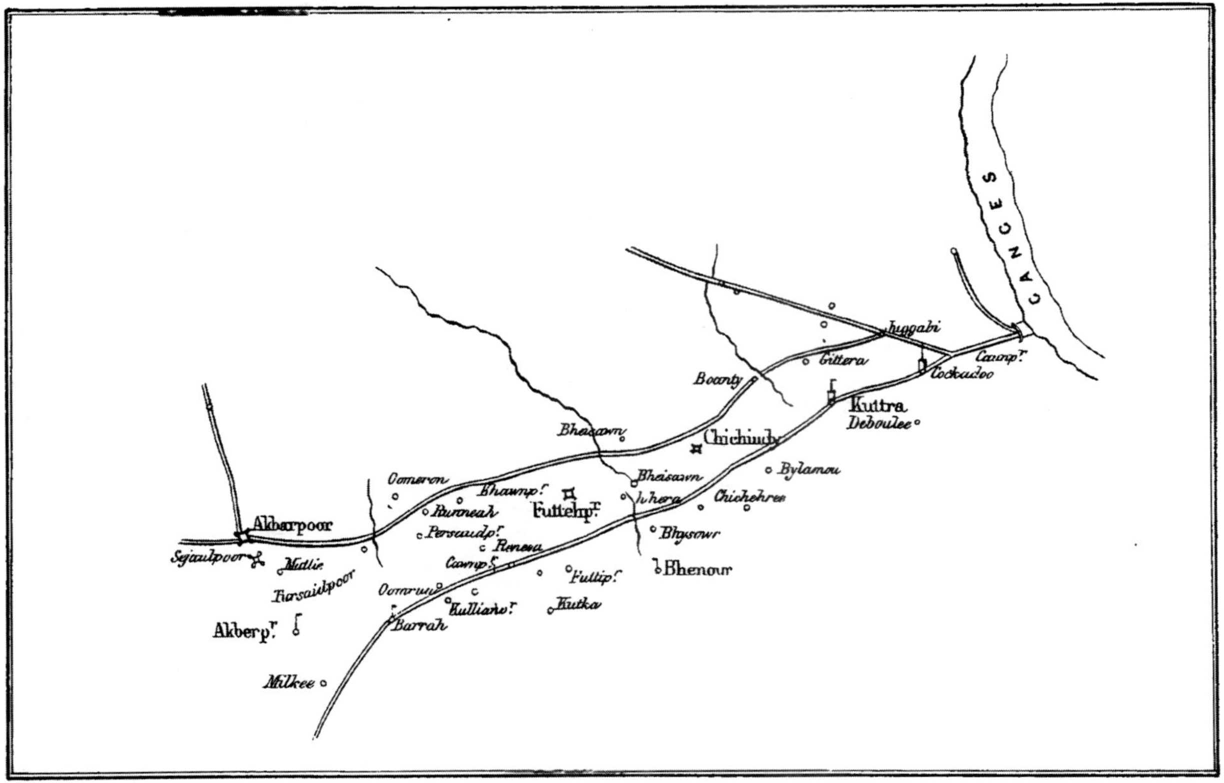

GANGES
Juggabi
Gittera
Caump:r
Cockadoo
Boanty
Kuttra
Deboulee
Bheaawn
Chichiuchy
Bylamou
Bhaisawn
Oomeron
Khaump:r
Juhera
Chichehree
Futtehp:r
Akbarpoor
Purneah
Persaudp:r
Renosa
Bhysowr
Sejaulpoor
Midlie
Caump:r
Bhenour
Tarsaidpoor
Oomrun
Fullip:r
Kulliano:r
Kutka
Akberp:r
Barrah
Milkee

Chichindy, and Kuttra as Gittera, when they stand in two maps in positions not exactly corresponding. The fault was in the employment of an officer to survey, without instructing him specifically how he was to write the names of his map. The revenue surveys, so far as they went, effectually corrected this error; and what is more, the maps constructed by the officers employed in this department are capable of being converted with confidence into any character, without each name being, as at present, an object of separate inquiry and research, whenever it is desired to publish a map in the Persian, the Hindee, or in any other character of the country.

But to return to our subject: the Record Committees, wheresoever they were established, succeeded entirely in reforming the orthography of names in the zila dufturs. That they did not do more, but after involving considerable expense failed to provide the desired land registers, was owing to many causes which need not be discussed here. The effect of these institutions in confirming the use of the Gilchristian system is all we have now to do with: that effect will, we presume, not be denied. The leaning had been to this system for thirty years before, but at last the act of Government, and the specific exertions of all public officers throughout the country, continued for nearly eight years consecutively while the Committees lasted, fixed and established this system of Gilchrist as the orthography of office and of business. Even though there were not in it any innate inherent superiority or grounds for preference, even were it the inferior system of the two, still this fact ought, one would think, to secure it from any hasty attempt at change. Except there be some obvious apparent defects pointed out, the undoubted ascertainment of which has been the result of actual experience, would it not be madness to think of discarding what had been so established? What then is to be thought of this new attempt of Mr. Trevelyan to set up again the rejected alphabet of Sir William Jones, and by the gratuitous circulation of thousands of copies to diffuse and disseminate, as if from authority, a system fully and formally tried and found wanting?

The Journal of the Asiatic Society, being a work of science conducted under the special countenance and support of that Society, will always be respected for the matter it contains; and it signifies little in what garb it may choose to present its Asiatic names. Allowance will be made for the consistency of the Society's adherence to the system of its venerable founder, and all that read its proceedings know well what they have to expect, and are prepared to encounter familiar letters applied to strange uses after the manner practised by this Society for half a century. But now that the Gilchristian method of writing has been so long established for record, for surveys, and for making familiar to the uninitiated public the sounds and names of Hindoostan, every official man and every man of sense must protest against the present attempt to introduce once more the discarded system, one too that from its use of the *a* for the short *u* would change the spelling of every word and name from one end of India to the other.

Let the Sir William Jones's system, his *a* and his *i í* and his long and short *u*, be reserved, like the Devanagree, for recondite science: there his alphabet has its footing, and no one desires to eject it from its stronghold: but for business let us have our current Nagree, the short *u* and the *ee* and the *oo*, which have grown into use from their ready adaptation to the ear, and from the preference secured for them by all the associations of sound to letters which we have been accustomed to from our infancy.

In the pages of the Journal there has appeared a notice laudatory of Mr. Trevelyan's attempt to effect by a *coup de main* a change in all the established methods of writing mofussil names. As this Journal has now for itself so wide a circulation in the interior, it is necessary that its pages should not be made to serve the party views of the advocates of any one exclusive system, but that the merits of each in its particular line should be fairly stated. The Sanskrit scholar will perhaps find his advantage in following the alphabet of Sir William Jones, which is that of the grammars and dictionaries, and of most of the translations from that language; but he that is content with the Persic, Oordoo, or the familiar literature of Hindoostan, the man of business and of the world, will find all the books, the dictionaries and grammars and vocabularies to which he is in the habit of referring, and all the records and public documents that fall under his observation, written uniformly in the character of Gilchrist. There is little fear that even the weight of the Journal's recommendation will be successful in superseding what is so established. If the world were not wide enough to hold both systems, — if the order had gone forth from Cæsar that one only should stand, and the issue were a *bellum ad internecionem* between the two,— then might the Journal fitly advocate the cause of its scientific mode of writing to save it from destruction and the sponge: but so long as there is no attempt to encroach on the ground it occupies, or to interfere with its peculiar province in literature; while it is suffered to luxuriate in the paradise of Sanskrit, without any attempt to foist in its rival, even as an humble companion of its pleasures in that Eden of joy; why should the votaries of this learned system strive to gain for it a universal dominion for which it has been found unfitted, and assume the offensive against the system in use for business? Let each retain its own, and both abide together in peace and good will and harmony; holding forth, in the facilities they jointly offer, an invitation to all people to adopt either the one or the other accordingly as they find either most convenient for their purpose; and under the assurance that the object, which is to obtain such a method of writing as shall afford a ready means of transferring the word back into its native character, will equally be accomplished, whichever may be the character adopted. Both systems represent perfectly to the scholar the letters used in the original languages, but it is contended that the Gilchrist alphabet, as now generally introduced and used in the public offices of this presidency, conveys to the uninitiated a more correct and true notion of the proper pronunciation, than the antiquated and rejected system of Sir William Jones, and therefore is the best adapted to business. Through the pages of the Journal let the European public of India be undeceived on this point. The attempt to dislodge the system of

Gilchrist is entirely a matter of individual speculation, and is certainly not the result of any inconvenience felt, or dissatisfaction expressed with it, by the Government, or by any class of public officers or persons whatsoever.

H. T. P.

(14.)

MR. C. E. TREVELYAN'S DEFENCE OF SIR WILLIAM JONES'S SYSTEM.*

It seems now to be admitted with scarcely a dissenting voice, that the plan of expressing the languages of the East

* This paper, as well as those numbered 15 and 18, was reprinted by Sir C. E. Trevelyan in 1854 (in a pamphlet entitled "Papers originally published at Calcutta, in 1834—1836, on the Application of the Roman Letters to the Languages of India"), under the circumstances described in the following Preface: —

"The recent International Conference, held under the auspices of His Excellency Chevalier Bunsen, for the purpose of establishing a standard Missionary Alphabet, required that information should be furnished relative to the undertaking commenced at Calcutta in the year 1834, to introduce into Asia the popular use of the Roman character, as a corollary and complement to the greater enterprise of making English the language of higher education and the fountain from which the nascent vernacular literatures of the East might be vivified and enriched; and with this view the three following papers have been selected for republication out of a much larger number published at the time in India. The course adopted in 1834 was a simple transliteration of the admirable Deva-Nágarí or Sanskrit alphabet, adding what was wanted to represent the peculiar sounds imported into the Indian languages from the Arabic (thus combining the elementary languages of the Japhetic and Shemitic races), and giving to the whole, as nearly as possible, the same powers as the Roman letters possessed in the original Latin and the derivative Italian, according to the system first advocated by Sir William Jones. During the twenty years which have since elapsed, this application of the Roman letters has made silent but steady progress; and, besides its increasing use by the natives of India, it has been extensively adopted by Missionary Establishments, by teachers of Oriental languages in this country, and, almost without exception, by authors of works relating to the East, who desire to express Asiatic words in an exact and uniform manner.

"*London*, 1854.

"[It will be seen from the above that the selections from the Calcutta Papers were first reprinted for the purpose of explaining what had taken place on this subject in India to the International Conference held at the residence of the Prussian Minister in London, in 1854, in order to settle a universal Missionary Alphabet.]"

in the English character offers the best and nearest prospect of fixing and enriching the native dialects, and of establishing a common medium of communication, epistolary as well as oral, between the people and their rulers; that great desideratum, the absence of which has always so much impeded the due administration of justice in this country, and stood in the way of our taking root in the affections of our subjects to the extent which the rectitude of our acts and intentions might entitle us to expect. The principle, therefore, that the languages of the East should be expressed in the character of the West, and that by degrees one written character should be made to pervade the whole world, has been admitted by a decided majority of those persons who from their education and habits of mind are qualified to give an opinion on the subject. The only question which remains to be discussed is the particular orthography, or, in other words, the particular mode of applying the European characters to the Asiatic languages, which it is most desirable to adopt. Hitherto public opinion has been divided between two systems; one of which (the Italian system), from its having been first introduced into the East by Sir William Jones, is generally known by that distinguished scholar's name, and the other system was invented by Mr. Gilchrist, and is called after his name.

It is necessary to premise, that, as far as the consonants are concerned, there is no discrepancy between the two systems worth contending about. The only difference between them is in the vowels and diphthongs, and even in this case only in some of them, while in others both systems exactly agree: but in order that the reader may have the subject clearly before him, we will subjoin a table of the vowels and diphthongs of both systems.

Sir William Jones's.

a	as in	*a*bove	á	as in	*a*rt
i	as in	*i*n	í	as in	pol*i*ce
u	as in	p*u*sh	ú	as in	r*u*le
e	as in	th*e*re	ai	as in	*ai*sle.
o	as in	n*o*te	au	as in	c*au*sa [Latin pronunciation]

Dr. Gilchrist's.

u	as in	cull*	a	as in	call.
i	as in	kill	e	as in	keel*
oo	as in	wool*	oo	as in	cool*
e	as in	there	ue	as in	chyle*
o	as in	cole	uo	as in	cowl*

Out of ten vowel and diphthong sounds, therefore, four are expressed alike in both systems, which reduces the field of contest between the two systems to within very narrow limits. Taking consonants and vowels together, there are about seventy different variations of sounds in Hindusthani, of which only six are expressed differently. This is the utmost extent of the quarrel between the shade of Sir William Jones and Dr. Gilchrist.

We shall endeavour to state as briefly as possible the relative advantages and disadvantages of the two systems.

Sir William Jones's Plan is systematic and complete in all its parts, so that in every case in which an analogy exists between different sounds, a corresponding analogy will be found to pervade the signs by which they are represented. Thus the long sound of *a* is *á*, of *i*, *í*; and of *u*, *ú*; and the diphthong *ai*, which is compounded of *a* and *i*, is represented by those letters and *au* (*ow*); which is compounded of *a* and *u*, by *au*. The consequence of this strict attention to preserve an analogy in the sign corresponding to the variations in the sound is, that the acquisition of the alphabet is greatly facilitated to the learner, who in fact has to make himself acquainted with only five elementary signs which are the representatives of as many original sounds, and the remaining five are only elongated forms or composites of these. He has to learn *a, i, u, e, o*; and *á* is only the long form of *a* distinguished by the usual mark, *í* of *i*, and *ú* of *u*, and *ai* is the composite of *a* and *i*, and *au* of *a* and *u*.

In Dr. Gilchrist's Plan, with a single exception, there

* The letters marked thus * are expressed differently in the two systems.

is no analogy whatever between the long and short forms of the vowels, and between the diphthongs and their component vowels. Thus in his system *a* is the long form of *u*, *ee* of *i*, and the diphthong *ai* is represented by *ue* and *au* by *uo*. It is needless to dilate on the confusion which this want of system must produce in the mind of every learner. No help is here provided for him; and instead of being guided from step to step by a change in the form of the character sufficient to distinguish the modification in the sound, while enough is retained of the original letter to mark the elementary connexion, he is perplexed by a variety of characters between which no kind of analogy is capable of being traced. In short, instead of having only five signs to get by heart, he has no less than nine. In tracing the analogy between corresponding modifications of sound, this plan is worse than if no assistance were afforded him. In this eccentric system of letters long vowels are actually divorced from their partners, and so disguised as to render it impossible to recognise the original connexion between them; and diphthongs are in like manner kidnapped from their parent vowels, and disfigured worse than gipsy children. Who would suppose that *u* is the legitimate husband of *a*, that *ee* is the devoted wife of *i*, that *ue* is the interesting offspring of *a* and *i*, and *uo* the eldest hope of *a* and *u*. This is not a system of *orthography*, but, if I may be allowed to invent a word, of *kakography*, of confusion, mystification, and absurdity. It is singular that when a man sat down with a *carte blanche* before him to invent a system of letters, he was not able to devise something better than this; and it is still more so, that, having the labours of his learned predecessor Sir William Jones to profit by, when he altered, he should have altered so much for the worse.

Another advantage of Sir William Jones's plan is, that besides being complete in itself, owing to the perfect analogy which exists between the different letters, it bears a strict correspondence throughout to the great Indian or Deva Nagari alphabet. All the alphabets derived from the latter are very systematic, and a scheme which is otherwise cannot properly represent them. But Sir William Jones does it exactly, as will be seen from the following table:—

अ *a*	आ *á*
इ *i*	ई *í*
उ *u*	ऊ *ú*
ए *e*	ऐ *ai*
ओ *o*	औ *au*

The natives of India are, therefore, already quite familiar with the idea of distinguishing the modification of sound by a corresponding modification of sign; and when they see the same plan adopted in the Anglified version of the alphabet, they immediately recognise the propriety of it, and enter into the spirit of the scheme. As the new orthography is mainly intended for the people of India, the circumstance of its being entirely coincident with their preconceived feelings and ideas must be allowed to be an advantage of no small importance.

It is hardly necessary to observe that no kind of analogy exists between Dr. Gilchrist's and the Indian or Deva Nagari alphabet. When an Indian reads Sir William Jones's alphabet, he sees a long *á* immediately succeeding the short *a;* a long *í* the short *i*, and a long *ú* the short *u* (the long vowel being in each case distinguished by a mark as in the Sanskrit), which is just what his previous knowledge would lead him to expect; but when he comes to Dr. Gilchrist's plan, he finds *a* following *u*, and *ee* following *i*. What therefore would be his opinion of the comparative merits of the two systems? Would he not say, that one is in every respect as complete as the Alphabet of the Gods (Deva Nágari), while the other is an inexplicable mass of confusion?

Another advantage attending Sir William Jones's system is, that it is not only analogous to but is the very system itself which is used in expressing Latin and all its derivatives; that is, Italian, Spanish, French, &c. It is true that in England we do not pronounce Latin in this way, but this is only because we have barbarised it, and made it accord with our Saxon pronunciation. Even in Scotland and Ireland, to say nothing of continental Europe, they read Latin exactly in the way in which it is now proposed to read Hindusthani. This entire coincidence of the new Hindusthani orthography with the orthography of the learned language of the whole of Europe, and with that of most of its colloquial languages, is a point of great importance. Even in the present age its advantage will be felt, in so far as the learned all over Europe, and in most cases the vulgar also, will by this means obtain direct access to our Indian literature ; and, what is still more deserving of consideration, a foundation will be laid for the establishment in due time of a uniform system of orthography throughout the world. This is an object which, however distant the prospect of accomplishing it may be, no man who has the slightest regard for posterity should ever lose sight of. Next to the establishment of a universal language, that grand desideratum of the philosopher and the philanthropist, the establishment of a universal system of orthography will most tend to the production of unrestricted freedom of intercourse between all the families of the human race; and the one has also a direct tendency to bring about the other. Now, if Gilchrist's plan were to be generally maintained in India, so far from having advanced a step towards this grand result, we should make a decidedly retrograde movement, and the proceeding would be tantamount to shutting the door on the possibility of a uniform system of writing and printing being ever adopted in the eastern and western hemispheres. Gilchrist's plan is utterly abhorrent from the Roman family of languages, and it does not even coincide with the English, as will be shown hereafter.

Sir William Jones's plan has a simple character for every simple sound, while in Dr. Gilchrist's simple sounds are in three instances expressed by double letters [ee, oo, and oo]. This, to say the best of it, is an extremely clumsy contrivance, and in the business of nations and course of ages it would lead to an immense unnecessary expenditure of time and money. That this is the case, may be seen by taking the example of a single sentence,

Jub soobh hoo-ee wuzeer-zadee bhee puhoonchee,

which in Sir William Jones's orthography would be

Jab subh hú-í wazír-zádí bhí pahunchí.

There are thirty-eight letters in this sentence written according to Dr. Gilchrist's plan, and only thirty if it be written according to Jones; that is to say, in only six words the former exceeds the latter by no less than eight letters. Apply this to a book, and conceive the waste of types, paper, and valuable time which must result from it. Supposing an octavo volume printed according to Sir William Jones's plan to consist of 500 pages, and each page to contain on an average 304 words, the total number of words in the volume would be 152,000; and if the same volume were printed according to Mr. Gilchrist's plan, then, at the rate of eight additional letters for every six words, the number of extra letters will amount to 190,000, which would make an addition to the book of 136 pages, and instead of consisting of 500 pages it would consist of 636. Apply this to the entire literature of half the world through a succession of ages, and conceive the result if you can. If this average is considered to be above the mark, I have no objection to suppose that every six of Gilchrist's words contain only half the number of double letters which those above instanced do, and at this rate the book printed according to Gilchrist's plan would exceed what it would be if printed according to Sir William Jones's plan by 68 pages.

Lastly, there are three characters in Gilchrist's alphabet which do not belong to English or to any other language under the sun which we have ever heard of. These are oo, *ue* and *uo*. With the exception of the pupils of Dr. Gilchrist, who, from early associations and respect to their master, may naturally be expected to be admirers of his scheme, these characters are utterly barbarous to every description of people; and it is therefore impossible for them to secure a general recognition for themselves in the breasts either of Englishmen, European foreigners, or Indians. Sir William Jones's plan, as has been before stated, contains no arbitrary sounds whatever, but is in every respect in strict accordance with the Latin and Latino-European languages. Even the *au*, of which no example is to be found in English, is perfectly familiar to every Scotchman and Irishman who knows Latin; and if a youth at Dublin College or the High School at Edinburgh were to pronounce *causa* like *cawsa*, he would be immediately corrected, and would be told to sound it *cowsa*, and the same, of course everywhere on the continent of Europe.

It will be proper in this place to say a few words in regard to the general principles of the two systems, and the causes which have led to their respective adoption. Sir William Jones well knew that the Romans and the Indians derive their origin from the same family of the human race, and that the analogy which is everywhere perceptible in their mythology and their language extends also in a high degree to their alphabets. The arrangement of both is exactly the same. In both, the same letters have exactly the same powers; and while one is the most perfect alphabet in the East, the other is acknowledged to bear the palm in the West.

Sir William Jones also knew that, when the barbarous Saxon monks came to apply this alphabet to their language, they did it without any regard to system, and took no pains to preserve the original powers of the letters. *i* was pushed out of its place by *ee*, and made to do duty for *ai; a* was generally superseded by *u;* and the services of *u* having been preoccupied in this manner, *oo* was made to officiate for it. Even this arrangement was by no means constantly adhered to, and thousands of instances might be mentioned of the application of the same letter to several different sounds, and of different letters to the same sound. The English system of spelling, in short (I protest against its being called *orthography*), is a labyrinth, a chaos, an absurdity, a disgrace to our age and nation. It forms the principal difficulty of our language (which is the more provoking, as there is nothing in the structure of English which calls for it), and causes annually to increasing millions, in all the four quarters of the globe, an enormous unnecessary expenditure of valuable time, and still more valuable temper. The amount of vexation and discouragement and loss of time which is caused every year, particularly to foreigners, by the extremely incorrect way of spelling now in use, is incalculable.

But to return to the subject immediately under consideration, Sir William Jones and Dr. Gilchrist had two systems of letters before them; one of which was acknowledged to be the most perfect which the wit of man had ever devised, and in every respect corresponded with the systems already in use in India, and on the continent of Europe; and the other was perhaps the most imperfect the world had ever beheld, and totally differed from those which prevailed both in the East and West, England and North America alone excepted. Sir William Jones was a noble philologist. He imitated the Universal Governor as far as it is permitted to man to do so, and, embracing the whole world in his view, married the East and the West by promoting by his sanction and influence the adoption in both hemispheres of the same mode of writing. As his object was to fertilise the whole world, he drew from the fountain head. But Gilchrist limited himself to the narrow circle of English spelling; and, by the adoption of that corrupt eccentric system, opposed an effectual bar to his system ever extending beyond his pupils and the readers of his own books.

It should be borne in mind that Sir William Jones and Mr. Gilchrist both drew from the mine of English letters, and that the only difference between them was, that one appropriated the dross, while the other culled the pure gold. Gilchrist chose the most corrupt and imperfect parts of our system, while Jones selected those which were consistent with true principles, and coincided with the most perfect alphabets both of the East and West. The *í* in *políce* is almost as well known in English as the double *ee* in *feel.* The *u* in *pull* is certainly better known than oo, which is pure Gilchristian. The *ú* in *rule* is as familiar as the *oo* in *cool.* The *ai* in *aisle* is assuredly far more common than *ue,* which is another arbitrary sign to be found nowhere except in the books printed by Dr. Gilchrist himself. The *au* in *causa* (Latin pronunciation) is also better understood than *uo*, which is another Gilchristian hieroglyphic; and even the short *a*, the stumbling-block of our Gilchristian friends, is quite as familiar to us as their favourite *u*, and anybody who will take the trouble to look in the English Dictionary will see it used at the commencement of 500 words like *above, about, abound,* and so forth.

It has fallen to the lot of our generation to introduce the English letters into India, and the simple question for us to determine was, whether we should choose that part of the English literary system which is corrupt and limited, or that which is complete and universal. Since most Europeans in India are from their youth thoroughly imbued with Gilchrist's system, if we had desired to obtain an ephemeral popularity, we should have chosen the least perfect plan; but this was not our object. We were not concerting plans for the satisfaction of a few hundred Europeans. The benefit of the hundreds of millions of our dark-faced brethren of Asia was our aim; and therefore, undeterred by the clamour which we foresaw would be raised by a portion of our countrymen wedded by education and habit to the system we felt ourselves called upon to reject, we adopted the notation which was most perfect in the abstract, and which most nearly corresponded with Indian and European feelings.

It will be satisfactory to our friends to know what we have ourselves but lately become acquainted with, that a few years ago, when the American missionaries first committed the language of the Sandwich Islands to writing, they adopted this same Italian orthography, the standard of which has now been raised in India. This is a remarkable testimony to the intrinsic excellence of the system. Two bodies of people, belonging to different nations, and situated nearly on opposite sides of the globe, were called upon to deliberate, independently of each other, regarding the choice of a system of letters which it was proposed to introduce into less civilised countries; and what was the result? In their selection both fell upon the Italian system, thus confirming what had previously been maintained regarding its superiority over all the other European systems.

Ought not this fact to encourage us to proceed with energy and zeal? The Americans are the natural allies of our nation for the diffusion of every good word and work throughout the world, and we joyfully hail their accession as our colleagues in the establishment of a correct universal system of letters. The following list of Sandwich Island words, expressed both in the old and new style, extracted from a History of the American Mission in those Islands, is annexed:—

NAMES OF THE ISLANDS.

Improved Spelling.	*Former Spelling.*
Ha-wai-i.	Hah-wye-e. Owhyhee.
Mau-i.	Mow-ee.
Mo-lo-kai.	Mo-lo-kye.
O-a-hu.	O-ah-hoo.
Kau-ai.	Kow-eye.

MISSIONARY STATIONS.

Ho-no-lu-lu.	Ho-no-loo-loo.
Wai-me-a.	Wye-may-ah.
La-hai-na.	Lah-hye-nah.
Kai-lu-a.	Kye-lu-ah.
Wai-a-ke-a.	Wye-ah-kay-ah.

NAMES OF PERSONS.

Ke-o-pu-o-la-ni.	Kay-o-poo-o-lah-nee.
Li-ho-Li-ho.	Lee-ho-Lee-ho.
Ka-u-mu-a-li-i.	Kah-oo-moo-ah-lee-ee.
Ho-a-pi-li.	Ho-ah-pee-lee.
Ka-pi-o-la-ni.	Kah-pee-o-lah-nee.
Ku-a-ki-ni.	Koo-ah-kee-nee.
Po-ki.	Po-kee.
Wa-hi-ne-pi-o.	Wah-hee-nay-pee-o.
Pu-a-a-i-ki.	Poo-ah-ah-ee-kee.
Ka-ma-kau.	Kah-mah-kow.
Ka-lai-o-pu.	Kay-lye-o-poo.
Pau-a-hi.	Pow-ah-hee.
Ke-kau-o-no-hi.	Ke-kow-o-no-hee.

It only remains to meet an argument of our adversaries which has been put forth by one of them with an air of anticipated triumph. "Sir William Jones's Plan," they say, "has been well known for these sixty years, and yet it has made no sensible progress;" from which they conclude that it never will make any. To this we reply, that God mocks at the short-sighted sagacity of mankind, by sometimes bringing to nought their best-devised schemes, and at other times He vindicates his own authority and proclaims to the world that the Most High ruleth in the kingdom of men, by bringing about mighty changes by means apparently the most inadequate, and at times the most unexpected. The use of gunpowder was confined to fireworks, and steam power was treated as a plaything, long before these great elements took their proper place in the system of human affairs: but, to pass over minor instances, was not Christianity, the system which is destined to bring back the world to its obedience to the Lord of the universe, and to make it that abode of purity and peace and unalloyed felicity which it was originally intended to be,—was not this glorious revelation confined for about 1500 years within the narrow limits of the Holy Land, until Christ appeared on earth and commanded his followers to make it known to all mankind?

There is no lack of scourges and blessings in the storehouse of God, and things can be turned by Him in his own good time and way to uses of which we can at present form no conception. Is it not conformable with our experience of the rules under which the divine government of the world is carried on, that the Christian Philosopher who consecrated his learning to the glory of his God and the good of his fellow-creatures;—that the Christian Scholar who did not hesitate to make the following solemn declaration, which will be recorded to the latest posterity: "I have regularly and attentively read the Holy Scripture; and am of opinion that this volume, independently of its divine origin, contains more sublimity and beauty, more pure morality, more important history, and finer strains of poetry and eloquence, than can be collected from all other books, in whatever age or language they may have been composed;"—that such a man should be blest in the work of his hands, and that the seed sown by him should, in God's own time, spring forth and cast its shoots far and wide throughout the East? Let who will gainsay it, Sir Wm. Jones laid a good foundation, and future ages will bless him as the father of the literature of the Eastern hemisphere. "Cast thy grain before the waters *, and thou shalt see it after many days."

To descend to secondary causes, Why has Sir Wm. Jones's system heretofore not made greater progress? Simply because nobody ever thought of making it a *popular* system. Where is the Primer, the Spelling-Book, the Grammar, or the Vocabulary which was ever published on this plan with a view to popular education? The utmost which its advocates have hitherto aimed at has been to fix it as the medium of *scientific nomenclature*, and in this they have *fully* succeeded. That it has not gone further is not the fault of the system, but of its admirers, who till lately never once attempted to extend it beyond these limits. As far as it has been tried, it has completely answered every expectation that was entertained of it, which is no small praise, and gives us promise of continued successful results. The system has completely obtained the acquiescence of the learned all over the world, and, if we mistake not, it will in the course of a few generations obtain the assent of the vulgar also.

On the other hand, Why has Gilchrist's system made the progress it has? Simply because he wrote, and taught, and published. What is his system, except his books and lectures? Without these it could have no existence. It is a remarkable fact, that Gilchrist's plan has never made any spontaneous progress; and we never heard of a single school except his own in which it is taught, or of a single book that was ever printed in it except by him. From this it would appear that it has no inherent virtue, no self-operating principle, calculated to seçure for it success independent of the exertions of the founder. It will apparently live and die with him. It has met with just that degree of success which might have been expected from the determined perseverance

* Alluding to the method of sowing in the East.

of its author, and from his personal and official influence, and it has not gone a step beyond this. The doctor himself is its moving principle. Let him relax his efforts, and it is nothing.

But what a different picture does Sir William Jones's system at this moment present? After having completely stood the test of learned criticism, after having gone through a probationary period of sixty years, and approved itself to the great body of scientific men throughout the world, it has been claimed for popular use. The jewel must no longer remain shut up in a casket, but must be brought forth to shine in the face of day. The money must no longer remain hoarded in the treasury; the time has come to spend it for the general advantage. The gold needs no assay; it has been well and thoroughly tried, and all that is required is to put it into circulation.

Three Printing-Presses, of which one enjoys a more extensive business than any other in Calcutta, and another is the most influential of the Provincial Presses, are at this moment actively engaged in preparing Picture Alphabets, Primers, Spelling-Books, Readers, Dictionaries, and Grammars; and two Lithographic Presses are employed in providing Writing Copies and Pictorial Illustrations. Daily assurances of support are received from all parts of India; numerous public officers, and almost all the leaders in the education of the country, are on our side; and if we make the same progress during the ensuing three months, which we have done for the last three, the system will become so firmly established that nothing short of a violent persecution would be able to uproot it.

C. E. T.

27th August, 1834.

[The following alphabet represents Sir William Jones' system, as applied to Hindustani books printed after this date, up to the period of Mr. Trevelyan's departure from India in 1838.]

THE ANGLO-HINDUSTANI ALPHABET,

WITH THE POWERS OF THE LETTERS.

A	a	woman	پَر	par	L	l	little	لباس	libás
Á	á	art	باپ	báp	M	m	man	ممکن	mumkin
AI	ai	aisle	پیدا	paidá	N	n	none	نماز	namáz
AU	au	our	دور	daur	N̲	n	sung	ہوں	hún̲
B	b	but	باغ	bágh	O	o	go	کو	ko
CH	ch	church	چا	chá	P	p	papa	پار	pár
D	d	duke	داغ	dágh	Q	q	quoit	قدم	qadam
Ḍ	ḍ	bad	ڈال	ḍál	R	r	race	راز	ráz
E	e	there	پیٹ	peṭ	Ṛ	ṛ	eternel*	پڑنا	paṛná
F	f	find	فضل	fazl	S	s	sin	سال	sál
G	g	go	گرم	garm	Sh	sh	she	شکر	shukr
G̣H	g̣h	ghostly	غم	g̣ham	T	t	pot	تخت	taḳht
H	h	here	ہزار	hazár	Ṭ	ṭ	fat	ٹٹو	ṭaṭṭú
I	i	in	اِن	in	U	u	bull	بت	but
Í	í	police	نیل	níl	Ú	ú	rule	خوب	ḳhúb
J	j	just	جَان	ján	V	v	vine	ولایت	viláyat
K	k	keep	کان	kán	W	w	was	وجود	wajúd
ḲH	ḳh	loch	خادم	ḳhádim	Y	y	you	یار	yár
					Z	z	zeal	زبان	zabán

* French

Note 1. The vowels, whether long or short, with the point under them (thus, ạ ạ́ ị ị́) represent the ạin ع, and have a guttural sound.

2. ہ and ح are represented by h, س ث ص by s, ط ت by t, and ز ذ ض ظ by z.

3. Bh, chh, dh, jh, kh, ph, ṛh, th, ṭh, are aspirated letters, and sounded together as the *bh* in ho*b*-*h*ouse by dropping the ho; thus, b,house.

(15.)

CIRCULAR LETTER ADDRESSED BY THE ORIGINATORS OF THE GENERAL APPLICATION OF THE ROMAN LETTERS TO THE LANGUAGES OF THE EAST, TO THE PRINCIPAL, TUTORS, AND STUDENTS, ESPECIALLY STUDENTS PREPARING FOR THE MINISTERIAL AND MISSIONARY WORK, AT THE DIFFERENT COLLEGES IN THE UNITED STATES.

Dear Gentlemen,

The attention of Christians of all denominations having been lately directed to the salvation of the heathen, we cannot but entertain the hope that the necessities of the *continent of India* will secure from different societies that degree of consideration and effort which its magnitude demands; and as almost all the colleges and theological seminaries of your highly favoured native country contain, we understand, young men in a course of education, who have generously determined to quit the endearments of home to labour for Christ in foreign lands, we trust that many such may be found among those to whom this letter is addressed, who in God's providence may be led to prosecute their benevolent efforts in this country. With this impression, allow us to draw your attention to a plan, which, if we mistake not, bids fair, under the blessing of God, greatly to facilitate their labours, and enlarge their usefulness. We allude to the general substitution of the Roman or English letters, for the various characters now used to express the numerous dialects of this vast continent.

In drawing your attention to this subject, we would first solicit your patient perusal of the accompanying volume, entitled, "The Application of the Roman Alphabet to all the Oriental Languages," of which we beg your acceptance. In this you will perceive fully exhibited the advantages of such a change, if it be practicable; and satisfactory proof, that, on the modified scheme of Sir W. Jones, it *is* easy to express in the Roman character, most accurately, all the sounds of all the Indian languages. Evidence in abundance has been since afforded, through the general acceptance which the scheme has met with from both Europeans and natives, that, even to the furthest extremity of our empire, its universal though gradual adoption may be safely predicted.

As to the several advantages of the scheme, we may briefly refer to the following. By the general adoption of the Roman letters, in lieu of the various characters now used to represent the dialects of the East,—

1st. The natives of India will be able to learn *our language* with much greater ease than they can at present.

2nd. We shall be able to learn *their language* with greater ease.

3rd. The natives of every province of India will be able to learn the language of every other province with greater ease.

4th. All the existing Muhammadan and Hindu literature will gradually sink into disuse, with the exception of such portions of it as are worthy of being turned into the new letters. This would produce a great moral change in India in the course of a generation or two. Nothing keeps India in a state of moral and intellectual debasement so much as the false religion, false morals, and false science contained in the sacred and learned books of the Muhammadans and Hindus; and by getting rid of these we shall stop the polluted stream at its source.*

* It will be seen from the following extract from Sir C. Trevelyan's evidence before the Indian Committee, that this opinion has reference only to the bearing of the learned Oriental languages upon popular education, and is given with a full reservation of their literary and antiquarian claims:—"Arabic is not spoken in common, nor is it learned to any extent, except a smattering of it for religious purposes by the Mahomedans. Sanskrit, no doubt, has higher claims, as it is the foundation of all the Hindoo languages; but it is a dead language, and it is a most difficult language. A whole life is required to learn it properly; and when, in consequence of the codification of the laws, there will no longer be any necessity for learning it, it will cease to be cultivated to a degree of which we are little aware; and I think it will seriously

5th. Just in proportion as Sanskrit, Arabic, and Persian go out, English will come in; and not only will our literature be extensively studied, but its beneficial influences will reach the people by a thousand channels, through the medium of the native language. It will be a grand thing to make English literature the model of taste, and the fountain of instruction, throughout India; and if Sanskrit and Arabic and Persian become confined to the learned few, and the English and the vernacular Indian languages are expressed in the same character, there cannot be a doubt that this object will be attained.

There are also other minor advantages which would result from the change of character, such as the much greater rapidity with which the Roman character can be written, the superior distinctness of both the printed and written characters, superior cheapness, &c., but it is not necessary to mention them here.

These advantages must be considered as important in the propagation of knowledge of *all kinds*. But there are one or two others which appear highly important to the Christian Church, in its attempt to introduce into this vast heathen country the blessed light of the glorious Gospel; and to these we beg particularly to direct your attention.

1. It offers remarkable facilities for the religious instruc-

become the duty of the State to found professorships and scholarships, with a view to preserve and cultivate it, as containing the ancient religious and social system of the country, and as being a key to the popular usages and opinions. The existing Sanskrit Colleges at Calcutta and Benares might be maintained for this purpose; but some change would be required in their plans of study, in order to adapt them to the object of preserving, and, as far as may be desirable, making more generally known, the whole of the ancient literature, science, law, and religion of the country. The Hindoo poetry and philosophy alone would require the attention of several literary men."—*House of Lords' Paper No.* 637—1 *of Session* 1853: *Mr. Hansard, Great Turnstile, Holborn.* This Report of the India Committee of the House of Lords is interesting much beyond the usual measure of Parliamentary Blue Books. It is entirely upon education, religion, and other cognate subjects; and, besides the evidence of Sir C. Trevelyan, contains that of Sir Erskine Perry, the Rev. Dr. Duff, Mr. Norton, Mr. Marshman, Dr. Wise, Mr. Wilberforce Bird, Professor Wilson, Mr. Cameron, the Rev. W. Keane, the Right Rev. Bishop Carr, the Rev. J. Tucker, and the Right Rev. Bishop Spencer.

tion of classes of society otherwise inaccessible to the missionary. It is a fact, that in *this character* the children of the most bigoted Hindus may be readily taught what they could not be taught in *their own.* It has been remarked by the most observant teachers of native boys, that those who have learned to read English *think* and *speak* on religious subjects, in that language, what they *dare not, cannot,* think and speak in their own. Now this is exactly the case in regard to Bangálí books in the English character. It occurred only a few days ago, that two most respectable Hindu gentlemen (one of whom is at the head of the bigoted Dharma Sabhá), who would *never have thought* of putting into a school a word spoken by or written about Christ in the Bangálí character, proposed of their own accord to put the Romanised version of the *Sermon on the Mount* (or "Instruction by Christ," as it is called) into a large native school, which one supports, and the other gratuitously superintends. They seemed to feel conscious that, in the Bangálí character, some opposing bigot would interfere, and raise against them the cry of apostasy; but that, if in the English character, the introduction of the work would be regarded as quite indifferent, and since it is requisite in the acquisition of a foreign character (as of the English language) to read the books usually employed, no scruple would be raised on the subject. Now, as we know the paramount influence of sentiments impressed on the minds of *youth,* and as for many years the circle of those who will learn their own language in the new character must be immeasurably greater than that of those who learn a foreign language like the English, it seems that by this plan Providence has supplied the Church with a powerful instrument for benefiting the bigoted part of the Hindu population, which it becomes its duty most diligently to employ.

2. There is also another consideration well deserving the attention of Bible and Missionary Societies. It furnishes the agents of both with new and most important facilities for the promotion of their labour.

A letter has just been received from an intelligent Missionary in the Bombay Presidency, well acquainted with the native languages in that part of India, in which he says that, when he was in Bengál, he brought round with him many books in different dialects of this Presidency, and that if the *characters* had been alike he should have easily mastered all, so as to make out the meaning of a passage as needed. He says, however, that the *variety of character* had rendered his progress so slow, that he had hitherto mastered only the Bangálí. "Send me," he says, "all you print in the *Roman* character in all your dialects, and I am persuaded that in this case I shall be able to understand a text in Bangálí, Hinduí, Uriyá, &c., as readily as now I can Mahrattí." To a *translator* of the Sacred Scriptures, who is anxious, in order to perfect his version in one language, to see what words or phrases have been used by preceding translators in all the other Indian languages, what an amazing advantage will be afforded when he has the opportunity of doing it without learning a new character, or being vexed or delayed by the innumerable letters, simple and compound, which otherwise must be acquired, ere the sense of a passage in any dialect can be ascertained!

Again, what a noble thing it will be for a Missionary, acquainted only with *one* language (be it Bangálí, Uriyá, Hinduí or Hindusthání), to read intelligibly and correctly the Sacred Scriptures and tracts in *all* these languages, when called to itinerate in the country; or when having at his own station, on different religious festivals, to converse with strangers or others acquainted with these languages. He may thus excite attention, may prompt inquiry, and may create an interest in his efforts, leading to the salvation of many souls!

It should be remembered too, that there is a large class of nominal Christians in the country, for which our Bible Societies have hitherto made no provision. We refer particularly to the descendants of the Portuguese and other Europeans; many of whom, though familiar with the spoken languages of the country, are unable to read them, and whose limited acquaintance with English renders it impossible for them to understand the sacred volume in that language. Let the Bible, in what may be called their mother tongue, be presented to them in the English character, and they will very soon be able to read with ease and profit its sacred contents. At present the Bible, whether in English or the native language, is to them a sealed book; and so it is likely to remain, until those who love the Scriptures shall come forward to remove the seal, and open the sacred treasure, by presenting its contents clothed in letters with which they are acquainted, or a knowledge of which they may very soon acquire.

The above advantages (besides others which we omit through fear of being tedious) are so important to the intellectual, moral, and religious improvement of the millions of India, that we feel persuaded you will now proceed with interest to our second inquiry.

Is the Roman alphabet a suitable medium for the representation of Indian words; and, especially, can all the letters of every dialect in India, great in number and diversified in shape as they are, be expressed in this character?

We answer unhesitatingly in the affirmative. The Roman, as originally applied to this object by the learned Sir W. Jones, and modified as proposed in the accompanying volume, is admirably adapted to this purpose, and in it all the letters of the numerous languages of Asia may be most readily and correctly expressed. Proof of this you will find in pp. 80 to 113 of the volume just referred to.

It has afforded us great satisfaction, since we have been led to advocate this scheme, to perceive that the American Missionaries had before adopted precisely the same system to express the language of the Sandwich Islands. This remarkable coincidence (which is more particularly dwelt on in p. 158, &c.) appears to us to afford most satisfactory evidence that the system is in a peculiar degree adapted to the power of speech, as possessed in common by natives of the remotest climes, and is therefore well adapted to form a character destined by degrees to become *universal.* We need not say that, next to a universal *language*, a universal *character*, by removing nearly one half the difficulties of his task, promises to a philanthropist the most glorious results.

We therefore proceed to our 3rd inquiry, Can an alteration so radical and extensive as the substitution of the Roman for all the Oriental characters be anticipated in any reasonable time?

To this we reply in brief, referring you to the accompanying printed documents for fuller information:—

1st. This change has been effected throughout almost all the nations of *Europe.* Excepting some of them who use Greek, Russian, and German characters, all have successively surrendered their original alphabets to that of Rome. They were governed or protected by the Romans, and the latter were their superiors in all kinds of knowledge. Now, as almost all the nations of Hindusthán stand in exactly the same relation to the British, and are deriving from them the same civil and intellectual advantages which the nations of Europe did from the Romans, why should they not follow the example of the latter, and relinquish their respective alphabets for that of the English?

2nd. Large classes of persons in the East have relinquished their original alphabets for those of their more powerful or better-informed native neighbours. Not to mention the thousands in Hindusthán who have adopted the Persian character, and the multitudes in the Malay Islands who have adopted the Arabic one, the Assamese, in our immediate neighbourhood, have lately discarded their own alphabet for the Bangálí, and the hill tribes on the frontier of Naipál for the Nágarí; and why should not the Bangálís and Hindusthánís in their turn do the same, when the corresponding advantages are confessedly more than equal?

3rd. The *present attempt* to introduce the Roman character has met with unexampled success. Only five months since, when the system now adopted was proposed to be used in gradual supersession of all the native alphabets, not more than four individuals* were friendly to the plan, while it had to contend with that large class of society who dislike all innovation, and that still larger one who dislike all trouble. Yet amidst the opposition of many, and the apathy

* The Rev. Dr. Yates, the Rev. W. H. Pearce, the Rev. Dr. Duff, and Sir C. Trevelyan.

of more, it has steadily progressed. Everybody who has acquired this system has become its advocate. At various stations between Calcutta and Dihlí, and even beyond the latter place, numerous gentlemen have declared themselves its friends. Christian clergymen and laymen, with Hindu and Muhammadan priests, teachers, and gentlemen, are engaged in preparing elementary books for publication. Various such works have already been printed in Bangálí and Hindusthání; two publications in Hinduí, and others in that language and Persian are passing through the press; and applications have been received to execute works in Uriyá and Burman. The system has been gradually introduced into schools in this city and elsewhere, both under native and European superintendence; and at Dihlí, where it has found its way into the college, 200 pupils in one branch, and 60 in another, are become quite familiar with it; and it is now so popular that native authors are preparing works which it is confidently expected will secure by their sale a *profit*, both to the editor and printer. Let the system proceed in this manner but six months longer, and its gradual establishment and general prevalence throughout India, with but moderate exertion on the part of its friends, may be considered as settled.

While we are thus privileged to see the rapid success of a scheme fraught with such blessings to India, we are particularly anxious that its advantages should be enjoyed by the *Christian Church*. It was commenced, and its success hitherto has been chiefly secured, by the unwearied exertions of friends to the evangelisation of India; and it is our most anxious desire that to this great object its advanced progress should be directed. We know not how this can be better effected than by its being made to assist, in their acquisition of the languages of India, that interesting class to whom we have before alluded; viz. candidates for Missionary labour; and, with the hope that among the numerous youth who are connected with your institution, there may be some of this class, we have done ourselves the pleasure of sending for your library a copy of each of the Bangálí, Hinduí, and Hindusthání works already published. We beg also to say, that should you favour us with a reply, and intimate in it your wish to be supplied with other books for the use of any of your students who are studying the Oriental languages with a view to Missionary labour, we shall esteem it a pleasure to send you copies of other works in the particular languages you may specify. A Grammar and a Dictionary, in both Bangálí and Hindusthání, are being prepared, and will be included among them.

Allow us to add, that we greatly need more Missionaries in India, and shall be delighted to welcome them, be they of what denomination of Evangelical Christians they may. We cannot but entertain the hope that our present address may *excite* in some, and tend to *cherish* in others, the generous desire to enter on the honourable work in the boundless field of labour which Hindusthán presents. The rapid spread of general education, which has shaken the faith in idolatry of thousands in our cities; the growing desire to acquire a knowledge of the English language, which renders most acceptable the Missionary who will establish a school to teach it; the conviction which is gradually pervading all classes of Europeans and many natives, that, to secure the formation of even a *moral* character, instruction in religious principles must not be neglected; with the approbation on the part of the British authorities of all judicious attempts to promote the moral and religious improvement of their subjects, and the toleration which may be safely calculated on in all the independent states, furnish to the Missionaries facilities for useful exertion hitherto unknown. O that the Church Universal would awake to its duty, and by the supply of devoted men, equal to the necessities of this vast continent, would secure (what from the ordinary operations of God's providence and Spirit we may reasonably anticipate) the speedy triumph of the Cross throughout its length and breadth!

Before we conclude, we will advert to a fact which we think has not yet been sufficiently attended to by persons who desire the welfare of India. We mean that the popular literature of the whole continent is yet in quite an incipient state. It may be said to be in the same condition as the

English literature was in the days of Chaucer. There are not more than twelve or fourteen books in Hindusthání fit for the education of the young, and not much more than twice that number in Bangálí. Does not this state of things present a noble field for Christian exertion? *An Indian literature,* that which will form the minds of one hundred and fifty millions of people throughout all their generations, has yet to be constructed; and where can we find a better foundation for it than in the word of God? The servants of Christ ought to esteem it an extraordinary privilege that such an opportunity has been afforded to them; and their vigorous and well-combined exertions should have no less an object in view than the gradual yet rapid formation of a CHRISTIAN LITERATURE for the millions of India, whence the spirit of it will become quickly diffused throughout the neighbouring countries, until the whole of Asia has been reduced to the obedience of Christ.* The first object will be to transfer the superior knowledge of every description possessed by the inhabitants of the Western into the vernacular languages of the Eastern hemisphere; and the whole should be done with a strict reference to

* The following passage, from Sir C. Trevelyan's evidence before the Indian Committee of the House of Lords in 1853, illustrates the influence which India has always exercised over the whole of Asia:— "India is the central country of Asia. It is an extremely rich country. It is rich in actual wealth, but it is still richer in undeveloped resources. It is inhabited by an acute, intellectual and partially cultivated people, among whom learning and learned men have, from the most ancient times, been held in high reputation. When our ancestors were clothed with the skins of beasts and were entirely destitute of literature, and indulged in wholesale human sacrifices, the Indians were a cultivated and learned people. India has in all ages exercised a considerable influence over the surrounding countries. We derive from India, our beautiful system of Decimal Notation, commonly called the Arabic numerals, but which really came to us through the Arabs from India, where it has existed from time immemorial precisely as it was transferred to us, the forms of the figures in Sanskrit being almost identical with those which we use every day. The Fables which have for ages been known to the Western world as the Fables of Æsop and Pilpay, were discovered, when Sanskrit literature began to be studied, under the name of Hitopadesa, the identity being beyond all question, although some of the stories have been clothed in a Western medium to suit Western ideas. Towards the East and North a yet more remarkable influence has been exercised by a reformed system of Hindooism (Buddism), bearing the same relation to the ancient

Christian principles; that is to say, everything which has a corrupting and debasing tendency should be carefully omitted; the truths of Christianity should be recognised and enforced; and, in all things, whether the subjects treated of relate to sacred or secular science, the mind should be led, by all practicable means, to a knowledge of God and of His will. The work of translation must, we conceive, be carried on almost entirely in this country; but there is another department of labour, in which any person of ordinary abilities in any part of the world may assist. We refer to the composition of original works suited to the capacity of the native mind, consisting for the most part of short stories, dialogues, and biographies, written so as to enforce the general principles of virtue, and to expose the real character of the prevailing Indian vices. Should any of the benevolent persons of either sex by whom this letter may be perused take up their pens in this holy cause, it is requested that they will forward the result of their labours, through the medium of the next post-office, to the booksellers mentioned below, by whom they will be transmitted to Calcutta; and after the necessary corrections have been made, with a

idolatrous system of India, unhappily still the prevailing system in that country, which the reformed Mahomedanism of the Wahabees bears to the ordinary Mahomedanism. This reformed Hindooism, which originated in the district of Behar, has spread over the countries to the eastward, over Burmah and Siam and China, and far among the Tartar and Mongolian tribes inhabiting Asiatic Russia, even to the shores of the Arctic sea; it includes among its votaries a larger number than any other existing religion; and the ancient vernacular language of Behar, under the name of Pali, and to a certain extent the Sanskrit language, have become the sacred language of many of those countries. If, therefore, the resources of this great Asiatic country are developed, so that it may acquire the strength which properly belongs to it; and if English education, and free discussion, and Christianity are firmly established there, it will work a change far and wide through the Asiatic countries and islands, which will be productive of the greatest blessings, and will, if I may say so reverently, subserve the designs of Providence. It will be one of the greatest distinctions of our posterity, that they belong to a nation honoured by Providence as the means of working out such a blessed change; and it is a gratifying fact that our brethren, the people of the United States of America, are effectually co-operating with us in this good work, by means of several strong missions, which use our common English language and literature for the instruction of the natives, in conjunction with their own vernacular languages."

view to adapt them to local circumstances, they will be published, with pictorial illustrations and translations in the different vernacular languages on the opposite pages, and distributed throughout the country from Calcutta to Kabul, by means of depositories which have been already established at the different stations. We conceive that there is scarcely any person who has received even a moderate education who is not equal to this task; and the ladies in particular, who know so well how to address those better feelings of our nature which are common to all mankind, are particularly well qualified for it. How exquisite will be the satisfaction to a person who has succeeded in writing a popular little book of this kind to know, that, while he is living in the retirement of his family in a distant country, he will yet be speaking to thousands of the heathen in different parts of India, and insensibly leading them by his interesting and affectionate appeals to a knowledge of their Saviour! We do not hesitate to affirm that a successful author might in this way be so blessed in his labours as to accomplish as much, if not more, as many Missionaries who have devoted their lives to the cause. In order that it may be clearly understood what is intended, we send, in the accompanying collection, the first number of the Library of Entertaining Knowledge, this day published; together with a copy of an Address which has been published on this subject in the Calcutta papers.

Begging that the person into whose hands this letter may be delivered will kindly secure its being heard or perused by *all* connected with the Institution, we remain, with best wishes for its prosperity,

Your faithful servants,

W. YATES,
W. H. PEARCE,
C. E. TREVELYAN,
J. THOMAS.

Calcutta, Nov. 1834.

Note.—Dr. Duff had gone to England for the recovery of his health when this letter was written.

(16.)

EXTRACT FROM THE MINUTE BOOK OF THE ROMAN LETTER PROPAGATION COMMITTEE.

Resolutions.

1st. Resolved, that it is desirable to establish a permanent fund for the extension of the plan of applying the Roman letters to the vernacular languages of India.

2nd. That Mr. Trevelyan having offered all the books belonging to him which remained unsold both in the Calcutta and Provincial depositories in addition to two small remittances lately received, and Mr. Pearce having offered on behalf of the Baptist Mission Press the remaining copies of the edition of the Hindustani Reader No. 1, just published, the same shall be accepted as a foundation for a fund for the above purpose.

3rd. That the proceeds of the sale of the above books, as realised, be carried to the credit of the fund, in the Savings' Bank, and be applied to the publication, or republication of such books as may appear to the Managers to be most required, and that these books be again sold and the proceeds applied as above, so as to form a permanent fund for the promotion of the Roman system.

4th. That no work be commenced until the sum necessary to complete it has been realised.

5th. That no work be published or encouraged by this Association, the whole of which is not unexceptionable in a moral point of view.

6th. That in case other persons should wish to republish any of the above works on their own account, this Association will most cheerfully give them permission to do so.

7th. That the Committee of Management consist for the present of the undersigned.

C. E. TREVELYAN.
W. H. PEARCE.
W. YATES.
J. THOMAS.

August, 1836.

(17.)

LIST OF BOOKS IN THE NATIVE LANGUAGES AND THE ROMAN CHARACTER, PUBLISHED, OR IN THE PRESS, AT THE END OF THE YEAR 1836.

(*Extracted from the* CHRISTIAN OBSERVER *of April*, 1837.)

Hindustání and Anglo-Hindustání.

	R.	A.
Yates' Introduction to the Hindustání language, comprising a Grammar, Reading Lessons, and Vocabulary	5	0
The Bâgh o Bahár	1	8
Hindustání Reader, No. 1, ...	1	0
Ditto ditto, No. 2, ...	1	0
Capt. Paton's Astronomy in English and Hindustání on opposite pages	1	0
D'Rozario's English, Bengáli, and Hindustání Dictionary	6	6
Thompson's English and Hindustání Dictionary, 2nd edition	3	0
Thompson's Hindustání and English ditto.		
U'rdu translation of the Field Exercises of the British Army, in Nágrí and Roman characters.		
English and Hindustání Student's Assistant, or Idiomatical Exercises in those languages, designed to assist Students of either language in acquiring an easy and correct method of expression, Part 1, Nouns	0	6
Student's Assistant, Part 2, Adjectives	0	4
Ditto ditto, Parts 3 and 4, Verbs and Dialogues .	0	8
Ditto ditto, Four Parts, complete, bound in cloth .	1	0
Ditto ditto, ditto; 2nd edition, now in the Press.		
Clift's Interlinear Instructor	0	5
Ditto ditto, another edition, published by the School-Book Society	0	5
Collection of Moral Precepts (interlinear)	0	3
Krishna Rau's Polygot, being the English Instructor in English, Hindustání, Mahratta, and Persian .	1	0

	R.	A.
Gospel of St. Matthew in English and Hindustání on opposite pages	0	10
Ditto St. Mark, ditto ditto	0	8
Sermon on the Mount, ditto ditto	0	2
Catechism on the Principles of Christianity (Tract Society's)	0	4
Another ditto, printed for the Rev. Mr. Bowley.		
Hindustání Hymns in English metre, by the Rev. Mr. Bowley	0	12
Primer, with a Frontispiece, by Sir C. D'Oyley . .	0	1
Ditto Hinduí	0	1
Picture Alphabet, per dozen	0	3
Copy slips (each book contains 38 copies) . .	0	2

Library of Entertaining Knowledge.

With Illustrations by Sir C. D'Oyley.

No. I. The Unhappy Mother who sacrificed her Infant, pp. 18	0	2
No. III. Cruelty to Animals, pp. 16	0	2
No. IV. Moral Precepts, pp. 18	0	2
No. V. Lucy and her Mother, pp. 18	0	2
No. VI. Little Girl and Butterfly, Shepherd's Boy, &c. pp. 18	0	2
No. VII. The Greyhound and the Mastiff; Virtue and Vice contrasted; and the Countryman and Snake, pp. 18	0	2
No. VIII. Ibráhím and his Happy Family, pp. 32 .	0	4
No. IX. History of Joseph, with cuts, pp. 88 . .	0	6

Bengálí and Anglo-Bengálí.

Gospel of St. Matthew in English and Bengálí on opposite pages	0	12
Sermon on the Mount, ditto ditto, 2nd edition . .	0	2
Níti-Kathá, Part 1	0	2
Ditto, Part 2	0	2
Animal Biography, No. 1	0	8

	R.	A.
English and Bengálí Student's Assistant, or Idiomatical Exercises, Part 1, Nouns	0	6
Ditto ditto, Part 2, Adjectives	0	4
Ditto ditto, complete in Four Parts—now in the Press.		
English Instructor, No. 2, interlinear translation, literal translation in native, and free translation in the Roman character	0	4
Bengálí Primer, with a Frontispiece, by Sir C. D'Oyley	0	1
Picture Alphabet, per dozen	0	3
Copy Slips (each book contains 38 copies) . .	0	2
D'Rozario's English, Bengálí, and Hindustání Dictionary	6	6

Uriya.

Reading Lessons, Roman and Uriya character . .	0	3
Níti-Kathá, Part 1, Roman character, pp. 18 . .	0	2
Ditto, Part 2, ditto, pp. 18	0	3
Natural Philosophy, Part 1, ditto, pp. 26 . . .	0	3
Ditto, Part 2, ditto, pp. 60	0	5

Asamese and Tai or Shán.

Spelling-Book in English, Asamese and Tai, prepared for the use of the Sadiyá Mission Schools.

The Parables of Christ in Asamese, ditto ditto.

Manipurí.

English, Bengálí, and Manipurí Dictionary, by Capt. Gordon, Political Agent at Manipur, in the Press.

The above books, being 57 in all, are to be had on application to Mr. Ostell, Bookseller, Tank-Square, Calcutta; and many others in the Roman character have been designed and will shortly be put in hand. All sums realised by the sale of the above books are employed in printing others in the same character.

(18.)

REVIEW OF THE ROMANISING SYSTEM, UP TO THE YEAR 1837.

BY MR. C. E. TREVELYAN.

I have read with much interest the discussions which have lately taken place on the subject of the general application of the Roman character to the languages of India. The superiority of this character over the other alphabetical systems at present in use in the East, its cheapness, its distinctness, its capability of compression, which so eminently fit it to be the organ of a national literature, seem now to be scarcely ever denied. This part of the subject is put in a very clear light by a letter lately published in the Agra paper, of which the following is an extract:—

"As to the character, I must confess, could I persuade myself of its practicability, I should by far prefer the Roman. It is so soon acquired, so easily read, so rapidly written, and its structure is so compact and uniform, and so well adapted for business: besides which, its stops, capitals, italics, and other expressive marks, afford so many advantages, that no character in the world can be compared to it. Hence it is not surprising, that it should have been adopted by the wisest nations all over the globe.

"Compared with this, the other characters are cumbrous and unmanageable. The Persian looks pretty indeed, but the letters are, for the most part, separate and very unsymmetrical in their structure; then there are numerous dots to be affixed, besides other marks to distinguish the vowel sounds. As to the Deva Nagri, it is almost as bad as the heavy old English or German text, characters which might have done very well in the dark ages for the scribes and copyists to waste their time upon, but are surely very ill calculated to meet the wants of these enlightened times, when so much writing is practised and such constant communication of thought is required."

Another great advantage arising from the general use of the Roman letters would be, that all the dialects of India being expressed in one common character, intercommunion of language and consequently intercommunion of thought, among the numerous races inhabiting the Peninsula, would be greatly facilitated. This position has been assailed by the *Friend of India*, by what appears to me to be a very illogical argument. He says that the majority of the European languages are expressed in a common character, but "has this happy circumstance produced any community of interest, any beneficial reciprocation of thought? Let the national jealousies, the perpetual wars of these nations, for many centuries, reply to this question?" Is it meant by this, that the wars which formerly raged among the nations of Europe are a conclusive proof that no "beneficial reciprocation of thought," no "community of interest," now exists between them? From the way in which the question is asked, this must be the inference intended, yet we all know that such is not the case. Among many causes which tend to unite nations, there are many others which have an opposite tendency. The study of the same languages and sciences, the similarity of the colloquial languages, and in our opinion the circumstance of those languages being expressed in one common character belong to the former, while conflicting commercial and political interests belong to the latter class. The wars which formerly prevailed merely prove that, as long as those wars lasted, the causes which produced disunion, whatever those causes were, predominated; just as the long peace which followed proves that those which tend to the existence of general harmony, whatever they were, have been since in the ascendant. Whether or not the use of a common written and printed character is one of the circumstances which assist in facilitating intellectual intercourse, and thereby in promoting a mutual good understanding, is a point which is left quite untouched by this argument.

The *Friend of India* goes on to state that "the most complete reciprocity of thought" does exist between the English, the Germans, and the Russians, notwithstanding their alphabetical characters are "perfectly distinet from each other," and that "this mental reciprocity springs from a corresponding elevation of mind, from that community of intellectual interest which pervades Europe." It did not occur to him, apparently, that the argument which he had just used about the wars is as conclusive against this cause of reciproeity as any other. "Has this happy circumstanee," we may ask in our turn, "produced any community of interest, any beneficial reciprocation of thought? Let the national jealousies, the perpetual wars of these nations, for many centuries, reply to the question." The unsoundness of the *Friend of India's* reasoning is, however, kept in countenance by the incorrectness of his assertions. Who does not know that the characters used by the English, Germans, and Russians, so far from being "perfectly distinct from each other," are very closely allied. Any body who can read the English, may learn to read the German character fluently in two or three hours, and Russian is written in the Roman character with a sprinkling of Greek. Of late years, also, German, as well as modern Greek, have been extensively printed in the Roman character. Thousands of German books which are annually imported into the United States for the use of that portion of the population whose native language is German, are almost entirely in this character.

"This mental reciprocity," says the *Friend of India*, "springs from a corresponding elevation of mind, from that community of intellectual interest which pervades Europe." These expressions are rather obscure, but we understand it to be meant, that the intellectual union of the natives of Europe is owing to the general agreement in their intellectual pursuits. This, it appears to me, is putting the effect for the cause. When people think and feel alike, when they have a "corresponding elevation of mind," a "community of intellectual interest" follows as a matter of course. The practical question is, how this much to be desired state of things can be brought about; how this "community of intellectual interest" can best be established.

It will be allowed that among the circumstances which conduce most directly to this result is the study by different nations of each other's languages: from which it follows, that whatever facilitates that study assists in producing the desired reciprocity. Now I ask, whether if English were expressed, as it is, in the Roman, French in the Arabic, Spanish in the Nagari, Italian in the Tamul, Dutch in the Bengali character, and so on, the study of foreign languages would be as easy or as common in Europe as it is at present?

Even this does not represent the full extent of the obstruction which the variety of different characters in India opposes to free mutual intercourse. As the vernacular languages of India are either derived from a common source or deeply impregnated by it, they are, for the most part, so similar to each other, that they ought rather to be considered as different dialects of the same language, than as different languages. If they were expressed in a common character, the same literature, with comparatively little alteration, would do for all; and every contribution to it, from whatever quarter, would be a direct addition to the common stock. Instead of this, almost every province has a separate character, and two, and sometimes more characters are current in every district. In the Upper Provinces, for instance, the Deva-Nagari, and several varieties of the Kaithi as well as of the Persian, are used by different classes of people in the same place. There is no use in urging that the Hindu Alphabets are derived from a common origin. No ordinary observer can trace any resemblance between the round characters of the South of India and of Arakan and Tenasserim and the square characters of the North*, and as for the Arabic character and its derivative the Persian, they are not only quite unlike the Indian letters, but have an entirely separate origin from them.

* In every case in which correspondence of arrangement and system now exists between provincial characters, it would be preserved in the Roman. The utmost extent of the change would be the substitution of signs of one shape for signs of another shape, but by this means the immense advantage of an easily learned, cheap, distinct, and a Europeanised and *uniform* alphabet would be obtained.

We need not dwell upon the evil consequences which must arise from the people of adjoining districts who speak different dialects of the same language (the people of Cuttack and Bengal for instance), and different classes of people in the same province who speak nearly the same dialect (the Hindus and Mahomedans, the Pundits and Bunyans for instance), being unable to correspond with each other, or to make any use of each other's literature, owing to the variety of characters in which they are expressed. If the south of England used one character and the north another, Scotland a third, Wales a fourth, Ireland a fifth, while the middle and upper classes throughout the United Kingdom used some the Deva-Nagari, some one form or other of the Kaithi, some the Persian or Arabic, and some the Roman character, would it not be considered a great national benefit if all these local characters could be superseded by the Roman? To say nothing of the obstructions to mutual intercourse, what an obstacle it would be to national improvement if every book had to be transferred into a dozen different characters before it became generally accessible, even if they were all equally good and cheap characters, which is not likely; and what small editions would be printed, and consequently how dear books would be, if the demand were split up into so many different sections! In many cases the limited number of readers in particular characters would prevent books from being printed at all in them. All these inconveniences are experienced in India, particularly in the Upper Provinces, where so many different characters pass current at the same place and time.

Another objection which has been urged by the *Friend of India* is, that, by reading the native languages in the Roman character, a child acquires a bad pronunciation of English. To this I reply that in Hindi, Bengali, and Uriya the consonants, with three exceptions each distinguished by a mark, are pronounced in every respect in the same way as in English; while, in words derived from the Persian and Arabic, there are only two additional consonants, which are also distinguished by marks; but, as these do not occur in English, they cannot teach a bad English pronunciation.

The objection, therefore, whatever it may be worth, is almost entirely confined to the vowels. Here, undoubtedly, it was impossible to establish entire uniformity, unless we had made the Indian mode of spelling as irregular as the English. The Roman letters were applied to the English language in so clumsy and unscientific a way, that the same vowel sign sometimes expresses half a dozen different sounds, and each in turn expresses the sounds of all. In applying them to the Indian languages, it was necessary to avoid this error, and to take care that each vowel sign had only one sound belonging to it. This was done by giving them the same power as they had in the Italian, and as they are supposed to have had in the original Latin.

But may not this use of them teach an incorrect pronunciation of English? By no means. Whenever a person learns English, whatever may be the nature of his previous acquirements, he has to learn to pronounce the same vowel sign in several different ways as occasion requires. If he was acquainted with one of these uses of it before, so much the better. He has so much less that is new to him to learn. It is as easy for him to distinguish between the use to which he has been accustomed to apply the letter, and the new uses to which he is now obliged to apply it, as it is to distinguish between each of those new uses. It is absurd to talk of puzzling a person who has to learn such different uses of the same vowel signs as *plough*, *enough*, *dough*, *through*, or who, when he has learnt *a-b ab*, is checked when he affixes the same sound to the vowel in *b-a ba*. Our knowledge of the powers of the Roman letters as they are used in English or Latin, does not prevent us from affixing the proper sounds to them when we learn French or Italian. We know that we have something to learn which we did not know before, and we keep the idea of our own and of the foreign language distinct in our minds. If there is any difficulty, it arises from the inability of our organs to pronounce sounds to which they have not been accustomed, and not from the different power of the same letter in different languages. This difficulty, we need not say, is not removed by the use of any character whatever. To the extent to which the powers of the Roman letters in Hindustani and English are the same, it must be allowed that their uniformity is a great assistanee both to the Englishman learning Hindustani and to the Indian learning English; while to the much smaller extent to which they differ, they both have to learn to affix new powers to the letters. In either ease, instead of having to learn an entirely new alphabet, they have to learn only a very few letters. There cannot be a doubt also, that English seientifie terms will be much more readily and aeeurately adopted into the vernaeular dialeets, and that both the words and spirit of the English language will become mueh more rapidly diffused through them, after they shall have been united with English in the bond of a common written and printed character.

The *Friend of India* admits that only one million out of the thirty millions of Bengal ean read. Why then does he talk about "every native in India relinquishing the native charaeter," and of "putting the people at onee in possession of our treasures" by translations into that charaeter? Sueh swelling phrases with so little meaning are of no avail.

And what sort of readers are this one million? How many of them understand what they read? How many can even pronounce fluently the mere words on a page they never saw before? Even Pundits and Munshees, and much more the common people, read with diffieulty, stopping to spell words, and repeating over and over the last two or three words while they are studying out the next. There are probably not five hundred persons in all India, not educated by Europeans, who could take up a translation in their own eharaeter of any work in philosophy, morals, or religion, and read it extempore with understanding.

The present state of the question seems to be as follows. The advantage of having only one eharaeter for the whole of India, and that eharaeter a eheap and easy one like the Roman, is very generally acknowledged. The practicability only is doubted, and the persons who have been deterred from giving their support to the plan by this consideration alone would have suffieed, if they had supported it, to place its ultimate success beyond all doubt. I shall therefore explain as briefly as possible my reasons for considering the plan *practicable.*

1. Their superior cheapness, which must give them the advantage of every other in popular opinion when they become sufficiently known.

Mr. De Rozario's English, Bengali, and Hindusthani Dictionary is comprised in one moderately sized octavo volume, and sells for six rupees but it has been correctly asserted* that if, instead of being printed entirely in the Roman character, it had been printed in the Roman, Bengali, and Persian or Nagari characters (that is to say, in a separate character for each language contained in it), it would have required more than three times the room, and have cost nearly three times as much as it now does. In the same way Mr. De Rozario's octavo edition of the Bagh o Bahar in Roman character of a large size sells for 1r. 8as., while the cheapest edition in the Persian character cannot be had for less than double that amount.

This remarkable difference of price is principally owing to the superior compactness of the Roman type, which makes it take up so much less room than any other, but not entirely. A fount of Nagari type cast at Serampore, which I have had examined, consists of no less than 700 letters, simple and compound †; and yet these only afford an equivalent for the thirty ordinary letters (including the accented letters) of the Indo-Roman alphabet, and make no provision for capitals, small capitals, italics, &c. After all this quantity of type has been provided, the vowel points must still be placed on various letters; and, owing to their resting on a thin strip of metal to allow of their being put above or below the consonants, they are very liable to be broken, and thus completely to embarrass the reader. If each consonant is cast with its proper variety of vowel points, which it has been already found necessary to do to a considerable extent, the size of the fount is increased to upwards of one thousand sepa-

* See *Christian Observer* for September, 1836.

† The great number of compound consonants in the Nagari character swells the types to this extent.

rate types! The same remarks apply in part to Bengali, although that type is somewhat less subject to breakage. Of the Persian it is not necessary to speak, as that character is already well-nigh abandoned, even by the enemies of the Roman system. The Burman fount lately cut in Calcutta requires above 900 letters; the Peguan more than 1000. Thus we might go on. Besides this, to procure a fount in a *new* character, or a smaller type in a character which has been already used, we are not, as in the Roman, at the mere expense of casting. A punch and a matrix must be made for each letter, at an expense of from one to two rupees each, without including the salary of the European superintendent; making a difference in the cost at once of from 1,000 to 2,000 rs. in a single fount, besides the cost of European superintendence. From all this any one may see how great a difference there must be, in the cost of type, between Oriental characters and Roman.

Add to this the greater space necessarily occupied by the native characters in the smallest size in which they have yet been cut, and then judge of the propriety of adopting for the purpose of national education a character so essentially defective, in contrast with one so eminently adapted for the purpose. The cost of paper and press-work alone for a book in Oriental letters would, on the average, be more than double what it would be in Roman, and the cost of binding would be in the same proportion. This evil is incurable. The number of double and triple letters, one underneath the other, with the arkaphola, &c., above them, render it impossible that the space now occupied by the native characters can ever be diminished so as to bear a comparison with the Roman.

2. The Roman character is likely to become more popular than the Nagari and Bengali, because it is so much easier both to read and write.

In the first place, it takes much less time to learn. In Nagari, when two or more letters come together, they are done up together into a strange kind of compound containing frequently very slight traces of either of the letters taken by themselves. These compounds amount to several hundreds. Without being familiar with them, it is impossible to peruse any book or writing, and they are each nearly as difficult to learn as a separate letter.

But when the same language is expressed in the Roman letters, each consonant retains its original form, however it may be placed in conjunction with others, and therefore, when the learner has mastered the thirty simple letters, he may at once commence reading.

This circumstance, much more than any difference in the mode of tuition, accounts for the extraordinary difference in the length of time taken by English and native children in learning to read. To read fluently in the native character is a still more difficult task than learning to read it at all. A native boy who is taught to read in the Roman character will in the course of two or three months be able to read, without stopping, anything that is put before him, whether he understands it or not, but a fluent reader in the Nagari or Bengali character is almost unheard of. We do not pretend to be able to explain all the causes to which this difference is owing, but such is undoubtedly the fact. It must be owing to one great cause, which is that the Roman character is a better one than the native. It is of course easier for the eye to become familiarised with only thirty, than with several hundred, separate signs; and something must also be attributed to the stops and other marks with which the eye is assisted in reading the Roman character. These causes lie on the surface.

When from reading we proceed to writing, the superior convenience of the Roman character is more striking than ever. The Nagari and Bengali have, in fact, no running hand.* To say nothing of the frequent occurrence of double consonants, which cannot be written without much delay and attention to exactness, the Nagari and Bengali alphabets consist of square-looking characters which are totally unsuited

* Some time ago one of the teachers of the Hindu College requested one of the best Bengali copyists he knew to write as rapidly as he could in the native character while he wrote in the Roman. In thus writing against time the advantage in favour of the Roman characters was two and half to one!

by their shape to be written in quick succession, and if this is attempted, they become unintelligible even to the writer himself, and still more to other people. It would be a much easier task to introduce the Roman running hand at once, than to effect such a change in the Nagari and Bengali as would admit of their being written quickly and intelligibly. In the one case, we should only have to teach the use of a character which has been adapted by gradual improvements, made in the course of many centuries by the most refined nations in the world, to the purpose of quick and legible writing, and which is already extensively used in India both by Europeans and natives; while in the other, we should have first to change the character itself, and then to teach it to everybody after it had been so changed. If the Nagari were to be modified to the extent necessary for the formation of a running hand, it would in effect become a new character. The Roman, however, is far from being a new character in the East, being already used by great and increasing numbers of the most influential classes in every part of India; and the Roman (viz. the English) running hand is likely to be much more easily acquired, and to be much better suited for quick and legible writing, than any which we should be able to form by a sudden alteration of the Nagari. The proper transaction of the judicial and other public business, to say nothing of private convenience, depends, it will be remembered, upon the adoption of a character which can be quickly and legibly written.

3. Owing to the common use of one character, the student will be saved the trouble of learning a new character for each language.

Thus, for instance, in order to make full use of Mr. De Rozario's Dictionary, which is in three languages, the student has only to learn the Roman character; whereas, if each of those languages were expressed in a separate character, which is what the opponents of our views wish, he would have to acquire, first the Roman; then the Bengali, and then the Nagari or Persian. In India, where so many languages prevail, the plan of having only one character must be allowed to be a great advantage. It is like having one master key to unlock a number of doors.

The student will now be able to turn at once from one language to another, without having first to perfect himself in a number of strange characters; and books which are printed in more than one language (which must frequently be the case in India for a long time to come) will yet be expressed in one common character. Though it does not take long to *decipher* a new set of characters, it requires long practice to be able to *read fluently* in them. All who have tried the experiment (let others say what they will) know and admit this. According to the new plan, as soon as a person has learned to read fluently in one Indian language, he will be able to read fluently in all, and he will also see at once how far each new language corresponds with those with which he is already acquainted.

"If a book in Latin, English, French, Spanish, and Italian were presented even to an unlearned Englishman, in the Roman character, he would readily perceive that numberless words, and roots of words, were the *same* in all; and would conclude that the study of one, two, or more of these might be a comparatively easy task, in consequence of this *palpable radical similarity*. But were the book presented in Roman, modern Gothic, old Gaulish, Visigothic, and Lombardic characters, he could scarcely be persuaded that under forms so wholly different there could lurk any similarity at all, and the study would be regarded a forbidding and difficult, if not a hopeless one. So actually stands the case in India; the number of *dialects* is immense, and each dialect has letters of a different figure. Let then a specimen of each be presented to an unlearned Hindoo: what must be his conclusion? What *can* it be, except that his country abounds with totally *different languages?* And if so, the attempt to hold any communication with natives not of his own province is likely to be abandoned as hopeless. Now were the whole presented in the *same character*, it would be *seen* and *felt* that the natives are not divided into so many sections of foreigners to each other; that they have *all fundamentally* the *same* language; and that without much difficulty a community of interest and a beneficial reciprocation of thought might be effected to an extent at present unknown, and from the repulsive aspect of so many written characters, deemed utterly impracticable."*

4. There is no accumulated literature in India which would be displaced by the general adoption of the Roman character.

If a new mode of spelling were to be adopted in Europe, it would affect millions of volumes printed according to the existing mode: but there is no such difficulty in India. The vernacular literature is quite in its infancy. It cannot boast of a single original work of any eminence; and the aggregate number of books composing it is so small, that they could early and easily be replaced by the existing presses. The present state of native literature, therefore, opposes no barrier to the execution of the plan. There is no sacrifice to be made. We must, at any rate, construct a native literature almost from the beginning. What is now proposed is, to do this in a cheap and effectual manner.

5. The young are for the most part the class of persons who are to be taught the Roman character, and it is manifest that they can have no prejudice against it except that prejudice be instilled into them by their parents. But the latter have no prejudice to instil. They invite us to teach their children our *language*, and it would therefore be strange if they were to object to their being taught our printed and written *character*. Repeated declarations have been made, that the spectacle of their children reading their native language fluently in the English character has excited the surprise and pleasure of parents. The prejudices and alarms of which we have heard so much are confined, as far as can be judged from anything that has appeared, to the breasts of the alarmists themselves.

The single fact that a child of three years old has no predilection in favour of the Nagari or Persian letters is worth

* "The Application of the Roman Alphabet to all the Oriental Languages, contained in a series of papers, written by Messrs. Trevelyan, J. Prinsep, and Tytler, the Rev. A. Duff and Mr. H. T. Prinsep, and published in various Calcutta periodicals in the year 1834."—From the *Serampoor Press*, 1834.

a thousand reasons. His interest and wishes (if he is capable of entertaining any on such a subject) can only incline him to learn the easiest character, whichever that may be. Now in teaching the youth of a country, we are really teaching the whole people. The children of to-day will be the men of twenty years hence. If we can only instruct the young (and among them the Roman system, when introduced, has been remarkably popular), it is of little consequence, as far as the progress of the plan is concerned, what the old learn or refrain from learning. Happily for India, the education of the most influential portion of her youth is at this moment in the hands of the English, either in their public or private capacity, and the education of the whole nation (a glorious charge) is rapidly coming under their superintendence. The formation of the native literature is also under their control. We may, therefore, teach what we like in our schools, and supply what books we like to the youth who have left them. The systems taught in the National schools will, there can be no doubt, in time become the prevailing systems of the country. Even one school at each Zilla station would be sufficient to secure this result. When we consider that these schools are situated in the great towns, the seats of wealth and intelligence, that they will furnish most of the masters for the subordinate schools, and that the persons educated at them are the children of the middle and upper classes, who will hereafter exercise the greatest influence in society, it is clear that it cannot be otherwise. The Kusba* and village schools, when they are established, will adopt the practice of the Zilla schools; the books printed in the Roman character will be generally read, and thus the system will soon pervade every part of the country. If it be admitted that the establishment of one character in every part of British India would be a national benefit, and that that character ought to be the cheapest and best, and that which will most closely connect the languages of the East with European literature, there can be no doubt of our having it in our power to effect it. The Government seminaries alone, to say nothing of

* A Kusba is a small country town.

those supported by Missionary bodies and private individuals, will be sufficient for the purpose.

6. Large tracts of country are entirely destitute of the use of letters of any kind, and in others they are used so sparingly as to render the introduction of the Roman letters a matter of the utmost ease. The great tract between the Brahmaputra and the Ningthi on the Eastern frontier of Bengal, and the great central space bounded by Bengal on the East, Hyderabad on the West, Cuttack and the Northern Sirkars on the South, and Nagpoor and the Saugor territory on the North, are instances in point. The obstacles which are supposed to be so formidable in other parts of India, have no existence here. As no letters are used at present, neither old nor young can be prejudiced against any particular alphabetical system, however they may be against letters in general. There are also no books in any other character which would be rendered useless by the introduction of the Roman. As regards districts so situated, the question is one of abstract expediency. Every character will be equally acceptable to the people. The only point to be determined is, which is the best. The superior cheapness of the Roman character, its superior distinctness, the ease with which it may be written quickly and distinctly, and the connexion which it establishes between every language expressed in it and the literatures of the West, naturally lead to a decided preference being given to that character. The great Eastern tract between the Brahmaputra and Ningthi has been already inoculated with it at two points. A dictionary will shortly be published in the English, Bengali, and Manipuri languages, all expressed in the Roman character; and a press has been established at Sadiya, in Upper Assam, at which the preparation of a series of works in the Roman character, in the languages of that quarter, has been commenced. A good press would print in one week ten times the number of books which are now to be found within 100 miles of Sadiya or Manipur. Whatever scanty literature there may be at present will soon be superseded by the productions of the English presses, or will be adopted into them, and the numerous hill languages in that quarter,

in which there are at present no books of any kind, will be expressed in one common, cheap, and excellent character, instead of being parcelled out among the Bengali, the Shan, the Burmese, or any others which may have their advocates as well as the Nagari and Persian. Except in the Cherokee language, for which a native Indian invented a new character, all versions of the Sacred Scriptures and other books published in America for the Aborigines (and they are by no means few) have been expressed in the Roman character; nor have any diacritical marks been used, though sounds more crabbed cannot probably be found in any language on earth. The same has been done in the Sandwich Islands, and, we believe, in all the islands in the Pacific Ocean and South Sea the languages of which have been reduced to writing by the Missionaries. It was particularly satisfactory to the originators of the plan in India to find, on a comparison of their system of orthography with that which had been adopted in the Sandwich Islands, that the two exactly corresponded. Both parties, though acting on opposite sides of the globe, without any communication with each other; arrived at the conclusion, that, in order to establish a perfect system, it was necessary to pass over the erroneous application of the Roman letters which had been made to the English language, and to return to their original powers in the Latin and Italian.

7. Our opponents are accustomed to argue as if we had undertaken an untried experiment. In fact, however, the experiment has not only been tried, but has succeeded, and that not in any foreign country, the circumstances of which might be very different from those of India, but in India itself. In the Upper Provinces the vernacular language is generally written by educated natives in the Persian character, which is not the original native character, but a foreign innovation. Persian was the language of education, and educated people therefore naturally used the Persian character when they wrote the vernacular language. Precisely the same cause which led to the introduction of the Persian character is now operating, not only in the same, but in a much greater degree, to introduce the Roman. The Maho-

medans had no system of popular education. Those who could afford to do so, educated their children; but printing was unknown, books were very expensive, and no facilities were afforded for obtaining instruction either by the Government or by the voluntary associations of private individuals. But as we have now all these advantages, there is every reason to suppose that in the course of a few years, fifty children will learn English for one who used to learn Persian, and the tendency towards the introduction of the English character will be in the same proportion. It is impossible that the Persian character can stand when it has once been disconnected with the Persian language. It is radically bad, both as a written and printed character; and the only circumstance which has given it currency is, that the Persian language is written in it, and that Persian was the language of education. When the educated classes, therefore, have ceased to use the Persian character, what character will they adopt? As before stated, the English language will not only take the place of Persian as the language of education, but will occupy a much larger space than Persian ever did. It follows, therefore, that the English character, which is every way worthy of adoption on account of its intrinsic excellence, will occupy the vacant place, and be extensively used by the upper and middle classes, and ultimately, it may with safety be asserted, by the body of the people.

Nor is this the only example of the successful introduction of a foreign character in the East. Amongst the numerous natives of Java, Amboyna, and the surrounding slands who embraced Christianity under the Dutch Missionaries, the Roman character has been successfully introduced, and is to the present day universally read. The number who use it is so considerable, that a few years ago a large edition of the Scriptures (3,000 copies of the whole Bible, and 3,000 additional copies of the New Testament) was executed for them at the expense of the Calcutta Bible Society.* The general use of this character in these regions,

* At Amboyna alone are 20,000 persons who universally use the Malay Scriptures in the Roman character. See letters of Dr. Carey, as per accounts of the Baptist Missionary Society, vol. v. 7.

so far as the influence of education is felt, must produce on the mind of every impartial observer the well-grounded conviction, that, in our position as the *national instructors of India,* the friends of education have but to unite in the effort to introduce the Roman character, and they cannot fail of success.

8. Lastly, we may fairly deduce the continued progress of the system from the progress which it has already made. Three years ago it was only an idea, a mere thought, undigested, unpromulgated, unreduced to practice. This germ has now grown into a system, which is actively supported by numerous persons in different parts of India. The first difficulties have been overcome. The public is daily becoming more and more accustomed to the new letters. Several thousand books expressed in them have been already put into circulation, and several thousand more are now in the press. All the books which were first printed were formed into a fund, the proceeds of which are employed in printing other similar books; and, which is the most satisfactory symptom of all, private speculators and benevolent societies, quite independent of the original projectors, have taken up the system and are actively engaged in the preparation of new books. The Government Education Committee has hitherto very properly remained neutral. It is always safest for Governments rather to follow public opinion in such matters than to attempt to lead it themselves. No obstacle, however, is opposed by the Education Committee to the progress of the plan; and if the local committees wish for books in the Roman character, they are left at perfect liberty to supply themselves with them.

The introduction of one character, instead of the many now used in the British territories in India, is acknowledged to be most desirable.

This being granted, the question arises, *which* shall be adopted? Of the native characters in this Presidency (to say nothing of Madras or Bombay) we must adopt the Bengali, the Deva, or some one of the many forms of the Kaithi Nagari, or the Persian, or Arabic, or the Uriya. As an *universal* character for India, no one has yet proposed to us to adopt the Bengali or Uriya; and some few who recommended the Arabic or Persian have now given that up. The only question regards, therefore, the comparative advantages of the Roman and the Nagari. Now regarding the Nagari character, it is a fact, that some years ago, when Government proposed to print an edition of the Regulations in the Hindui language, they sent to the principal officers of Government throughout the Upper Provinces specimens of Deva Nagari and of Kaithi Nagari printing in the most approved types, and requested them to ascertain which of these characters was generally understood by the people under their authority. The general reply to the circular was to the following effect: that while many individuals, for the most part Brahmins, were found in each district and large town, who could read with comparative ease the Deva Nagari character, it was used by the people generally in no district whatever; that the written character employed in the transaction of business was the Kaithi; but that this was so different in different districts, (as any one may ascertain for himself who will compare chits and hundies* procured from different parts of the country,) that they could recommend *no form of the character whatever* which would be generally understood. Under what obligations, then, are we to introduce a character possessing none of the advantages of association, either with the rulers of the country or with the great majority of the population, when we have the opportunity of teaching in our schools whatever character we please.

The truth is, that the Roman character not only is the best of those which are at present used in India, but may be brought into general use with much greater ease than any of them. We have seen that, even in those British provinces in which Deva Nagari is most prevalent, it is confined to a small minority of the educated class. The great majority of those who can read and write use the Kaithi, Persian, or other characters. In any case, therefore, before one character can become general, the majority must learn some character of the minority; and, of all the different characters which are now used, the English is the easiest to learn, and is the one to which the influential classes (who formerly learned Persian

* Native Letters and Bills of Exchange.

but now learn English) will soon become most attached. A Persian Amla *, and still more an English schoolboy, would certainly prefer the English to the rugged intractable Nagari character. In Bengal and the whole of India south of the Nerbudda, the case is still more decidedly against the Nagari. Here it is not used by any class of persons. Both the vernacular and the learned languages are written in a provincial character, which in most cases bears no resemblance to the Nagari. An attempt, which was supported by all the wealth and learning of the College of Fort William, was once made to introduce the Nagari letters into Bengal, but, as the plan was not recommended by any practical benefit (the Nagari letters being rather less, than more, convenient for printing and writing than the Bengali), it ended in failure.

But how stands the question regarding the Roman character? English is rapidly becoming the language of education from one end of India to the other. This character, therefore, is everywhere known. It is the character used in keeping a great proportion of the public records and accounts. It is used in all the higher order of schools. It is used by all persons who have received a liberal education. There is little occasion, therefore, for teaching or propagating this character. It is already taught and propagated, and is every day coming into more general use. Every native who receives a tolerable education learns it by learning English, and it would be a saving of time and labour to him to use it also in writing and reading his native language, instead of learning other, and more difficult, and less convenient characters for that purpose. All that is required to be done is to prepare books in the native languages and Roman character, and to introduce them into our schools. Provided this is done, the convenience of the educated classes, who everywhere determine the nature of the literature of a country, and the real superiority of the Roman letters over every other at present in use in India, must ultimately settle the question in their favour.

The only hope, it appears to me, of the people of India ever becoming an united people, is by their being inoculated

* An administrative officer of the Courts of Justice who transacts business in Persian.

at all points by English literature, by their all being recast upon the English model; and if this be admitted, it must also be allowed that the general adoption of the English character would be a very essential aid. This character admits of the introduction of European terms, and consequently of European ideas, much more easily and correctly* than any other. As there would be only one character for the whole of India, those terms would be everywhere uniformly spelt. The new literature of India would commence, as far as possible, upon a common basis. All its different tribes would have the same learned language, the same written and printed character, the same scientific terms. The tendencies of this state of things would all be in favour of uniformity. The vernacular languages very much resemble each other at present; and when they are expressed in a common character, and enriched from a common source, they will every year become more and more like each other. The mass must certainly become leavened and amalgamated more speedily after all its different parts shall have been united by the bond of a common character, both among themselves and with the source whence they are to be enriched; to which must be added the advantage of having a cheap, an easily learned, an easily written, and a distinct and easily read alphabet, to serve as the medium of the national literature, instead of others which are very deficient in most or all of these respects.

I am aware that there is much repetition and desultory writing in this paper, for which I hope I may be excused, but I think that those who have had patience to follow me, must allow that it would be a great national benefit if *one* character could be brought into general use in India; that the Roman character not only offers greater advantages, but

* In the account which the Burmese ambassadors wrote of their mission, English names were disfigured in such a way as to render it difficult to trace them; in explanation of which Colonel Burney observes that "it is impossible to write many of our names in the Burmese character, particularly those having double consonants. It will at once be allowed that if the Burmese language were expressed in the English letters, which admit of no double consonants, this difficulty would be in a great measure removed, and the same would be the case in a greater or less degree in regard to every other Eastern language."

might be more easily diffused than any other; and that if the European community would only assist to the extent to which they find that they carry the native feeling with them, its general introduction is perfectly feasible. The *Friend of India* calculates (not incorrectly, I think) that there are about one million of persons in Bengal who are able to read; and as the population of the Upper Provinces is supposed to be about equal to that of Bengal, there would, at this rate, be about two millions of persons in the British dominions on this side of India who are able to read. These, it will be remembered, are all grown up people, and the place of those who die off is supplied by the newly educated youth. But the education of the youth is already in a great measure in our own hands, and is daily becoming more and more so. If the children be taught for a few years the Roman character, those who are ignorant of it will become the minority. Even now there are about six thousand youths educated at the Government seminaries alone. When a school is established at each Zilla station, there will be sixty thousand; and when, proceeding a step further, we establish Kusba and Village schools, there is no saying how many we shall have under instruction; and to these must be added those who will be educated at the Missionary and private establishments, and those who will be instructed in their own families or at native schools, by masters and books supplied by us. In one way or another, nearly all the readers of the forthcoming generation will be taught by European benevolence; and it is therefore preposterous to say that we cannot, if we like to do so, generally introduce any character, and still more one which has so much to recommend it from its cheapness and intrinsic excellence, and from the opportunity which it affords of closely connecting all the native literatures, both among themselves and with the literature of Europe. Nobody can be the worse for the change. The number of persons who will use the old characters will annually diminish; and as every good book will be printed both in the old and new characters as long as there is a demand for it in both, even they will not be subjected to any inconvenience. Were it otherwise, it would not be right to condemn posterity to the perpetual use of an inconvenient and expensive character for the sake of a portion of the present existing generation which is annually diminishing in number, and will soon entirely pass away. But, in fact, the general introduction of the Roman character will deprive nobody of anything. It will be a free gift without any corresponding sacrifice.

The advocates of the Roman character ask but little. They prefer no exclusive claims. "Fair play and no favour" is their full demand. Let the native character of each province be taught to all the youth in our schools, that they may be qualified to read and understand anything either written or printed which may fall in their way; but let them be *also* taught the Roman character, as applied to the Indian languages, and furnished with books in that character, (they will always be twice as cheap as in any other,) as rapidly as they are needed and prepared. To this the advocates of the native characters ought not to offer any objection, since, while it gives the pupil a knowledge of a character which must be acknowledged desirable for him to acquire, it also affords him the opportunity of deriving every advantage as to bodily support or mental improvement which a knowledge of the old characters can afford him. A process of this kind would shock no feelings, would inflict no injury, would entail no expense, and yet would gradually melt down all the native characters into the Roman, the "consummation devoutly to be wished."

Are we *always* to have, even in the countries under British influence and government, so many characters? Are we *never* to make the approximation to union of language and feeling which a common character affords? Must literature and literary men to the remotest ages be subject to all the confusion, difficulty, and expense that now embarrass us? All will reply: No; in time we must do as in Europe. But many say, we must wait a fitting season. What season so fitting as the present; when an entire literature is to be formed, and almost an entire population taught to read? When nothing is to be lost, and when scarcely any are to be incommoded.

This being granted, which character shall be adopted?

The whole tenor of this paper goes to answer that question. Indeed it will seem a marvel fifty years hence that ever it could have been made a question. Let us then adopt that character which will multiply Oriental scholars, smooth the path of learning, save an expense of millions, and hasten by ages the spread of science, morals, and religion.

C. E. TREVELYAN.

November 1, 1836.

(19.)

LETTER FROM THE REV. R. C. MATHER TO SIR CHARLES TREVELYAN, SHOWING THE PROGRESS MADE IN APPLYING THE ROMAN LETTERS TO THE LANGUAGES OF INDIA UP TO THE COMMENCEMENT OF THE GREAT MUTINY IN 1857.

Waterloo Cottage, Tonbridge,
January 16, 1858.

Dear Sir Charles,

I was surprised, but delighted, to learn in the course of a conversation I had with Dr. Duff two years ago, when, having returned to India, he passed through Mirzapur on his way to Calcutta, that you continued to cherish all the interest in the Romanising system which you had so signally displayed twenty-four years previously. At that time I was new to India; but, shortly after making your acquaintance, I left Calcutta for Benares and Mirzapur, and commenced the study of the Hindústání and Hindí languages, and have ever since been engaged in communicating, through those vernaculars, both our religion and our science orally, and by publications from the press, to the natives of the North-west Provinces. From the first I was highly impressed with the advantages connected with the general introduction of the Romanising system of Sir William Jones, as modified by yourself and the Rev. Dr. Duff and Mr. Pearce, and have all along laboured to promote its diffusion.

I am happy to say that our labours have been crowned with a success which, at the beginning, we did not dare to anticipate. The Roman character has spread to that extent, that not only those who have learned English prefer to read the vernaculars in it; but, in addition, it is at the present time *the Christian character of the North-west Provinces*, since it is used by the great majority both of our missionaries and their converts. We have in it a body of general and religious literature of many volumes and of thousands of pages; and the saleableness of works in that character is progressively increasing, and now far exceeds what it was even five years ago, and much more what it was at the commencement of our efforts. As an instance, I may say that we printed a revised and simplified edition of Miss Bird's Geography, as one of our first school-books. That edition consisted of only five hundred copies; but it took ten years to sell them at two shillings each. We have since printed a second edition; and within two years nearly all have been disposed of at the same price. To a person conversant only with the educational book-market at home, this will seem a very small result. It should be understood, however, that in the present state of the Indian mind geography is regarded not as a necessity, but a marvellous luxury; and that Miss Bird's work is only one out of several compilations used in our schools. So viewed, the fact is important, as showing progress of a sure character; for no native will buy what he does not believe is good and necessary for him. And here it will be well to add, that all our publications in the Roman character, of which I propose to give an account somewhat in detail, have been originated in the *bonâ fide* conviction that they would sell, and more than clear the outlay incurred in their preparation. This conviction experience has shown to be well founded, as, in the case of the Mirzapur printing-office, one important source of support has been the sale of vernacular books printed in the Roman character.

A still more signal proof, however, of the hold the system now has on the minds of our missionaries in the North-west Provinces of India, who, it should be remembered, form a body of 102 persons, is the resolution adopted at a Conference of Missionaries held at Benares in January of 1857, in respect to the continued use of the character. They say, "While thankful for what has been done towards providing a literature suited to the wants of native Christians and the Hindú and Mussulman population at large, the Conference at the same time feels the importance and need of using the utmost endeavours to enlarge and improve it. The Conference is generally of opinion that it is desirable to continue the use of the Roman character, more especially for native Christians; but at present sees no reason for supplanting the native characters in general use." It should be noted that in this Conference thirty missionaries and two chaplains of the Hon. East India Company were associated, and, with one exception, all were unanimous in the support of the resolution.

On the day previous to the meeting of the Benares Conference, there were assembled in the same hall 150 native youths, Hindú, Mussulman, and Christian, who had come from all parts of the Benares division to stand an examination on the Sacred Scriptures, with a view to obtain certain prizes of considerable value, which had been offered to those who should show the most extensive acquaintance with Scripture truth. On that occasion, in a class of 152, 26 prizes were awarded, of the aggregate value of 1,252 rupees. Of the answers submitted in writing, 76 were written in Urdú-Persian; 12 in Urdú-Roman; 18 in the English language; 46 in Hindí and Nagarí. Respecting these comparative results the editor of the *Khair-Khwáh-i-Hind* observes: "It is worthy of observation, that while the candidates using the English language were few compared with those using the Urdú and Hindí, they have carried off the majority of prizes. The competitors using the Urdú language, but writing the Roman character, come next in the order of success. The only explanation we can give of this remarkable fact is, that on them European teachers had bestowed a larger measure of attention, and that their minds had consequently been better trained. The Urdú and Hindí competitors have, perhaps, as a whole, given a larger measure of fact and quotation ; but in original composition, in independent thought indicative of an understanding of the subject, in grasp of mind, they have, as a class, been left far behind." You will be pleased to read this statement, as demonstrating what was long ago asserted as a probable result,—that the Roman character would be an important help in the communication and reception of knowledge in its clearest and most exact forms.

The system current amongst us is that which you originated, with two exceptions. Instead of expressing غ by gh, we express it by g ; also for the ع we write the vowel represented by it, with a comma before or after the letter; but on the top of the line, instead of below it, as اعمال we write *A'amál.* The system of Romanising has been applied amongst us only to the Hindústání as current in the North-Western Provinces: or, if to the Hindí at all, only in the case of a Hindí Primer. The library of Urdú-Roman school-books, originated by yourself and Messrs. Duff and Yates, formed the basis of the school and general library since issued from the press. Before you left India, Henry Martyn's four Gospels and Acts had been printed in the Roman character by the Bible Society, at your suggestion and under your superintendence. Since then, two separate translations of the entire New Testament have been Romanised and printed. After these had seen the light, the whole Bible appeared in the Roman character, under the editorial care of the Rev. J. A. Shurman. This edition consisted of 3,000 copies, and has since been exhausted. A second edition of the Old Testament left the press a short time ago, partly under the care of Mr. Shurman, and subsequently under my care. This, too, consists of 3,000 copies. The New Testament, uniform with the Old, is now being completed at Mirzapur under the care of the Rev. M. A. Sherring. The four Gospels and the Acts have also been recently published by the Rev. Mr. Lewis in the language of the inhabitants of the Khasia Hills.

Next to the Scriptures, in order of time, was commenced our native newspaper, the *Ḳhair-Ḳhwáh-i-Hind.* This was started in September, 1837; and, up to the time of the mutinous outbreaks of May last, has been regularly printed both in the Persian and Roman characters. The new series alone, commencing with the year 1845, forms a volume of 1,200 closely printed pages. This periodical is taken by all the missions in Northern India, and aims to be the organ of the native Christian community. It has often been suggested to us that it would be well to reprint large portions of the work, that continuity might be imparted to subjects which have been treated in sections written at different periods; and a plan was submitted to the Agra government to reprint the natural history articles with illustrations, both woodcuts and lithographs; and it was then estimated that the first volume on the Mammalia would extend to 500 duodecimo pages.

The Pilgrim's Progress, abridged by the Rev. W. Bowley, next appeared in Urdú-Roman; then a volume of Hymns in Hindústání by the same author was passed through the press by yourself. Of this little work there have been two or three editions, and it is in universal use by our native Christians. After this came Miss Bird's Geography, simplified and enlarged by the Rev. Messrs. Mather and Glen, of the Mirzapur mission. What have subsequently appeared I will insert in a tabular form, arranging the publications, not in keeping with the order of time, but similarity of subject, or the classes of persons for whose benefit they have been written.

SCHOOL-BOOKS.

Urdú-Roman.

		PAGES
1. History of India. (Marshman.) *Duodecimo.*	about	300
2. Moral Precepts in Verse. (Capt. Paton.) .	„	150
3. Mirzapur Picture-Books, eight Numbers. By Mrs. Mather	„	140
4. The Peep of Day. By Mrs. Leupolt . .	„	150

	PAGES
5. Ancient History. By Rev. J. A. Shurman . about	300
6. A Treatise on Astronomy. (Paton.) . . „	80
7. The Bágh-o-Bahár.	
8. The Gulistán.	
9. A Catechism of the Principles of the Christian Religion.	
10. The Assembly's Shorter Catechism.	
11. Gallaudet's Book on the Soul. By the Rev. J. Wilson.	

MANUALS FOR NATIVE CATECHISTS.

Urdú-Roman.

12. A Manual of Theology. By Rev. Messrs. Mather and Glen . . . . „	310
13. A Companion to the Bible. By ditto . . „	386
14. A Manual of Church History. By Rev. J. H. Budden, W. Muir, Esq., and Rev. Messrs. Mather and Glen . . . . . . „	298
15. A Commentary on the First Ten Chapters of Genesis. By Rev. J. Owen . . . . „	300
16. Dr. Hodges' Way of Life. By the Rev. J. Warren . . . . „	300

A LIBRARY FOR THE NATIVE CHRISTIAN COMMUNITY.

Urdú-Roman.

17. Gallaudet's Ruth. By Rev. J. Wilson.	
18. A Volume of Sermons by various Authors. Edited by Rev. J. Warren . . . „	300
19. Jesus, the Child's Best Teacher.	
20. Flavel's Fountain of Life. By Rev. J. Warren. Abridged . . . . . . „	350
21. Watts and Henry on Prayer. Abridged by Rev. J. Warren.	
22. True Wisdom: Eight Sermons. By Rev. J. Warren.	
23. Mrs. Sherwood's Little Henry and his Bearer. By Rev. J. H. Budden.	

PAGES

24. One Hundred and Fifty Hymns. By the Rev. W. Bowley.
25. Four Hundred and Forty-five Psalms and Hymns. By Rev. W. Bowley and others.
26. Rev. J. A. James's Anxious Enquirer. By Rev. W. Buyers.
27. Legh Richmond's Dairyman's Daughter. By Rev. J. Warren.
28. Legh Richmond's Young Cottager. By Rev. J. Warren.
29. Life of Africaner. By Rev. Messrs. Mather and Glen.
30. Life of the Egyptian Martyr, Muhammad Sha'abán. By Rev. Messrs. Mather and Glen.
31. Moffat's Forsaken Mother. By Rev. Messrs. Mather and Glen.
32. Mrs. Sherwood's Indian Pilgrim. By Harí Babú. Revised by Rev. R. C. Mather.
33. Bunyan's Pilgrim's Progress. Parts I. and II. Translated in full by Baboo Harí John.
34. The Narrative of the German Cripple. By Rev. W. Glen.
35. The Narrative of the Man that killed his Neighbour. By Rev. W. Glen.
36. Little Louis. By Rev. P. Sandberg.
37. Little Anna. By Rev. P. Sandberg.
38. Our Lord's Last Command: or, Communicant's Manual. By J. Mackay, Esq.
39. A Threefold Cord: or, A Precept, Promise, and a Prayer for every Day in the Year. By Rev. R. C. Mather.
40. A Sermon on the Sins that do so easily beset us. By Rev. R. C. Mather.
41. The Confession of Faith. By Rev. Dr. Campbell.
42. The Book of Common Prayer. By Rev. W. Smith.

PAGES

43. The Qurán (Koran). With Introduction, Notes, and Index. By the Rev. J. Wilson and E. Frazer, Esq. . . . about 550
44. Hindusthání and English, and English and Hindusthání Dictionary. By De Rozario.
45. Thompson's Hindusthání and English Dictionary.
46. Nathaniel Brice's Hindusthání and English Dictionary.

The above list contains, I think, all the works that have been published in Urdú-Roman. Probably the matter would fill 11,000 to 12,000 duodecimo pages, were it all transferred to that form. This is a result which, were it now only a possibility in the future, instead of an actual fact, would seem to us very important.

Before closing this letter, I will suggest a most practicable mode of rendering the Romanising system popular amongst all classes of the natives of India. It is only necessary that Government should announce its willingness to receive petitions in the vernacular, but written in any character. The natives naturally wish that their petitions should be read, and their real meaning understood; and, as they suppose that their English rulers understand their own characters best, they would of their own accord get their petitions written in those characters. How much good such an usage would accomplish in putting a check on the duplicity and frauds of the native officials, it is easy for any one who has been in India to understand. What an amazing benefit would result, also, were all the accounts of Government kept in the Roman character! The despatch of business would be immensely facilitated, and the perpetration of frauds would become proportionately difficult.

It has always seemed to me most unwise to permit the use of the Shikasta (Persian running-hand) in our law courts. Next to the benefits arising from the introduction of the Roman character, would be the benefits that would result, were it made imperative that all legal documents should be executed by Ḳhush Nawíses (engrossing clerks) writing in the Nastálíq form (answering to our round hand); or if in the Hindí language, in the well-made Deva Nágari letters.

I am, &c.
(Signed) ROBERT COTTON MATHER.

Sir C. E. Trevelyan, K.C.B.
&c. &c. &c.

(20.)

ON THE DIFFICULTY OF THE ORIENTAL CHARACTERS, AND THE ADVANTAGES OF APPLYING THE ROMAN ALPHABET TO THE LANGUAGES OF INDIA.

(*Extracted from the* TIMES, *November* 10, 1858.)

One of the greatest difficulties with which we have to contend in the government of India arises out of the fact that there we are, in a peculiar sense, aliens in language. After a full century of possession the complaint has been heard that the representatives who hold this empire for us nowadays know less of the native dialects than those who built it up in the bygone time. The traditionary nabob, who was supposed to have with all his wealth a miserable conscience and a diseased liver, and the more recent "old Indian," who came home, generally a bachelor, to end his days among expectant relatives, could speak with the natives, and therefore sympathised with them more than the cadet who in these days of the overland route goes to India scarcely feeling that he has left England, and who counts the weeks till he shall obtain furlough or leave the country for ever. It is surely a curious result of bringing England nearer to India, that it should be the means of severing the Englishman from the native, of widening the vast gulf that separates the European from the Indian. Yet such is the fact, and it is to our ignorance of the native dialects, it is to the want of intercourse which that ignorance involves, that we must in great measure attribute the tremendous surprise with which we had to face the mutiny of last year. Now, if we were to ask, where is the great difficulty of learning a native language during a residence of some twenty years,—of learning, say, Hindustani, which is throughout India what French is throughout Europe,—we should be told that the difficulty lies at the very threshold of the study; it is in the alphabet. So great is this difficulty, and so urgent is the necessity of surmounting it, that—as we had some time ago occasion to point out—it has been proposed, and we think wisely, to substitute for the complicated Oriental alphabets the Roman letters which are in use throughout Europe. Nor is this a measure of utility proposed merely for ourselves. It is of still greater importance to the natives, as without it they can have but little education, and no literature. And when it is understood that the alphabet it is proposed to adapt to the Oriental languages as the standard of pronunciation is not the English alphabet, which especially in its vowel sounds is exceedingly anomalous, but the Italian or Roman,—the same which the American missionaries have employed with most perfect success in reducing the languages of the South Sea Islands to writing, and which the Dutch have in like manner introduced into Java and Amboyna,—it will be evident that the suggested improvement is to be regarded, not as the yoke imposed by victors upon a conquered race, but as a necessity of civilisation, and as the homage which the most useful alphabet in existence demands from others that are deficient and impracticable. As from India we obtained through the Arabs those numerals which are now in use throughout almost the entire globe, so it is proposed to give India in return the benefit of those letters which we ourselves obtained from our Roman conquerors.

The various languages of India are so nearly allied, that, properly speaking, they are but different dialects of the same language; and, if they were all written in the same character, the unity of speech would be apparent, while with but trifling alteration one literature would do for all, and a contribution to any particular dialect would be an addition not, merely to the literature of that variety, but also to the common stock. Where every dialect, however, has its separate alphabet, and every province is distracted by the currency of two or three alphabets, the utmost confusion prevails, and people who understand each other in speaking—Hindoos and Mahomedans, Pundits and Bunyans—are unable to correspond with each other in writing, or to make use of each other's books. Even were it possible out of the fourteen current alphabets of India to select one for universal use, the difficulties in the way of adopting it would be almost insuperable. There is not one of them which it is not extremely difficult to read, difficult to write, and difficult to print. As for reading, it is well known that the natives themselves cannot read them fluently. Even the pundits and moonshees are continually obliged to stop for the purpose of spelling the words. A fluent reader of any of the native characters is almost unheard of, while a mere boy who is taught the Roman characters will in the course of a few months read anything that is given to him without stopping. Writing, it may well be imagined, is still more difficult. As a general rule, it is impossible to write fast in the native alphabets without making so many blunders and omissions that the manuscript becomes an unintelligible scrawl. Taking a most favourable example, however, we may mention an experiment which was tried by one of the teachers of the Hindoo College. He asked one of the best Bengali copyists to write as rapidly as he could in the native character, while he himself wrote in the Roman; and the result of the competition was in favour of the latter by two and a half to one. This is bad enough. The greatest difficulty of all, however, occurs in printing. For one dialect a fount of type is required consisting of not less than 700 letters, simple and compound; another requires 900 letters; a third, 1,000, and so on. Apart from the cost of preparing such a fount, consider the difficulty which the compositor has to contend with in having a "case" before him with this prodigious collection of characters, which, after all, makes no provision for such convenient indications as we have in our capitals, small capitals, and italics. Consider the labour, not only of selecting all these letters, but of placing now above and now below the consonants those incomprehensible vowel points, which, as resting on a thin strip of metal, are very liable to be broken, and to embarrass compositor and reader alike. Consider the enormous space, too, which these characters must occupy, and the waste of paper and press-work which follows. Consider the impossibility of producing those varieties of large and small type which are so useful in books printed in Roman letters. The wonder is, that, having to surmount these enormous difficulties, it has ever been possible to print in the Oriental character. Our Indian cadets are recommended to buy Shakespear's *Hindustanee Dictionary*, but the cost is five guineas; they are advised to buy his grammar and two other works, but the cost is four guineas more. No doubt they are cheap, if the labour bestowed upon them be taken into account; but to the young cadet they are dear, they are bulky, and they are by no means inviting. The dictionary might be sold for half a sovereign if it were printed in the Roman character; it would be intelligible at first sight, and it would be reduced to respectable dimensions. There is, indeed, nothing like the Roman alphabet for utility, — easily read, easily written, with a thousand little conveniences in print which no other can boast of, as no other can be compared with it for compactness. By slightly increasing the number of its sounds, and this is easily done by accenting in various ways the existing letters, it is capable of being substituted for the most copious of the Oriental alphabets. The strange multiplication of characters in the Oriental orthography is created by the compound sounds; a compound being formed by the union of two or more letters which, when written together, bear but slight traces of what they originally were, and to all intents and purposes form a new letter. No such difficulty presents itself in the Roman alphabet, the simplicity of which so commends itself even to the natives of India that not only is it used in writing by great and increasing numbers of the most influential classes, but also Hindustani newspapers are actually printed in it and preferred by those who understand it.

These facts prove what we have said, that the introduction of the Roman letters into India would not only be useful to ourselves, but is the condition on which alone the education of the natives and the growth of a vernacular literature are possible. If we desire the personal influence of Englishmen to be brought more strongly to bear upon the Mussulman and the Hindoo; if we desire to bridge over the chasm that now separates the victor from the vanquished, the ruling from the subject race; if we desire to educate the natives, and to bring them under the dominance of European ideas and a Christian civilisation; if, too, we would wipe away the reproach which has been so often brought against us, and raise a monument of ourselves in that land, less imposing it may be, but certainly more enduring than the most magnificent of public works, then the best thing we can do—the stepping-stone to all else—is to set about this very simple work of establishing the use of the Roman alphabet throughout India. A good deal has been done already in this direction. The proposal was originally made nearly a quarter of a century back; and, though at first received with opposition, it has gradually come into favour, especially since the terrible event of last year aroused the English public to the consideration of Indian affairs. As a first-fruit of this movement, the British and Foreign Bible Society have undertaken to publish a large edition of the New Testament in the Hindustani language, but in the Roman characters, the English version being printed in parallel columns, as in the polyglot bibles; and what is the object?—to induce the soldiers in the Queen's army, as well as others now in India, to study the language and to acquire the ability of associating with the natives. It is hoped, also, that the Government of India may be induced to give some encouragement to the scheme, the promoters of which are certainly modest in their expectations, if it be true, as we believe, that they limit their requirements to the three following points, namely, 1st, that Government would simply *permit* petitions and other documents in the Roman character to be received in their courts and offices; 2nd, that they would publish a set of the Acts of the Indian Government in the Roman character; and, 3rd, that in the same character they would publish an edition of the vernacular Government *Gazette*, including, of course, projects of law and other documents relating to current legislation.

These demands are so moderate, and the object to be attained is so desirable, that we trust it is only necessary to propound the scheme in order to bespeak for it the favourable consideration of the Indian Council.

(21.)

ON THE HIGH PRICE OF INDIAN BOOKS PRINTED IN THE NATIVE CHARACTERS.

(*Extracted from the* TIMES *of Nov.* 13, 1858.)

To the Editor of the Times.

Sir,—In an article which appeared in your issue of yesterday under the above heading, reference is made to the cost of Shakespear's *Hindustani Dictionary* as five guineas, and to his *Grammar* and two other works as costing four guineas more. We beg to say that an advertisement has several times appeared in your columns and elsewhere during the last six months, showing that the whole of Mr. Shakespear's works can be purchased for 6*l.* 14*s.*; viz.:—

	£	*s.*	*d.*
Hindustani Dictionary	3	3	0
„ Grammar	0	14	0
„ Introduction	1	1	0
„ Selections (2 vols)	1	16	0
	6	14	0

The prominence given to the erroneous statement of the cost of these works is so calculated to injure their sale, that we trust to your giving equal prominence to this communication.

We remain, Sir,

Your obedient servants,

RICHARDSON BROTHERS.

23, Cornhill, E.C., Nov. 18.

(22.)

ON THE HIGH PRICE OF INDIAN BOOKS PRINTED IN THE NATIVE CHARACTERS.

(*Extracted from the* TIMES *of Nov.* 18, 1858.)

To the Editor of the Times.

Sir, — In the *Times* of Saturday, Messrs. Richardson state that the whole of Mr. Shakespear's works can be purchased for 6*l.* 14*s.*, as follows: —

	£	s.	d.
Hindustani Dictionary	3	3	0
" Grammar	0	14	0
" Introduction	1	1	0
" Selections (2 vols.)	1	16	0
	6	14	0

I lately procured these works from my son's outfitter, who made a favour of obtaining them for me bound, at the price of the books in boards at the booksellers'. The charges in the outfitter's bill were as follows: —

	£	s.	d.
Dictionary	5	5	0
Grammar	0	14	6
Introduction	1	10	0
Selections	1	16	0
	9	5	6

I am, &c.,

London, Nov. 17. PATERFAMILIAS.

(23.)

ON ROMAN TYPES IN INDIA.

(*Extracted from the* LEADER *of November* 20, 1858.)

The extension of the Roman types in India has reached a further practical stage in the shape of an article in the

Times, a stage of importance in all measures, but more particularly in reference to this, because it not only makes it known to the great mass of the English public, but brings the public mind of England to bear on the public mind of India,—an influence very much wanted, for greater conversance with the subject on the part of Indian officials is not necessarily attended with the formation of sound opinions, inasmuch as local prejudices are too often brought to bear against general conclusions, and to warp the judgment. We have already brought the subject forward as one of no mean importance in connexion with the progress of India, because it will smooth the way to the acquisition of Western knowledge, and facilitate the intercourse of the Indian nations.

The system of vowels to be adopted is, we consider, of less importance than the determination to introduce the Roman type and script, for these will adjust themselves. It is certainly desirable that the best system should be adopted at once; but while we wait for the determination of this and the agreement of men's minds, the opportunities are being lost of going to work. We would let each Presidency and each jurisdiction adopt its own system of representation if it liked, whether Sir W. Jones's, advocated by Sir Charles Trevelyan, or Dr. Gilchrist's; whether Professor Newman's, or the system of following wholly and bodily English spelling.

We have already referred to the exposition of the Jones or Italian system, advocated in the well-known papers of Sir C. Trevelyan, Mr. W. Yates, Mr. W. H. Pearce, Mr. J Thomas, and the Rev. Dr. Duff at Calcutta, in November, 1834, and which were republished by Longmans in 1854. This system depends chiefly on the adoption of Italian sounds for the vowels, and it has great prospects of success, though it is ill suited for the accomplishment of one important purpose, namely, preparing the Hindoo student for reading English. It is one known in India from the time of Sir W. Jones, and adopted by a large section of Indian scholars; and, since its promulgation for the representation of Indian dialects in 1834, it has made steady progress, being adopted by natives of India, by teachers of Oriental languages in England, and by authors of works relating to the East. It has this recommendation, that it is, as well expressed by Sir Charles Trevelyan, a simple transliteration into Roman of the Deva Nagari, or Sanskrit alphabet, adding what was wanted to represent the peculiar sounds imported into the Indian languages from the Arabic. Professor Newman's system is of the same class, but he employed another mode of pointing. Dr. Gilchrist's does not depend on any preconceived system, but is the concoction of the learned author, and very difficult to follow out. It has, however, the support of a large section of Indian officials, trained in his system. This method cannot stand, for it is wearing away under the silent influence of the Trevelyan system, and, though it shows a bold front now, it has no vitality in it.

The great advantage of the Trevelyan system is *that it well represents the Indian dialects and is truly a transliteration.* This is its stronghold, for it is a great help to the European student of the Indian dialects, and is useful for natives wishing to refer to other Indian dialects. It has naturally received the adhesion of Continental scholars because it is conformable to their own pronunciation. Where it fails is, that, so far from assisting the native in the study of the English language, it creates a special impediment. The system of spelling for the English language unfortunately adopted in the middle ages, in preference to the Flemish system or a modification of the Anglo-Saxon, has placed English spelling in a class by itself. This spelling, however, is a broad fact which we must admit, for there is no immediate likelihood of England and the United States adopting any other method. The phonetic type has been consigned to oblivion, and even such a simple amendment as Webster's spelling has been little adopted, and is set at defiance by the printers. We have, therefore, two courses in which to work, one to comply with the requirements of the Indian languages, and another to comply with the requirements of the English language.

When we consider of how little importance for imparting knowledge are the vernacular languages of India, we may be induced to place less stress on their development. Although Persia has a literature, it is now yearly falling more and more into the status of a foreign language, and within a few years it will get out of use in India; but, further, no particular regard need be paid to Persian or Arabic, because neither possesses the literature of progress, nor is the language of large masses of the people.

With regard to the vernacular languages, although they are now required to be written for legal purposes, for correspondence, for translations from English works, and for native newspapers, yet they cannot be regarded as of such importance or such permanent interest, that their requirements are to be preferentially consulted. The result of Indian administrative reform must be to extend the use of the English language for legal purposes, to suppress native written documents and apparatus for perjury, to conduct the examination in English, and to create English court records. The best evidence points to these results, and in all new arrangements for non-regulation districts they are being realised. For mercantile correspondence English will become of more use, and as the vernacular literature will not supply the demands of the population for knowledge, so English books will be more consulted and native books less. Many of the Indian languages and dialects prevail over small areas, and they will never obtain a competent literature, any more than the Finns, the Frisians, the Welsh, the Irish, the Basques, or any small nationality of Europe.

Thus everything tends to the increased use of the English language, and instruction in the vernacular schools must be looked upon, not as opening the whole curriculum of education to the student, but as preparing him for the study of English. The grand end and aim, therefore, should be to facilitate this result, and to make Indian spelling conform as near as possible to English spelling, and not to create a fresh barrier after abolishing the Deva Nagari, the Persian, and the other characters. It is of no importance for Indian purposes, or for English purposes, that a Frenchman, a German, or an Italian can read Bengalese or Canarese with facility, or that a Bengalee or Malabar will have greater facility in acquiring French or German; these are not objects to be consulted, and are of no practical use. What has to be done is to facilitate intercommunication between England and India, and to make the literature, civilisation, institutions, and commerce of the English race available for India. This is the end to be accomplished, and the acquirement of the Indian languages by Englishmen will be facilitated by any system based upon such principles; for the English student will be facilitated by English spelling rather than by the Trevelyan method.

With regard to the measures to be adopted for establishing Roman spelling, various propositions have been made. An able writer in the *National Review*, whose article on the Zouave and kindred languages was noticed in the *Leader*, took occasion, while discussing the application of the Roman character to Arabic and Kabyle, to make some remarks on its Indian application. He very well observes that to adapt systematically a Roman type for extra-European languages would not only add great facilities to comparative grammar and ethnological linguistry, but would be of service to us politically in India, religiously in every missionary station. He proposes that the Indian Government should appoint a committee of three to report on the best mode of adapting the Roman alphabet to the Indian languages, the committee to consist of one printer, one person acquainted with several Indian languages, and one English man of letters. His object in naming a printer is, of course, to have a practical judgment on the relative value of diacritical points, accents, and other marks as affecting type-founding, composing, and correcting; because it will be desirable to mark some of the vowels, and necessary to distinguish such consonant sounds as are not to be found in English, and require new combinations of the Roman alphabet for their representation. We doubt whether an English man of letters would be the best member of the committee, for he would have literary prepossessions like the Indian member, and we think it far better that a merchant or man of business should be appointed, who can appreciate the inconveniences of a new system of pronunciation and of a special script. As the Trevelyan method is worked through the missionaries, so the *National Reviewer* proposes to take advantage of the railway, and that the committee should request every Indian railway board to set up every notice at every station in a twofold type, first in the Indian, next in the Roman. In Wales, the notices of the *Rhylffordd* are set up in English and Welsh, but the English first; and very curious specimens of composition are *Rhylffordd* notices in Welsh, being half English terms turned into Welsh; and in Bengalee the like notices will be half English. The reviewer then urges that all Government proclamations shall be printed on the like system; but, as we think, it will be far better and simpler to print the proclamations all Roman, without any local type, and in parallel columns of English and the local language, because the Roman alphabet can be readily taught to adults and youths who can read, and there would be the greater encouragement to read the Romanised publications.

The Trevelyan method, as announced by "Indophilus" in the *Times* this week, has been put in a very effective shape by the adoption of a measure for the publication of cheap books in this country in the Roman type. The Bible Society has sagaciously aided in this movement, and is about to produce thirty thousand Roman-Hindostanee Testaments at a low price. These the religious public will buy up, and give as presents to every official, emigrant, and private soldier proceeding to India, many of whom will acquire a readier knowledge of Hindostanee, while the greater proportion of the books will, on their arrival in India, be got rid of and dispersed among the natives, and become a further means of propagating Roman type. This will be a useful step for the introduction of Roman type and script for all regimental orders in corps where Hindostanee is used.

Mr. Jarrett has put himself forward as an opponent of "Indophilus," and presents but a sorry case.

(24.)

LETTER FROM SIR CHARLES TREVELYAN ON ROMAN TYPE IN INDIA.

To the Editor of the Leader.

Sir, — I beg to submit for your consideration the following points in reference to your recent able and interesting article on the application of the Roman character to the languages of India: —

1. In expressing Oriental languages in the Roman character, literary and scientific men throughout the civilised world have, after the example of Sir William Jones, adopted that application of the Roman letters which comes nearest to their powers in Latin and the languages derived from it.

2. The Roman letters, according to the same application of them, have become firmly established as the missionary and Christian character of Upper India, as will be seen in detail from the accompanying letter from the Rev. R. C. Mather, of the London Missionary Society.

3. The Roman consonants have the same power, according to this application of them, in the Oriental languages as in English, the exceptional sound which some of them have, in addition to their ordinary use, being distinguished by a diacritical mark; and —

4. As the five Roman vowels are applied to the English language in an extremely irregular manner, so that the same letter often represents several different sounds, any attempt to follow the English practice, in this part of the system, would have tended rather to mislead than to assist.

The consonants, therefore, are substantially identical; while, although the vowels represent only one of the different powers of the same letters in English, and that not always the most usual, yet, having been adjusted to the symmetrical scale common to Sanskrit and Latin and their derivatives, they can never be confused, in their application to the Oriental languages, with any of their various conventional uses in English; and the superior compactness, cheapness and distinctness of the Roman letters, the various sizes and forms of type, the capital letters, italics, stops, and other aids to modern printing, equally apply to vowels and consonants. This intrinsic superiority of the Roman character, and the facilities it affords of bringing all the languages and dialects of Asia into a closer relation with each other and with the languages of Europe, constitute the essence of the change which was commenced twenty-five years ago at Calcutta.

I have the honour to be, Sir,

Yours very faithfully,

C. E. TREVELYAN.

London, 22nd November, 1858.

[We shall resume the subject to which Sir Charles Trevelyan refers at an early period, for it is one of the most important subjects connected with the advancement of civilisation in India.—ED. *Leader*.]

(25.)

THE NEW ALPHABET FOR INDIA.

(*Extracted from the* HOMEWARD MAIL *of Dec.* 6, 1858.)

The Persian running-hand is, as is well known to all Indians, hard to decipher, and by no means such that he that runs may read. Some may think that it is called *Shikastah,* or "the broken," because he that attempts to read it will rend the collar of patience and break the strings of perseverance. India was long afflicted with the curse of this inscrutable character, and only grey-bearded *munshis,* who in learning it had forgotten all else, could penetrate its mysteries. At length Time, the great mediciner, produced the decree which swept it, for ever it is to be hoped, from the offices of the *Sáhibán i 'A'líshán,* that is, of the English gentlemen, and from general use. Unfortunately, the same decree substituted a dozen curses for the one defunct, in prescribing the use of the vernacular dialects. Of these the Urdú is the least formidable, being a very mild approach to the terrible Shikastah. The written character of the Hindí, however, compensates amply for all that is gained by the comparative facility of the Urdú. It is called the *Káithí*, from the Kayasths, or writing class of natives, who use it, and who, if they can read what they write, must be men of extremely subtle parts. The difficulty of the Kaithí, again, is barely equal to that of the written character in the South of India, where the Telugu, Kanarese, and Tamil rejoice in a system of scratches which can be made revoltingly obscure. All these, however, must hide their diminished heads before the *Mod*, or letter character of the Maráthí. This ingenious mode of torment is said to have been invented by one HIMAR PANT in the end of the eighth century A. D., who, if he was really sensible of the miseries he was about to inflict by it on a large family of mankind, must, indeed, have been a fiend in human shape. Some ingenious persons, with more imagination than etymological truth, have supposed the name *Mod* to come from a word signifying "an ant," and to imply that the character is such as if ants, escaping from an inky grave, had run over the paper and blotted and scrawled its fair surface. But *Mor*, "ant," is a Persian word, and the odious *Mod* is Márathí, from a Sanskrit root which signifies "to twist or break." *Mod*, therefore, in Maráthí, corresponds in sense to *Shikastah* in Persian, and hopelessly illegible as it is, it sinks into utter insignificance in that respect when compared with the Márwárí and Sindhí. Concerning these latter scribblings many strange tales are told; as of a pleasant gentleman, who having received a letter announcing something undecipherable that had happened to his son, went through the ceremony of lamenting for his decease in the morning, and gave a *fête* in honour of his nuptials at night, not knowing which of the two events had occurred.

The above is a very frigid and tame account of some of the difficulties which attend what may be called the *Inshá i Harkaran*, or general correspondence in India. Now as life, leisure, and vision are all limited, it does seem an utter absurdity to hesitate about the adoption of an easy substitute for the abominable scrawls used by the natives.. The English alphabet, properly adapted to express the Indian letters, is that substitute, and to INDOPHILUS is due the gratitude of all parties for recommending it. This is not a question as to the disuse of the Indian languages in business transactions and official proceedings. Such a proposal would be preposterous; but it is simply a suggestion for an alteration which would be as convenient and beneficial to the natives as to ourselves. We are well aware, indeed, of the difficulty attending all such changes; but, in the meantime, we give to the proposal of INDOPHILUS our heartiest good wishes and support.

(26.)

THE NEW INDIAN ALPHABET.

(*Extracted from the* GLOBE *of Dec.* 10, 1858.)

Philanthropists and philosophers will trace civilisation to many origins, but amongst the most powerful instruments have been the most simple; and perhaps familiarity prevents us from sufficiently estimating the profit that we have derived from one of them. It is nothing more than the letters which we teach our children when they are infants, that Roman alphabet which Sir Charles Trevelyan is so perseveringly and so sagaciously striving to introduce into India. Probably no obstacle to the introduction of civilisation, with all the ideas that the word implies, is so serious as the various kinds of alphabets which the races of India employ for recording and transmitting their thoughts. Caste itself is not more powerful. It is an obstruction alike to the communication and to the growth of ideas. Any man who has studied the working of the mind will observe, that except with relation to tangible subjects, which themselves serve the purpose of memoranda, the mind is scarcely capable of establishing one set of ideas, and passing to the next, until the former shall have been written down. But how can a man handle thoughts who pillories them in characters like those upon a Chinese tea-chest?

We have not specimens of the characters at hand, or the thing would be apparent. One of the commonest alphabets in India is the Nagari, the first letter of which is like a Roman capital A, the two legs standing wide apart, with three beams radiating downwards, from the cross bar; the figure then being set upon one of its beam ends, and looking somewhat like a monstrous letter F turned the wrong way. But the same letter *a* in its broader sound has the same cumbrous character, with the addition of something like a capital I following it. The letter *i* is like the capital letter T with a very elaborate worm-like substitute, tail curled upwards, for the upright stem. The *e* is like a capital U, with a tail to it; *u* like a figure 3, with a tail rising up to the top, and a broad cross-bar at the top; *o* like the elaborate A aforesaid, with a large comma laid horizontally over it, and a capital I after it. All the letters of the alphabet are of the same elaborate construction. For the purposes of writing there is no running hand. The combination of letters to express different sounds is as cumbrous as the simple characters are; so that, for purposes of printing, the individual characters are multiplied by a process almost like permutation. Thus a "fount" of Nagari type consisted of no less than 700 letters, and these only equivalents for the 24 letters of the Italic alphabet, and six more which are required for an Indo-Roman alphabet. The set of 700, however, makes no provision for capitals, small capitals, italics, or the other adjuncts of printing. Nor is the Nagari the most elaborate; the Birman fount requires 900, the Peguan more than 1,000.

Even yet we have not exhausted the causes of complication. In India "the number of dialects is immense, and each dialect has letters of a different figure." The effect in preserving severance of nation between races identical in origin is complete. In Europe, with a common character, we readily perceive that most of the languages have in common many words radically the same, and the study of tongues is comparatively easy. In India, Dutch and German, — Tuscan, Neapolitan,

Genoese, and Venetian, — English and lowland Scotch, are, by their alphabets, separate languages. But dialect prevents the growth of national *thought* as well as language; even idiom has a tendency to compel stereotyped forms of thought; and with the progress of ideas our own language is becoming less idiomatic.

While there are these solid reasons for the adoption of a common and a simple alphabet, the reasons against it are futile and imaginary. It would not, — as the "phonetic" reform would have done with us if it had established any claims to notice, throw the whole library out of use, for the vernacular literature of India is still a literature of the future. Already the efforts to introduce the plan have been to some extent successful; and it is an instructive fact, that of the prize students examined at the last Missionary Conference at Benares, in January, 1857, although the candidates using the English language were few, they carried off the majority of the prizes, and that those using Urdú language and the Roman character came next in efficiency. If the Roman character be adopted, *of course*, as Sir William Jones advised, the Italian powers would be adopted also, simply because in Italian those powers are fixed, without any such variations of value for the same characters as in our words, *ought, bough, cough, dough, rough*, and *through*, with the surname *Gough*, and the poetic *sough*, — the last as unascertained in sound as the thing it represents, the big sigh of the wind among the trees. And if Sir Charles Trevelyan were to be the final Cadmus for endowing India with letters, one of the first improvements we might expect would be, fixed modes of spelling native proper names, with intelligible "Telegraphic Intelligence" from India.

(27.)

LETTER OF MR. W. EDWARDS, OF THE BENGAL CIVIL SERVICE, ON THE ADVANTAGE OF USING THE ROMAN CHARACTER INSTEAD OF THE NATIVE, IN ALL OFFICIAL DOCUMENTS AND PETITIONS.

(*Extracted from the* TIMES *of Dec.* 15, 1858.)

To the Editor of the Times.

Sir, — As a proposal to introduce the Roman printed character into India has lately formed a subject of remark in your columns, I am anxious, through you, to draw attention to the great advantage likely to accrue from the adoption of the written character in supersession of the difficult and crabbed native ones now in use. Our Indian Government must always be more or less one of record; and, from the difficulty of the character in which the proceedings of all departments of our internal administration are at present recorded, a vast amount of power and influence falls into the hands of our native officials termed "Amlah."

These functionaries, well aware of the advantages they thence derive, perpetuate the evil by writing systematically so illegibly that few, save their own immediate brethren similarly employed under the state, can decipher the writing without great pains and difficulty.

I can read both Urdú and Hindee characters with considerable facility, and often would I have gladly taken up the proceedings in cases pending before me as collector, magistrate, or judge, to find out for myself the important points therein, but the writing was prohibitive, and, in the multitude of cases to be disposed of, I could not spare the time to spell out the manuscript, but must content myself with listening to it read out by one of the "Amlah."

As long as the native characters remain in use for recording all our proceedings we must remain an "Amlah-ridden Government," and a greater misfortune could not happen to us, or a more prolific source of weakness be conceived.

I think the present time affords a very favourable opportunity for introducing a change, as almost all our Mofussil offices have to be reorganised, in consequence of the defection of nearly all our old "Amlah" to the rebels and the destruction of our records. Orders might with advantage be issued for recording all proceedings of our Courts in future in the native languages in English running-hand,—there are plenty of persons duly qualified for this duty procurable for all our Mofussil offices and for our most important police posts,— for it would be of incalculable advantage to magistrates to have their daily as well as particular reports written in English character, so as to be at once readable by themselves wherever or whenever they may reach them. Writers should, as now, be attached to our offices, who could give in their own character copies of all official documents to parties duly applying for them. Petitions also should in future be written in the English character. Petitioners, it is well known, never write their own petitions, but employ persons who make a living by writing them. No greater expense would be incurred in having these documents written in the English character than in Hindee and Urdú, as at present. I always had a box, of which I kept the key, for petitions at my gate, and generally returned from my rides or walks morning and evening with many in my pockets. How advantageous would it have been had I been able to read through these petitions myself; but the time which would have been consumed in deciphering them could not have been spared!

What confidence would it give the people, and how much more should we Mofussil officials know of the real state of the country, if petitioners felt assured that the presiding authorities would themselves read their petitions, without the intervention of "Amlah," who have at present so much real power in their hands that the people regard them with the greatest dread! They are generally fixtures in a district, while the European officers are constantly changed. They contrive to surround themselves with a number of relations and dependents dispersed through all the offices in a district, so as to keep themselves constantly informed of whatever occurs. The real power thus falls into their hands, and they use it, of course, for their own purposes. The change I advocate would effectually turn the tables, and deprive them of all undue influence and power. District officers would be able to read for themselves, and also — which is most important — pass and record their own orders in their own handwriting, in the English character in Urdú, on each document as it was placed before them.

I really believe, from my own pretty extensive experience in all departments of the State, that if the change I advocate were introduced, it would give us a hold over the people and an intimate knowledge of the country equal to 40,000 men at least. Now is the time to act. All that is wanted is an order of Government directing the change. Six months or a year hence we shall be all in the old track; establishments will have been reappointed to each office, records will have accumulated, and the opportunity will have been lost.

Could the new Indian Council be moved to send out the necessary instructions?

I remain, Sir, your obedient servant,

W. EDWARDS,
Bengal Civil Service.

Dec. 13.

(28.)

THE BATTLE OF THE ALPHABETS.

(*Extracted from the* WATCHMAN AND WESLEYAN ADVERTISER, *Dec.* 15, 1858.)

Not long ago, it was often said that if the English were driven out of India they would leave behind no lasting monument of their dominion. That reproach is seldom heard now, and, if the rule of the Crown continue only for as long a period as that of the Company, lines of telegraphs and railways, if these were all, would memorialise the British name as lastingly as the camps, the walls, and the Roman roads in this country, do the sway of the Cæsars. But it is a more lofty ambition to leave an imperishable record in the mind of the remotest generations, and to bequeath to those whom we have subjected a higher civilisation, a nobler and purer literature, and the one true religion. Something of this it is doubtless in our power to do, as the education of the people is under our direction, and our presses supply the books which they read. From the same causes we can certainly give them the best medium of literature and science in the alphabet which we ourselves employ; and however presumptuous it may be thought to speak of displacing the "alphabet of the gods" (the Sanskrit or *Devanagari*), and the many other characters, whether of native invention or borrowed from Persian and Mohammedan invaders, which are used in India, the proposal is held by competent authorities to be perfectly feasible, and those of us who are not Oriental scholars may easily enough see that its accomplishment would be an incalculable benefit. Twenty or thirty years ago it was but a proposal or rather the revival and popularisation of the idea of Sir William Jones; but now it is so far actually represented that a small library of valuable works has been published in the vernaculars of India, but in the Roman character, which has been called the Christian alphabet of the North-West Provinces.

The Chinese, it is well known, employ symbolic or hieroglyphic characters, which, being addressed rather to the eye than to the ear, become an intelligible medium of communication to all the literary classes, however their dialects may vary, who inhabit the continent and the islands between Tartary and Japan; a fact which so much impressed the earlier missionaries that they supposed this species of abbreviated delineation — not word-painting but idea-picturing — might be accepted as a universal means of writing, intelligible at sight, all over the world. They did not sufficiently allow for the difficulty of first mastering the multitude of signs. Such are the advantages of phonetic characters, which represent not the infinite variety of objects of sense or thought directly, but those few primary sounds of the human voice by the various combinations of which we arbitrarily denote them, that there can be little doubt the Chinese themselves will in time abandon their clumsy alphabet, and Romanise like other people. The Indian alphabets, of native or foreign origin, are all phonetic; but are so cumbrous and difficult, that in several instances it is nearly as hard to read fluently as it is to master the language; and they are so many and so various, that dialects which, when spoken, are as near kin to each other as the Italian and Spanish, look when written as little allied as Russian and German. Sir Charles Trevelyan has lately republished the letters in which he, in concert with Dr. Duff and others, discussed this subject two and twenty years ago; and has added to them that interesting statement of the Rev. R. C. Mather, (first communicated to the Reviewer in the *London Quarterly*,) in which the progress made in applying the Roman letters to the languages of India is traced up to the present time. In this pamphlet we are told that it is with much difficulty, and never without stopping to spell, that the educated Hindu himself reads his own language in his own characters. If the case is so bad when the book is printed, it may be imagined what the confusion must be when it is attempted to throw the native characters into a running-hand. In a letter published this morning by a contemporary from a gentleman of the Bengal Civil Service, giving the results of his own experience, the writer says: "I can read both Urdú and Hindí characters with considerable facility, and often would I have gladly taken up the proceedings in cases pending before me as collector, magistrate, or judge, to find out for myself the important points therein; but the writing was prohibitive, and, in the multitude of cases to be disposed of I could not spare the time to spell out the manuscript, but must content myself with listening to it read out by one of the 'Amlah.' As long as the native characters remain in use for recording all our proceedings we must remain an 'Amlah-ridden Government,' and a greater misfortune could not happen to us, or a more prolific source of weakness be conceived." Surely the Government, both for its own sake and for that of the natives, will be induced to make the change which intelligent and practised officials in its service urgently recommend.

In giving to Oriental races, and to the inhabitants of islands where missionaries are sent, the Roman alphabet, it is understood that we do not spoil the boon by coupling with it our peculiar English pronunciation of the vowels, or our still more abnormal spelling. With us the one is too well fortified by use, and the other by an immense literature, to be the subject of experiment. The orthography of an English word often points to its etymology, and only children are sensible of the inconvenience of modifying the power of a letter by placing one or two others, themselves silent, before or on each side of it. It is no trouble to the English student of an Indian language, which he has presented to him in the easy dress of his own alphabet, to remember that the vowels and diphthongs are to be sounded as they are in all European languages which are derived from the Latin, except his own; but to the Hindu it would be utterly disheartening to begin with our barbarous double vowels, which have no accordance with anything in his own alphabets, while the Italian system is strictly analogous with that of the *Devanagari*. Even in this country we commonly accept the Italian spelling of the names of persons and places belonging to the East, or to the islands of the Pacific where the missionaries have introduced it. Feejee, so pronounced, we now spell as we should have done at first, *Fíjí;* Owhyhee, *Hawaí;* Hindoo, *Hindú;* and this not only in missionary publications, but in our literary journals. Thus in the *Athenæum* of last Saturday we find *Ajmír, Jaypúr, Rajpút,* and also *Sanskrit,* though in the last word our English C is not so intolerable as Mr. Grote has found it in the spelling of classical names, in which it sometimes deceives both eye and ear. One can imagine a person in this country old-fashioned enough to be offended with the better spelling, but it is strange that it should be rejected by well-informed men in India. Yet we have before us a recent letter, (too long, we beg to inform our friendly Correspondent, for republication,) in which the names of the first four successors of Mohammed are so written, very much on the inelegant and barbarous plan of Gilchrist, that they are scarcely recognisable; for which there is the less excuse, as Gibbon and the French authorities whom he followed had made the precedent of a more convenient orthography perfectly familiar to English readers. This branch of the question, however, is certain to rectify itself spontaneously. The method of Romanising the written and printed languages of India is one so convenient to the Government, so useful to the student, so propitious to the native mind, so conducive to the spread of the science and ideas of the West, and so likely to be subservient to Christianity, that, though no one wishes to obliterate all the native alphabets, we hope it will, in the course of another century, gradually supersede them in popular use. The prejudices against it are fast disappearing, and both in public and private we find it warmly advocated and applauded.

(29.)

THE ROMAN ALPHABET APPLIED TO EASTERN LANGUAGES.

(*Extracted from the* LONDON REVIEW *of October* 1858.)

If the reader wishes to beguile an hour of leisure or indisposition, let him turn over the leaves of the *Bible of Every Land*, published by Messrs. Bagster and Sons. Those spirited publishers have presented in one quarto volume specimens of the Holy Scriptures in nearly all the languages into which they have been translated, together with notices of the ancient and modern worthies who effected the translations, and a summary of the labours of the several benevolent and religious Societies, by whose aid and patronage many of the versions have been obtained. The maps, prepared and coloured specially for the volume, form a complete atlas, enabling the eye at once to trace the spread and prevalence of each family of languages in past and present times; and the wonderful variety of alphabets by which it has pleased human ingenuity to express the sounds formed by the organs of speech is fully illustrated by beautiful lithographs, or types, some of the latter having been lent for this publication from the Imperial Printing-Office in Vienna.

Specimens of the languages of all Asia, and especially of those of India, are given with great success. But to confine ourselves to those of India, we find at least twenty various alphabets in which those languages are written. We have given some attention to these alphabets; the most pretentious of them all is the Dévanágarí, which may be called a most splendid system of short-hand, difficult to write, and still more difficult to read*; with such a copious variety of combinations, that, according to the testimony of the Boden Professor of Sanskrit at Oxford, one word of three syllables may be written in one hundred and eight different ways.†

The *Grant-ham,* in which Sanskrit is written in the South of India, is said to have no less than eleven hundred and twenty-eight different combinations of the letters of the alphabet, each combination requiring a separate and distinct character, which the student must learn before he can read the

* The manner in which the vowels are joined to the consonants in forming syllables is one great difficulty in the way of a learner. One vowel is stated to be *in* the consonant; another is placed *after* the consonant; one is placed *over* it; another *under* it; and a fifth is placed one half *before* it, and the other half *after* it. Thus:—

                                    i
k spells ka; ka spell kã; k spell ki; k spell ku; ek spell ke; aik spell
                                                  u
kai; eka spell ko; and ekl spell kou!

                                                                  i i   i i
In Tamul the word *Kristu,* or Christ, is written k, r, s, t, krst (Kristu).
                                                                        u   u

                                                                  i   i
In Telugu and Canarese the same word is written k, su, ksu (Kristu).
                                                                  r t   r t

In Sanskrit it is written i, k, s, iks (Kristu).
                                  r t rt
                                    u   u

The time will come when these puzzling ingenuities will be left to the Brahmans, who probably invented them to make learning difficult; and Englishmen will have every language of India written straight on in their own clear characters. [This note has some errors for which I do not hold myself responsible.—M. W.]

† The derivatives of the compound of *sam,* '*cum,*' and *kri,* 'to make,' may be written in a variety of manners: *sanskartá,* for instance, may be written in a hundred and eight ways. These are, however, matters merely of orthoepical conceit.—*Professor Wilson's Introduction to the Grammar of the Sanskrit Language,* p. 22. [The writer of this article has misapprehended Prof. Wilson's meaning.—M. W.]

language.* Whether we adopt the Dévanágarí, or the Grantham, it is a heavy task to learn to *read* Sanskrit; and we are prepared to believe the assertion of a learned Brahman in Madras, that of one thousand Brahmans who profess a knowledge of Sanskrit, not more than one hundred can read it; and that of one hundred who can read, not more than three can understand it! A friend of ours in India, an Englishman, well versed in one Indian language, informed us that he was unable to read the Dévanágarí after two years' hard study. Even the Tamul, which is the simplest alphabet of India, has had its sixteen original characters so amplified by the example of the Sanskrit, that it has two hundred and sixteen combinations of characters in its ordinary style.

Is it not time that the students of the languages of India should agree among themselves to write them in the Roman character, and that for all ordinary purposes the English alphabet should be made to suffice?

When the Messrs. Bagster issue a second edition of their book, which we understand is in progress, they will add greatly to its value to students of the languages of India, if they will accompany each original specimen with a version of the same in the Roman character.

Sir William Jones employed a method of writing the Sánskrit in the Roman character which was considered to be an improvement on that of Wilkins.† More recently, Dr. Lepsius and other Continental scholars have written Sanskrit in Roman characters.‡ Bopp, at the end of his Sanskrit Grammar, gives

* "Quare eodem sedulo Operas dirigente, hujus idiomatis elaborati typi et characteres conflati nunc primum sunt in hac typographiæ nostræ officina regio plane sumptu et apparatu; quandoquidem cum LI. radicales litteræ censeantur, XVI. nempe vocales, et XXXV. consonantes, ex quibus dein aliæ, veluti secundariæ procedunt, quas compositas, seu potius litterarum nexus appellaveris, eo sane processit characterum seu typorum copia, ut MCXXVIII. numerentur, atque ex ea non leve etiam typographis in perquirendis ac simul etiam nectendis singulis harum litterarum formis confletur negotium." —*Alphabetum Grandonico-Malabaricum sive Samscrudonicum* (Romæ, MDCCLXXII. Typis Sac. Congregationis de Propag. Fide), p. vi.

† The Works of Sir William Jones, 4to. edition, vol. i. p. 206.

‡ Standard Alphabet for reducing unwritten Languages and foreign graphic Systems to a uniform Orthography in European Letters. By

several half-pages of Sanskrit in the Roman or Italic character on a very neat and compact system, accompanied by the original Dévanágarí.* Dr. Caldwell, in his Comparative Grammar of the Drávidian or South-Indian languages, eleven in number, uses only Roman letters throughout his admirable work †; an example which may be profitably followed by those who wish to make the native languages easy of acquisition and use to mere English readers. As already intimated, Professor Bopp's system of expressing Sanskrit sounds, and especially those of the aspirated consonants, is more compact than any other, and may come into general use. For instance, the word Bhaváni, he writes B'aváni, making the inverted comma express the aspirate; and the two syllables, achchha, which appear barbarous, he writes aç'ça, using the French or Spanish ç to express ch.

It is necessary here to note the history of a change which is likely to lead to great results. Sir William Jones's object was limited to expressing in an uniform manner, in the Roman character, such Oriental words as might be used by European scholars. The application of the system to the purposes of national literature and popular instruction is of modern date. It was only in the year 1834, that Sir C. E. Trevelyan, with Messrs. Duff, Yates, and Pearce, adopted Sir W. Jones's orthography with some modifications, for printing books in the vernacular languages, as the foundation of a new system of national literature and popular instruction. The pamphlet entitled "Papers originally published at Calcutta in 1834 and 1836, on the Application of the Roman Letters to the Languages of Asia," explains the nature and objects of this

Dr. R. Lepsius, Professor at the University, and Member of the Royal Academy, Berlin.

Dr. Max Müller, of Oxford, has also published a system in which all accents and diacritical marks may be dispensed with, by using *italic* letters for those accented on other systems.

* Kritische Grammatik der Sanscrita-Sprache in Kurzerer Fassung Von Franz Bopp, Berlin, 1845, pp. 369—375.

† A Comparative Grammar of the Dravidian or South-Indian Family of Languages. By the Rev. R. Caldwell, D.D., Missionary of the Society for the Propagation of the Gospel in Foreign Parts, at Edeyenkoody, Tinnevelly, Southern India.

undertaking; and Mr. Mather's letter given towards the close of this paper describes the progress which had been made in it to the time of the mutiny. Professor Wilson has adopted the same modifications of Sir William Jones's orthography, and there is no substantial difference between Sir C. E. Trevelyan's and his.*

The comparison of the several versions of the Holy Scriptures in the languages of India would be an easy task if those translations were given us in the Roman character, and the desired uniformity in the adoption and use of theological terms would become practicable. For an instance, in illustration of this subject, let us take one verse of the Gospel according to St. John. The word "beginning" is rendered by Dr. Carey into Sanskrit, *ádi;* the same word, *ádi,* is used in the same sense in Tamul, Telugu, Canarese, Malayalim, and many other languages. Let the word *ádi* be retained for that special rendering in every language in which it is found, and the advantage is obvious. The particle "in" is expressed by an affix denoting the case, which differs in the several languages. But whether we read, "In the beginning," *ád-ou,* as in Sanscrit; *ádi-andu,* as in Telugu; *ádi-illa,* as in Canarese; *ádi-il,* as in Malayalim; or *ádi-ilé,* as in Tamul, &c., the difference is only inflexional, the word "*ádi*" expresses the meaning of our word "beginning." So also the word *vák-yam* is used to express the meaning of "the Word," in Yates's Sanskrit translation. It is used in the same sense in the other languages enumerated; but the translators have

* SANSKRIT ALPHABET IN ROMAN CHARACTERS.

BY PROFESSOR H. H. WILSON.

Vowels.

a, ā, i, ī, u, ū, ri, rī, lri, lrī, (e) ē, ai, (o) ō, ou.

Consonants.

Gutturals . . .	ka, kha, ga, gha, ṅ.
Palatals . . .	cha, chha, ja, jha, ṅ.
Cerebrals . . .	ṭa, ṭha, ḍa, ḍha, n.
Dentals . . .	ta, tha, da, dha, ṅ.
Labials . . .	pa, pha, ba, bha, m.
Semivowels . .	ya, ra, la, va.
Sibilants and Aspirate .	sa, sha, sa, ha.

To these may be added, an and ah.

not uniformly adopted it, as they might have done. The Telugu and the Canarese use *vák-yam;* and the other versions use *váda*, Sanskrit; *vardai*, Tamul; *wáchanam*, Malayalim; *wáchana*, Singhalese. This unnecessary and undesirable variation in the use of terms will probably begin to disappear when all the versions shall be rendered into the Roman character. So, also, for the word "God," *Déva, Dévam*, or *Dévanu*, is known in all the languages alluded to; but the Sanskrit versions use *I'swara* and *Mahéswara;* the Tamul, *Parábaran;* while the rest use *Dévudu*, Telugu; *Devaru*, Canarese; *Devam*, Malayalim; *Deviyan*, Singhalese. We commend the Romanising of the several versions of the Scriptures in India to the attention of Bible and Missionary Societies, as one grand step towards the perfection and uniformity of the translations, an object greatly to be desired.

Had the several translators of the Holy Scriptures possessed in the Roman character the labours of their fellow-labourers in other Indian languages, their several versions would have come much nearer to each other than they now do. It may be conceded that much advantage has resulted from the independent action and unrestrained research of the several translators, each in the language he cultivated; but it is now practicable to give to all the translations the benefit of these wide-spread labours. It will be seen at a glance that the following versions of John i. 1 might have been so nearly alike in each language as to reduce the labour of the European student and Scripture reader very considerably:

John i. 1: "In the beginning was the Word, and the Word was with God, and the Word was God."

TELUGU.

'Adi-andu Vákyamu kaddu; 'A Vákyamu Dévunitó undenu; Marinni á Vak-yamé Dévudai undenu.

CANARESE.

Old Version.

Adiyalli vakeavembavaniddanu; a vakeavembavanu Devarasangadaliddanu; a vakeavembavane Devaru.

New Version.

'Adiyalli vákyavū ittu. A vákyavū dévara beliyalli ittu. 'A vákyavū dévará gittu.

MALAYALIM.

'Adiyil wachanam undáyiruu, á wachanam Deivattóda kúde áyirunu, á wachanam Deivavum áyirunuu.

SINGHALESE.

Patangammehi wachanaya wuyeya. E wachanaya dewivanwahanse samagaya. E wachanaya dewiyanwahanseya.

TAMUL.

'Adi-yilé Várttei irundadu. Av-Várttei parábaranidattil irundadu. Allámalum av-Varttei-yé, Parábaran.

We have no wish to see the various alphabets now used in India entirely abolished. They are monuments of human ingenuity, and as such should be respected and preserved. But while the natives should be taught each to read his own language in its own character, they ought to be taught it also in the Roman character, as one step toward their acquisition of the English language. Every language in India, if for no other reason, yet as one token of British rule, ought to be reduced into the Roman character, in its grammar and dictionaries: and, above all, in its version of the Holy Scriptures. The direct benefit would be great to the natives themselves; and the indirect benefit, by enabling Europeans to acquire and use the languages with greater facility, would soon tell, with good effect, on the interests of India. If we wish to diffuse among the masses in India a knowledge of Divine truth, we must employ an agency much more extensive than that of the missionaries and their assistants: we must make it possible for English ladies to read the Scriptures to their domestic servants; we must place the Bible in a form in which they can read it, in the hands of the thousands of educated East Indians of European origin, who all speak the vernacular, but, with few and rare exceptions, never learn to read the native characters; and make pious British soldiers also Scripture-readers to the poor heathen who are employed to wait upon them and drudge in their service.

The English-speaking population of India deserve special mention in this place. They are, for the most part, descendants of the English in every grade of the two services. They are professors of the Christian religion; and, with rarely an exception, highly value the minister and his work. Many of them are devotedly pious, and are even zealous for the truth among their own people and among the natives. They generally marry young, and have moderately large families. In Madras and many other large towns they form the bulk of the English congregations of the missionaries; in some cases they support their own missionary, and build their own chapels. These estimable people are not eligible to the higher departments of the service of the government; they are, however, employed in the arsenals as artificers, and as musicians in the army. They are clerks, traders, merchants, printers, bookbinders, watchmakers, and of any other occupation not of a servile character. The comfort and respectability of their style of living command the admiration of strangers; and, as the material and moral interests of India advance, this class will also advance in position and influence.

The moral conquest of India is to be effected by a process less rapid and less obvious to public view, than that of its subjugation physically and politically by the courage of our soldiers, and the wisdom of our legislature. We have never despaired of British interests in India; much less have we despaired of the interests of Christianity. But our hopes are dependent on the diffusion of Divine knowledge by means of the Holy Scriptures.

At the renewal of the East India Company's charter forty-five years ago, (in 1813,) British India was reluctantly, and under certain vexatious restrictions, thrown open to Christian teaching. So recent are the facilities which have been so largely improved by Societies and individuals zealous for the spread of Divine truth! There were, indeed, Protestant missionaries in India previous to the year 1813; but they were to be found, not under the government of the Honourable Company, but in the Danish settlements of Tranquebar and Serampore, or under the patronage of the Rajah of Tanjore and other native chiefs. Within the last forty-five years, there has been more attempted and effected for the improvement of our Indian fellow-subjects by private benevolence, without the aid or patronage of Government, than in the previous 3000 years during which India has been known to Europe. The Brahmans, the Jews, the Nestorians so called, the Mahommedans, and the Jesuits, have in their turn penetrated India, each claiming to be teachers of religion; but it is the undisputed glory of British Christians to have given to India, in its several languages, the whole Word of God, which is *a light to them that sit in darkness and in the shadow of death.*

Dr. Caldwell is correct in his opinion that the dark-complexioned, Tamul-speaking, devil-worshipping aborigines of India gained little advantage in religion and morals by their subjugation to the fair and learned Brahmans of Central Asia. The Brahmans brought with them the Sanskrit language, the Dévanágarí character, and the Védic hymns. That language has enlarged and improved itself by its contact with the Tamul *; and in return has expanded the sixteen original rock-inscription letters, which tradition assigns to the Tamul, into the *Grant-ham,* or *book* alphabet, containing, as noticed above, eleven hundred and twenty-eight different combinations. The Brahman has taught the native the existence of a supreme God, who is *not* to be worshipped; has withheld from him the Védic hymns,—no great disadvantage,—and has given him a literature exquisite in its grammar, but worthless in respect to real knowledge and mental improvement. We find less that is objectionable in religion, and more that is commendable in morals and corrective of the faults of human nature, in the poems of the low-caste Tamul natives Tiruvalluver and the woman Avveiar, in the imperishable *Kural* annotated by Parimelazager, and in other popular poems, than in all the Puranas and other Brahmanical compositions professed to be founded on the Védas.

It would be too much to expect from the Israelites of the first dispersion, who found their way from Assyria or Babylon to India some centuries before the Christian era, that they should have contended successfully against the polytheism of India. Some of their descendants, and those of their pro-

* "The [Tamul] language retains an alphabet which tradition affirms to have heretofore consisted of but sixteen letters; and which, so far from resembling the very perfect alphabet of the Sanskrit, wants nearly half its characters, and has several letters of peculiar powers [such as r cerebral, r hard, l cerebral, &c.]." — *Benjamin Babington, Madras Civil Service, Gooroo Paramartan*, p. ii.

selyted slaves the black Jews of Cochin, are found still adhering, in outward profession, to the law of Moses; but great numbers of the Beni-Israel, still retaining that distinguishing appellation, are worshippers of Hindu idols, and in appearance and customs differ little, if at all, from the Pagans around them. We have no evidence that the Israelites gave the law of Moses to the Hindus in their own language.

If the Christians of St. Thomas, who can be traced back to the fourth century, met with any success in the conversion of the Hindus, it was necessarily limited to the results of oral instruction; as it does not appear that they ever translated either the Holy Scriptures, or their Liturgy, into the language of the natives.

We may pass over the wonderful story of the early Jesuit missionaries. They gave to the astonished Hindus the refinements of the schools, and the marvels of Romish tradition, with here and there fragmentary portions of the Word of God, accommodated to their own immediate purposes.

To Ziegenbalg, the first Protestant missionary to the Hindus, belongs the honour of having first given to India a translation of the Holy Scriptures into a native language. We have seen a copy of this great man's translation, printed with types which he himself cast, on paper of his own manufacture, and bound in several thick quarto volumes under his own direction. Ziegenbalg's history presents an example of labour and success which may be studied to advantage by every man who aspires to the honour of taking part in the evangelisation of India.

Ziegenbalg, with commendable singleness of purpose, directed his attention to the natives only. He left it to his colleague, Gründler, to labour for the benefit of the Portuguese-speaking population. It is for his successors, after a lapse of one hundred and fifty years, to be witnesses of a numerous and wide-spread population in India, European or of European origin, mixing with the natives in everyday life, and in every department of it, speaking their several languages,—a possible agency for the diffusion of the knowledge of truth in religion and science, such as does not exist in any other pagan country. What are the objections to furnishing this peculiar class of East Indians, as well as the natives themselves, with the translations already made, in the Roman or English character?

We may grant that each people in India prefers its own alphabet to any other: but is that a sufficient reason why they should not be accustomed to read their own language in the simple and useful character now used by more than half the civilised world? We may also admit that each alphabet expresses precisely the sounds of its own language: but the same sounds can be also represented in the Roman character. The German, the Frenchman, and the Spaniard equally express the widely different sounds of their own languages by the Roman alphabet. Why should not each Hindu be taught to follow the example? It may be objected that an Englishman attempting to read an Indian language in Roman characters will only make himself ridiculous. The remark will equally apply to French or German. The system is adapted for persons who know the language conversationally, and require only a little practice to enable them to read it.

This whole subject is fully discussed in a volume which issued from the Serampore press in 1834, consisting of a series of papers written by Messrs. Trevelyan (now Sir Charles Trevelyan, the "Indophilus" of the *Times*), J. Prinsep, and Tytler, Rev. Dr. Duff, and Mr. H. T. Prinsep; which shows that the system at that time was in successful operation.

Since this article was commenced, Sir Charles Trevelyan has placed at our disposal a letter from an eminent missionary in the North-West of India, which cannot fail to afford satisfaction to those who take an interest in the welfare of India; and which we earnestly commend to the attention of all missionaries in India, to the Committee of the Bible Society, and to all who are practically engaged in missionary and educational pursuits for the benefit of our Hindu fellow-subjects.*

We hope it will no longer be matter of doubt whether the whole of the languages of India ought not to be Romanised forthwith. We have found the objections to this proposal to

* The letter here alluded to is that of the Rev. R. C. Mather, which has been already given *in extenso* at p. 202.

be comparatively trivial, and the advantages to be of the greatest moment. If, by reducing these languages into the Roman character, we can enlist a large body of Indo-Britons into the *corps* of instructors of the Hindus in the Word of God; if, at the same time, we can afford the greatest facilities to translators and missionaries for perfecting their labours; and if, by the use of the Roman character, we can elevate and encourage the natives of India in civilisation and general knowledge, and especially such portions of them as profess the Christian religion; it appears to us that there is a work to be done which invites the cooperation of all the true friends of India. Let missionaries transcribe for the press in the Roman character the translations which have been made into Indian languages; let the vernacular-speaking descendants of Europeans, as well as the natives themselves, be supplied with Romanised versions of the Holy Scriptures; let the use of the Roman character be encouraged in the courts of law, and in the transaction of Government business throughout India; and an impulse will be given to the native mind which cannot fail to be most beneficial in its operation and final results.

(30.)

FIRST LETTER OF PROFESSOR JARRETT.*

To the Editor of the Times.

Sir,—Allow me to suggest that the writer of an article in the *Times* of November 10th, on "The Native Languages of India," has somewhat overstated his case against the native alphabets. All these alphabets are modifications of two—the Devanágarí or Sanskṛit and the Arabic. The nature of the former is such that any person who has learned the forms and

* This letter appeared in the "Times" of November 12th, before the papers numbered 21—28.

sounds of about sixty characters, mostly of a very simple form, can pronounce with certainty any word he meets with, provided no contractions are used. It is these needless contractions that cause the whole of the difficulty referred to in that article. If, then, the rule were laid down by authority that no contractions would be allowed in legal documents, the 700, 900, or 1,000 types spoken of by the writer would be reduced to 60. The Arabic alphabet contains 28 characters, and four marks to determine the vowels, and by means of additional diacritical points it is adapted to the sounds of the Persian, Turkish, Hindústání, and Malay languages. The great fault committed by those who use the alphabet is the common omission of the vowel points, in which case no one can read a word if he does not know its meaning. If, however, the very simple system invented by Professor Shakespear is employed, the greater part of these vowel points may be omitted without causing any ambiguity in the sound of a word. The difficulty experienced by the moonshees in reading arises either from the careless omission of diacritical points, or from the silly habit of using ornamental writing; but the difficulty itself is not greater than that which you, Sir, must daily have to encounter in reading English correspondence.

The author of the article is a little mistaken in supposing that by using the Roman alphabet "unity of language would become apparent" among the natives of India. There is, I believe, no sort of connexion between the dialects of Northern and Southern India, although the latter borrow words of a technical character from the former, so that the identity which would be seen would resemble the likeness between English and Greek if the King of Greece were to enjoin the use of our alphabet. However desirable, then, a common alphabet for all languages may seem, there are grave objections to its use, for every language that has been long written possesses prescriptive right to its own alphabet, and in most cases all attempts to transcribe it in any other will fail to attain accuracy. On this account it is to be feared that the British and Foreign Bible Society will be disappointed in the result of their publishing the Hindústání New Testament in Roman characters. Their funds would have been better employed in printing that work in the Niskhí character, with Shakespear's vowel system.

I am, Sir,
Your obedient servant,

Nov. 10th. THOMAS JARRETT.

(31.)

LETTER OF INDOPHILUS.

To the Editor of the Times.

Sir,—In my former letters I adverted to the objectionable nature of some, and the expensive character of all, the usual Indian class-books. Considerable progress has now been made in the preparation of an improved series, which I will briefly describe.

The first is *An Easy Introduction to the Study of Hindustani,* by Mr. Monier Williams, late Professor at the East India College, Haileybury; including Reading Lessons, Dialogues, and Vocabulary, by Mr. Cotton Mather, Assistant Professor of Hindústání at Addiscombe College. This has just been published by Messrs. Longman at the remarkably low price of half a crown.

Owing to the simplicity of the style and to the circumstance that the meaning is already generally known, the New Testament and Psalms are superior to every other book, even as a manual for learning a foreign language; and the Bible Society has, with much liberality, determined to print, for the common use of Europeans and of the natives of India, an edition of 20,000 copies of the New Testament and Psalms in Hindústání and English in parallel columns, and another edition of 10,000 copies in Hindústání only. These will shortly be published at a very low price; and a separate edition of the entire Bible in folio, with copious references, is in an advanced state. All three are being edited by the Rev. R. C. Mather.

A *Clavis* of the New Testament and Psalms, in Hindústání and English, is also being prepared concurrently with the principal work, and a foundation has been laid for the publication of other books of the same general nature as soon as these have been put out of hand.

These books are all in the Roman character, the use of which removes the first and greatest difficulty in the acquisition of a foreign language; and if the tastes or necessities of the student should afterwards induce him to acquire any of the other characters by which Hindústání is expressed in different provinces, or by different classes of people in the same province, he will bring to the task the great advantage of a familiar acquaintance with the words. There is no reason now why Hindústání should not be taught to every recruit going to India, or why every English lady there should not be able to learn enough of the language to read the Bible to her servants. These are only some of the results of the application of the Roman character to the numerous languages and dialects of India, the advantages of which may be summed up as follows:—That it substitutes a cheap and legible, for an expensive and indistinct character; that it facilitates the acquisition of the native languages by the English, and of the English language by the natives; and that, by making one character serve for many languages and dialects, which have already more or less in common, it will greatly assist general intercourse and create a tendency towards a common Indian language, of which English will be the connecting link and the Christian religion the source of inspiration.

As I wish to avoid controversy, I had not intended to answer Mr. Jarrett's letter which appeared in the *Times* of the 12th inst.; but I find that, owing to the want of correct information, his letter has made a certain impression. My answer is, that his remedy would be worse than the disease. The 700, 900, or 1000 separate types alluded to by him as required for the Devanágarí and its derivatives are intended to reduce the excessive diffusiveness of the character, by representing in a more compact form different combinations of letters; and if no contractions were allowed, as Mr. Jarrett proposes, the expense and bulk of printed books, which is already too great, would become intolerable. In like manner he suggests that, in order to render the Persian character intelligible, the vowel points should be inserted, and "the silly habit of using ornamental writing" should be discontinued. A degree of legibility superior to that which belongs to ordinary Persian writing would, no doubt, be attained by these means, though it would still fall far short of the clearness of Roman writing, in which the vowels are inserted in the lines; but writing would become as slow as a schoolboy's copy. The Persian letters are subject to this unfortunate condition, that if written quickly they are illegible, and if written legibly they require too much time, and in printing, too much expense and space, for the vowel points must be put either above or below the line.

As regards the connexion between the different Indian dialects, the short statement of the case is, that, setting aside barbarous hill tribes which have no written character, the languages north of the Kishna and Godaveri bear the same relation to Sanskrit as Spanish and Italian do to Latin; and the languages south of those rivers bear a closer relation to Sanskrit than English does to Latin and its derivative Norman French, because the Brahminical invaders communicated to those Southern people their religion, their literature, their science, and, to a great extent, their governmental, artistic, and social terms.

What does Mr. Jarrett mean by saying, in reference to Hindústání: "Every language that has long been written possesses prescriptive right to its own alphabet, and in most cases all attempts to transcribe it in any other will fail to attain accuracy"? Is he not aware that the same language, with only a difference of dialect which is less than prevailed when I was a boy between Somersetshire and Northumberland, is expressed by one set of characters in the Punjab, by another in Rajpootana, by another in Behar and Benares, and so on; and that the Mahomedans and those who have been educated in the Mahomedan fashion use, in writing the same language, the Persian character, which is different from all the rest? Even this does not represent the full extent of this Babel of letters, for in the same district and place the Pundit uses one character, the local shopkeeper (Bunyan) another, the general merchant another, the person who has received a Persian education another different from them all, and so on. To which of these alphabets has the Hindústání language a "prescriptive right"? And if "in most cases all attempts to transcribe it in any other will fail to attain accuracy," how has written intercourse been carried on at all among these tens of millions of people speaking the same language? Lastly, to what character have the 99 people out of every 100 who cannot read or write at all a "prescriptive right," and what is the system of letters specially applicable to the rising generation of this great population, which it is our high duty and privilege to train to a knowledge of better things? Mr. Jarrett has, I fear, failed to appreciate both the facts of the case and the true nature and scope of the mission of this country in India.

In the *Times* of Saturday, Messrs. Richardson complain that Mr. Shakespear's *Dictionary*, *Grammar*, *Introduction*, and *Selections* are stated to cost nine guineas, whereas they can be purchased for 6*l.* 14*s.* Many parents, who could ill afford it, know to their grief that the alternative was between the first-mentioned price and depriving their sons of the means of professional instruction; but I am quite satisfied with the standard of comparison which Messrs. Richardson's modified statement affords. As no private soldier, and but few persons going to India in the mercantile, indigo, railway, public works, and other occupations, can afford to give 6*l.* 14*s.* for books which, however desirable, are not absolutely necessary; and a considerable proportion even of those who go out in the military, medical, and marine services are obliged to confine themselves to indispensable articles of outfit; it follows that the key of this most important knowledge for themselves, for the people of India, for our whole nation, is taken away from the great majority of our countrymen proceeding thither. But by the simple expedient of the adoption of those letters to which the art of printing was first applied, and which have been elaborated by the ingenuity of successive generations to a degree of distinctness, compactness, and simplicity which belongs to no other, this difficulty has been overcome. Professor Williams' and Cotton Mather's *Easy Introduction*, for instance, which comprehends grammar, reading lessons, dialogues, and vocabulary, is to be had for 2*s*. 6*d*. Any person of moderate education and ordinary intelligence might, with the help of this, acquire a fair practical knowledge of Hindústání in three months; and when to this is added the Bible Society's Anglo-Hindústání New Testament and Psalms for say 1*s*., and the *Clavis* or Dictionary for perhaps 2*s*., the outfit of the ordinary student will be completed.

I am, &c,

London, Nov. 15. INDOPHILUS.

(32.)

SECOND LETTER OF PROFESSOR JARRETT.

To the Editor of the Times.

Sir,—Having admired the wisdom shown in the letters that have appeared in your paper under the signature of "Indophilus," I feel some hesitation in appearing as in any degree his opponent; but since he has, in your impression of to-day, appealed to me by name in consequence of my letter of the 12th, I must request you to allow me to reply in a few words.

The object of my letter was to show that the difficulty of acquiring an Indian dialect is not necessarily increased to any great amount by the labour of learning the native alphabets; that the long array of such alphabets might be reduced to two, the Sanskrit and the Arabic; and, lastly, that unity of language does not really exist throughout India.

"Indophilus" says: "I had not intended to answer Mr.

Jarrett's letter; but I find that, owing to the want of correct information, his letter has made a certain impression. My answer is, that his remedy would be worse than the disease."

My reply is, that the disease consists in the use of numerous alphabets in writing the various dialects; the remedy is, to employ only two, from the one or other of which they are all derived, and to write each of these in the simplest possible form. This last condition excludes about 100 contractions employed in writing the Sanskṛit character, some of which are of a very complicated nature. It is true that by laying aside these contractions we should employ more paper, but we should secure perspicuity, the most important element in every composition, and thus gain time, which is of more worth than paper. To this it may be added, that the disuse of contractions would lead to the employment of smaller types, and thus the "bulk of printed books" need not become intolerable.

As to the Arabic character, I did not recommend that all the vowels should be inserted, but that Shakespear's method should be adopted, which allows of the omission of nearly half the vowel points.

"Indophilus" assumes that I am mistaken in supposing that by using the Roman alphabet unity of language would not become apparent throughout India, and in saying, as I did, "There is, I believe, no sort of connexion between the dialects of Northern and Southern India, although the latter borrow words of a technical character from the former;" while "Indophilus" says, "The Southern bear a closer relation to Sanskrit than English does to Latin and its derivative Norman French." I must, however, demur to this last statement; for, unless we are misinformed by those who have studied the relations existing between the so-called A'ryan and Drávidian languages, the primitives in these two families of tongues are wholly different. The reasonableness, moreover, of my thinking that the use of the Roman alphabet would not bring to light the asserted unity of language will be seen by comparing the languages of England and Wales. These are written in the same character, and are, to a great extent, founded on the same primitives, and yet very few Englishmen can identify many words in a Welsh book with those he himself employs.

"Indophilus" inquires: "What does Mr. Jarrett mean by saying, in reference to Hindústání, 'Every language that has long been written possesses prescriptive right to its own alphabet; and, in most cases, all attempts to transcribe it in any other will fail to attain accuracy'?" What I mean is this: Greek words are best written in Greek letters, and consequently the Greek patriots were not a little astonished, some years ago, at being invited by a Philhellene to adopt the Roman alphabet. Hebrew Bibles are best printed in the Hebrew character; the Persians and Turks having long used the Arabic alphabet, it would be something like presumption to ask them all to lay it aside; the Sanskṛit character, in its various modifications, having been for many ages employed inwriting A'ryan words, it would be unwise to replace it by another; while the Hindústání being derived mainly, in various proportions, from Sanskṛit, Persian, and Arabic, should be written in the simplest form, either of the Sanskṛit or Arabic character, and in no other. "Indophilus" asks further, "To what character have the 99 people out of 100 who cannot read or write at all a prescriptive right?" I reply, to that character which best suits their language, and least separates them from the rest of their nation, without reference to their present ignorance.

I am, Sir,

Your obedient servant,

THOS. JARRETT.

The College, Ely, Nov. 16.

(33.)

FIRST LETTER OF PROFESSOR MONIER WILLIAMS ON THE NATIVE ALPHABETS OF INDIA.

*To the Editor of the Times.**

Sir,—I have watched with interest the controversy relative to the Indian alphabets. The subject is most important as connected with the progress of European civilisation in the East, and you have earned the gratitude of every friend of India by opening your columns to its discussion. This question, however, like every other, has two sides, or rather is multilateral, and it is characteristic of the cautious Englishman to weigh and balance conflicting views before committing himself to the adoption of any new theory. The truth is, we are not naturally a crotchety people. If crotchety men there be among us, they are not trusted. They are looked upon with almost as much suspicion as monomaniacs. No scheme will "go down" with the English public, which is not founded on plain practical common sense. If, therefore, the theory of introducing one simple alphabet throughout India be the conceit of an enthusiast, we have only to leave it alone. Its doom is inevitable. If, on the other hand, it rests on sound principles of reason and feasibility, its adoption becomes a mere question of time. Truth is too strong for prejudice, and though the battle be long, the victory must come at last. The whole matter is safe in the hands of a shrewd, matter of fact, discriminating British public.

As, however, all sides have now had their say, I may, perhaps, be permitted to pass briefly in review the various phases which this question has assumed.

And first, let me observe that the principle on which "Indophilus" and the other advocates of the Roman alphabet found their arguments seems to be absolutely incontrovertible. No one can dispute the desirableness of one common medium of expression for the Babel of languages current in our Indian

* This letter appeared in the "Times" of December 31st, 1858.

empire; and no one, I presume, will call in question the comparative simplicity of the Roman alphabet, and the superior facility it affords for cheap and easy printing.

Accordingly the opponents of Indophilus have not attempted to contravene these propositions. Their tactics have been different. Some have tried ridicule. This is always a popular method of attack. No weapons are so easily wielded as those which meet arguments by sneers. But steel yourself, "Indophilus." George Stephenson, before you, bore the brunt of a whole nation of sneerers. Fortunately he was not troubled with too sensitive a cuticle, and the world is now blessed with railroads. A few have resorted to personal scurrility, and have imputed mercenary motives to the originators of this movement. These are even less deserving of notice than the last.

Our business is more with those antagonists who assume what may be called the orthodox attitude. These deliver their opinion with temper and courtesy, and are worthy of deference.

First, then, we have had it asserted by one of your correspondents that there are only two principal alphabets in India, the Devanágarí or Sanskṛit, and the Arabic, and that all the others are modifications of these two. The most that can be said of this statement (though no one, by the by, has yet contradicted it) is that it conveys a very inadequate, if not erroneous, impression of the fact. Instead of two principal alphabets there are at least five, as follows: — 1st. The Devanágarí, or Nágarí, read from left to right, for the learned Sanskṛit, and all the Hindú dialects founded on Sanskṛit, such as Hindí, Maráthí, Gujaráthí, Bengalí, Uriya, Sindhí, and Kasmírian. Each of the latter, however, has its own modifications, or rather corruptions, amounting in some cases to almost separate alphabets, so that even in the Bengálí, which is the most nearly allied to the Sanskṛit, some of the letters are totally different in shape.

2. The Arabic, read from right to left, for Arabic, and modified considerably for Persian, Hindústání, and Pushtu, being all Muhammadan languages. As the Arabic and Sanskṛit languages are utterly distinct, and have nothing what-

ever in common, so no two systems of writing could possibly be imagined more opposed to each other in every particular than the Devanágarí and Arabic.

3. The Telugu, for its own language and for Kanarese (the former being spoken in the Nizám's country and the Circars, the latter in part of Mysore and Kanara). This is quite a distinct character, though, like the Devanágarí, it is read from left to right, and has equivalents for all the Sanskṛit sounds. As the square symmetry of the Nágarí and the flowing curves of the Persi-Arabic symbolise the characteristic peculiarities of the Sanskṛit and Persian languages respectively, so the rounded shape of the Telugu letters is typical of the softness of this Italian of the East.

4. The Tamil, for its own language (spoken at Madras and southwards to Cape Comorin). This, again, is quite a distinct character from any of the preceding, and differs also from the Telugu in being too scanty to represent all the sounds of the Sanskṛit alphabet.

5. The Malayálam, for its own language, called also Malabar (spoken in Travancore and Malabar). This, also, is quite a separate character, although, like the Telugu, it has equivalents for all the Sanskṛit sounds.

Whatever may be said about remote affinities, each of the above five alphabets has an individuality of its own so decided, that a knowledge of any one of the five would not lessen the amount of labour required for the mastery of any one of the others. Moreover, the first, or Devanágarí, has so many corruptions, that a description of them with anything short of the unlimited range of your columns would be impossible. Suffice it to say that they differ in every province, and that in most instances the debasement is so complete as to create a nearly distinct alphabet. For example, let a Sanskṛit scholar be asked to read for the first time a sentence either in the Kaithí or Mahájaní as commonly written by the natives. Not a word would he be able to decipher, although these are said to be nothing but modifications of the Nágarí.

Again, it was stated by the same correspondent that every language has a prescriptive right to its own character. The Greeks, it is said, would be rather astonished at being asked to adopt the Roman character. This is specious enough. The answer, however, is plain. The Greek character being quite as simple as the Roman, and equally convenient for printing and reading, no one would of course think of supplanting it by the Roman, especially as the difference between European alphabets is so small. But if in Europe there were 22 languages, each with a character to all practical purposes distinct from the other; if most of these, again, had their two or three corrupt forms, and if one and all, from the peculiar structure of the letters, from the number of compound forms and the total absence of punctuation, were quite unadapted to meet the demands of a growing civilisation for an abundant supply of cheap, clearly printed, readable books, then I think this orthodox notion of "prescriptive right" must give way to other considerations of infinitely greater moment. The Hindú has a prescriptive right to his own religion with its million gods, to his own science, his own mechanical arts and usages of all kinds. But does any one in his senses hold that this is any reason why we should not give him the advantage of our superiority in all these respects by any means in our power, if, at least, our mission in India is to be anything but a mockery?

But it is said: "Every language has its own character, which properly belongs to it, and must therefore suit it best, and all attempts to transcribe it into any other must fail of accuracy." This sounds very just and sensible; but a more untenable proposition with reference to Hindústání could scarcely have been advanced. Hindústání (or Urdú, as it is sometimes called) is a dialect which cannot be much older than the 14th century of our era. In one respect it resembles all other languages. It reflects exactly the history of the people who speak it. These, like ourselves, are a mixed race, formed by the conglomeration of successive immigrants, such as Brahmins (or A′ryans), Arabs, Moguls, Persians, Portuguese, French, and English, with an aboriginal tribe of inhabitants. The natural result of this jumbling together of dissimilar races has been a very patchwork mosaic-like dialect, even more composite in its structure than our own mother-tongue. This mixed language, then, taking its origin in the court and camp of the Mogul emperors at Delhi, and settling down into the vernacular speech of the north-western districts, has within the last two centuries diffused itself all over India as a common medium of communication, which educated people acquire, like French in Europe, as a supplement to their native tongue. When, however, the English appeared in the East, Hindústání was hardly a written language. The question then arose, What alphabet was to be employed in writing it? Arabic, Persian, Sanskṛit, all claimed it as their own. Was it to be the Arabic?—but this alphabet wanted four letters which are common enough in Persian words viz. p, ch, zh, and g. Was it, then, to be the Persian (i. e. Persianised Arabic)?—but this alphabet again wanted three letters much used in words purely Hindú, and denoted in Roman type by ṭ, ḍ, and ṛ. Lastly, Was it to be the Sanskṛit?—but this was the most unsuitable of all, for it could not express nine very common letters, some of which must occur in every line of Hindústání, viz. the four z's, the Persian zh, the three guttural consonants ḳhe, 'ain gain, and the labial fe. The difficulty, therefore, of finding a suitable alphabet ended in a compromise. It was decided that, as four new letters had been added by the Persians to the Arabic alphabet, so three others should be invented to adapt the Persian to the expression of Hindústání. This was a necessary concession to the Persian element in Hindústání; for in those days Persian was the language of education and the vehicle of higher learning among Indian Musalmáns. But a similar concession had to be made to the Hindú element; and the Devanágarí, which wanted nine letters, was forced to adapt itself to Arabic and Persian words by the employment of various awkward diacritical marks. Hence it came about that Hindústání, which had no alphabet of its own, was written sometimes in Persian, sometimes in Devanágári characters, according to the prominence given to the Musalmán or Hindú element. Now, however, that our own language is gradually winning its way to the position formerly occupied by Persian, and the influences which once operated in favour of the usages of the Musalmán conquerors now act more strongly in the direction of the English,--so much so, indeed, that the ideas, speech, literature, and laws of Hindús and Musalmáns are daily becoming more Anglicised,—it follows that the mixed dialect which is meant to be the medium of intercourse between the races (whether called Hindústání, Urdú, Rekhta, or by any other name) has as much right to be written in the Roman as in the Persian or Nágarı alphabets. And since, *cæteris paribus*, the Roman alphabet is by far the most simple and flexible of the three, being more easily adapted to Persian and Nágarí words than either Nágarí to Persian and English, or Persian to Nágarí and English; and since, moreover, it has already been employed increasingly for twenty-five years in expressing this mixed dialect, it does not seem too much to predict that our good old English A B C is likely ere long to establish its claim to be considered *the* Hindústání alphabet.

But the correspondents of some journals have demurred to the assertion that the Indian alphabetical signs are wanting in simplicity, and deny that they need cause any difficulty either to the printer or the reader. The mastery of these alphabets, say they, is "an affair of twenty-four or at the most of forty-eight hours." * Those who make such allegations can have had small experience of teaching Englishmen to read Oriental characters. Nor would their statements have passed unchallenged, did they not shelter themselves under cover of the ignorance that prevails on the subject of Indian writing. Permit me, then, in consideration of the vast moment of the topic under discussion, to trespass further on your space by a brief account of the Arabic and Deva-nágarí systems, as the two most important of the five I have described as current in India.

* Diligent and apt scholars may perhaps acquire a certain knowledge of the Persian letters in that time; but mere knowledge of the letters is one thing and fluent reading is another. Even in English we should be much hindered by the absence of all vowels. Much more so in Persian or Hindústání, where the dots which constitute the sole distinction between many of the consonants are also often omitted or displaced. As to the Nágarí alphabet, my own experience of teaching it to 600 or 700 students at Haileybury enables me to affirm that it requires at least two months for the most apt scholar to read it fluently; that the majority do not master it in twice that time, and that some, though they know all the letters, never acquire the power of reading it without hesitation.

And first as to the Arabic. It is a mistake to suppose that the Indian Musalmáns make use of the regular Arabic character, commonly called Naskhí. What they do use is the Persianised Arabic, called Ta'lík; a beautiful flowing character, which, though derived from the Naskhí, differs from it even more than round-hand from print. Let the merely Arabic scholar be presented with a book lithographed in this type (in the manner of all Indian Musalmán books), and he could read little or nothing of it. But the character in vogue for common correspondence is neither the Naskhí nor the Ta'lík, but the Shikasta, or "broken" writing, which stands in the same relation to the Ta'lík that the most frightful scrawl of some overworked M.P. might be supposed to bear to the broad text-hand of his secretary. Years of practice are necessary to enable a man to read this character readily. But the difficulty of reading both the Ta'lík and the Shikasta is not caused by the number of letters in the Persian alphabet, though this is greater than in the Roman, and complicated, moreover, by no less than four *z*'s, besides duplicates and triplicates of other symbols. What creates the difficulty is, that every letter has four separate forms, according as it is initial, medial, final, or detached; and that groups of three, four, five, or even six letters are shaped exactly alike, being only distinguishable from each other by the number and position of their dots. Further hindrance to the reader is caused by the omission of the vowel-points, which do, in fact, court neglect, for the simple reason that they are not written continuously with the other letters of a word, but added afterwards above and below the line. A Musalmán leaves out his vowels much as an Englishman leaves out the dots to his *i*'s, only more systematically. Furthermore, he has far less scruple about amputating, decapitating, or otherwise mutilating his consonants than we have; and this looseness is not confined to handwriting, but is often carried into printed or lithographed books. Nor could the case be well otherwise, when, by the very nature of the character, nearly all the vowels and consonants depend for their distinction on supplementary points or marks, like our two letters *i* and *t*. The less broadly marked the differences of alphabetical signs, the more, of course, will any inaccuracy or omission affect legibility. What confusion worse confounded would result in English if the vowels were formed by strokes above and below the line, and if many of the consonants (as, for example, *b*, *p*, *t*, *n*, *y*, *s*) had no distinction of shape excepting in the position of minute dots, which in printing were liable to break off or run into each other, and in writing were perpetually omitted or displaced! And yet this is exactly what takes places in the Persian character, shortening, it may be, the process of writing, but reducing it to a species of hopelessly difficult stenography. But further, the Musalmán being forbidden by his religion to paint animals, is forced to develope his æsthetical tendencies in the direction of calligraphy. For every-day purposes he pens the vilest scrawl; but on other occasions he makes a picture of his writing; he sets about it as he would about drawing or miniature-painting; every stroke is studied; he dispenses with all vowel points because they offend the eye; he groups his dots as he would the figures in a landscape; he allows himself unlimited license in the way of curves and flourishes; he cares nothing about legibility; his sole object is to carry out his ideas of "the beautiful" in penmanship.

For these reasons, then, the Persi-Arabic character, however pleasing in appearance, can never be anything but very unreadable, very unprintable, and wholly unadapted to meet the requirements of advancing knowledge and civilisation in the East.

And now a few words in explanation of the Deva-nágarí or Hindú system. This, although deficient in two important symbols (represented in the Roman by *z* and *f*), is on the whole the most perfect and symmetrical of all known alphabets. The evil is, that, like Lord Ellenborough's Bill for the government of India, it is too perfect for the practical purposes of this utilitarian age. The Hindús hold that it came directly from the gods (whence its name); and truly its wonderful adaptation to the symmetry of the sacred Sanskrit seems almost to raise it above the level of human inventions. One main feature of this system is that the vowel *a* is never written, unless initial. This sound is supposed to be inherent in every simple consonant, so that to denote its absence consonants have to be linked together into one compound. For example, in writing such a word as "kártsnya," to prevent the sounding of "a" excepting at the end, the letters "rtsny" require to be tied together in a sort of complex knot or monogram. Hences arises the necessity for 400 or 500 compound letters in addition to these 60 simple ones. Indeed, no Sanskṛit fount of types is complete without 600, 700, or even 800 different sorts, simple and compound. One of your correspondents proposes to deal very summarily with these troublesome compounds. Without more ado he would oblige the natives to get rid of them altogether, and content themselves with the moderate allowance of 60 simple letters. I submit, however, that these conjunct consonants are essential to the integrity of the Deva-nágarí system, and to ask the natives to dispense with them is to ask them to do rather more than to accept the Roman character. It is to tell them to abolish everything which makes their own revered system of writing the most perfect and elaborate in the world. Unfortunately, in this instance perfection is associated with utter unsuitableness to the common necessities of the age; in further proof of which it may be mentioned that in this character the vowel *i*, when not initial, has to be written before the letter after which it is pronounced. Thus, such a word as the English "innings" would have to be written "iinnngs;" again, in such a word as "armed," the *e* and *r* would have to change places. Good reasons might be given for these alphabetical niceties, but if we are to infuse any of our practical spirit into the Hindú mind, it is impossible that such a system of writing, however theoretically correct, can long be applied to the expression of the vernacular dialects.

We have no need to meddle with the sacred Sanskṛit. This time-honoured and venerable language, the repository of all. the learning and literature of the Hindús, may be allowed undisputed possession of its own "divine" character, to which it has the exclusive right. But Sanskṛit, be it remembered, is now a dead language. Nay, more; it was never spoken and never intended to be spoken in the way it is at present written. The spoken Sanskrit, which is found on the rock-inscriptions of 300 years B.C., and which is the direct source of all the languages now current among the Hindús, was a kind of *patois*, as different from the learned Sanskṛit as Italian from Latin; and this *patois* had its own written character quite distinct from the present form of the Deva-nágarí.* As for the common purposes of speech a less artificial language was required, so for ordinary writing it was necessary to employ a less elaborate character. And if this was the case in olden times, why should not the vernaculars of the present day be more suitably expressed by the simpler Roman alphabet? Even the majestic Sanskṛit condescends to bend to this unpretending, yet all-embracing character. In Oriental books printed in England and Calcutta English types have been applied with complete success to the expression of Sanskṛit words. But our concern is not with the dead. Let Sanskṛit lie embalmed in its hallowed Deva-nágarí. For the living languages alone we ask a commoner alphabet, more suited to a workday age.

A great deal has been said about the danger of "disgusting the susceptibilities" and offending the tastes of the natives of India, as if the attempt to introduce the Roman character might bring about a second mutiny. Be it known, however, that there is no more wish to force this alphabet on our Indian fellow-subjects than there is to force them to adopt our views of religion and science. The only desire we have is, that every opportunity be taken of placing the Roman character before them, and of inducing them to use it†; that

* Although no traces of the present Deva-nágarí are discoverable till about the 10th century of our era, yet it must have existed long before; for how could the imperfect inscription characters have expressed the perfect Sanskṛit, which had its Pánini, its Manu, its Rámáyana, &c., in the 3rd century B.C.? The Sanskṛit-speaking immigrants must have brought with them their own character, or invented it very early, reserving to it the exclusive privilege of expressing their sacred language. The Brahmins themselves never addressed the people in these inscriptions, as they never sought political power. Those who did so would of course employ the spoken *patois*, and the vulgar characters current among the people.

† What could be more reasonable than the suggestion which has appeared in the *Times*, that natives should be allowed to write their petitions in the Roman character? They would thus insure the perusal of these documents by the authorities to whom they were addressed.

after convincing themselves of its practical superiority to their own, they may voluntarily adopt it.

The talk about the impolicy of encouraging Englishmen to neglect the study of the native characters, as if that involved a neglect of the languages, is equally superfluous. Let it be plainly understood, that, by printing the Indian vernaculars in English letters, we have no intention of subserving the indolence of a number of young men, who are bound, as the future rulers of the country, to acquire a thorough knowledge of these languages. What we hold, however, is, that we are likely to have more good scholars by rendering the study of the Oriental dialects easier and less repulsive to Englishmen at first, than by disgusting them with a strange and difficult tongue, and a still stranger and more difficult character, simultaneously; and that while we aim at the adoption of our own alphabet by Hindús and Musalmáns, we do not therefore desire the neglect of the native alphabets by Englishmen. On the contrary, as long as the inhabitants of India use their own systems of writing, it is the plain duty of all Anglo-Indians to study them. We only affirm, with the great Dr. Gilchrist, that the pronunciation and inflection of words, with the general construction of Indian languages, are more obvious to Englishmen in an English dress, and that "there is nothing to prevent learners from afterwards making themselves masters of whatever character they find most essential."

In short, we have no wish by this movement to encourage negligence in the study of the native dialects, but the reverse. Nor have we any hope, for generations to come, of fusing the twenty-two languages of India into one common tongue, or of ever supplanting them by English. We cannot change the organs of speech; but what we can do let us do by all means, and with all speed consistent with discretion. Let us gradually, and in a Christian spirit of conciliation, induce our Indian fellow-subjects to adopt our views of religion and science, to study our language and literature, to benefit by our mechanical knowledge and our various appliances for economising time, labour, and money. As a principal means to this end let us take every opportunity of commending to their use a common character, adapted to the expression of all their languages, and bringing all those languages into community, so far, with our own; a character which, insuring cheap and rapid printing on the one hand, and easy reading on the other, may be made a potent engine, not only for promoting intercourse between the European and Asiatic races, but for diffusing education among the millions of Hindús who have never yet learned to read and write.

As surely as railroads, electric telegraphs, steam-printing, penny postage, and every other European improvement, must in due time find their way into the remotest corners of our Eastern empire, so surely must the simple Roman alphabet, with Christian instruction in its train, take the place of the complicated symbols which now obstruct the path of knowledge and enlightenment.

I have the honour to be, Sir,
Your faithful servant,
MONIER WILLIAMS.

Cheltenham, December 29, 1858.

(34.)

THIRD LETTER OF PROFESSOR JARRETT.

To the Editor of the Times.

Sir,—Two letters from me on this subject appeared in the *Times*, one on the 12th of November, and a second on the 18th of that month, the former being occasioned by an unsigned article which appeared November the 10th, and the latter by a letter signed "Indophilus" in your paper of November the 16th, in which I was called on by name to explain my first letter.

Professor Monier Williams, in a letter published in the *Times* of December the 31st, calls in question the accuracy of my statement as to the essentially different alphabets used in India. I said on the 18th of November: "The object of my letter was to show that the difficulty of acquiring an Indian dialect is not necessarily increased to any great amount by the labour of learning the native alphabets; that the long array of such alphabets might be reduced to two, the Sanskṛit and the Arabic; and, lastly, that unity of language does not really exist throughout India."

Professor Williams remarks: "The most that can be said of this statement (though no one, by the by, has yet contradicted it) is that it conveys a very inadequate, if not erroneous, impression of the fact. Instead of two principal alphabets, there are at least five." The three additional alphabets mentioned by Professor Williams are the Telugu, Tamil, and Malayálam. In answer to this charge of inaccuracy I may be permitted to quote, first, the Rev. R. Caldwell, the best authority I know on the subject, and then Professor Williams himself. The former gentleman, in his most valuable *Comparative Grammar of the Drávidian or South-Indian Family of Languages*, has this passage, page 93:—

"There are three different Drávidian alphabets at present in use, viz. the Tamil, the Malayálam, and the Telugu-Canarese." These, "together with their older, but now obsolete shapes, and the 'Grantham,' or character in which Sanskrit is written in the Tamil country, have all been derived, I conceive, from the early Deva-nágari, or from the still earlier characters that are contained in the cave inscriptions, — characters which have been altered and disguised by natural and local influences, and especially by the custom, universal in the Deccan, of writing on the leaf of the palmyra palm with an iron stylus. Thus, there is reason to conclude that all the alphabetical characters which are used, or known, in Southern India have a common origin, and that their origin is the same as that of all the existing alphabets of Northern India, namely, the system of characters in which Sanskrit was written by the ancient Brahmans." Thus far Mr. Caldwell. Professor Monier Williams has prefixed to his very useful Sanskṛit Grammar what he calls, "a table of the various modifications of the Deva-nágarí alphabet, both ancient and modern, from the date of the earliest inscriptions to the present time." This table, then, teaches us to consider the modern character (which Professor Williams calls perfect) as the best representative of 13 different forms, among which are those which Mr. Caldwell pronounces to be the origin of all the Southern alphabets. Surely, then, I did not say anything very inaccurate when I affirmed that the modern Deva-nágarí might be conveniently and advantageously used for all of them, seeing that they all are modifications of the same characters, and were meant to express the same sounds. Professor Williams says, also: "No Sanskṛit fount of types is complete without 600, 700, or even 800 sorts, simple and compound. One of your correspondents proposes to deal very summarily with these troublesome compounds. Without more ado, he would oblige the natives to get rid of them altogether, and content themselves with the moderate allowance of 60 simple letters. I submit, however, that these conjunct consonants are essential to the integrity of the Deva-nágarí system, and to ask the natives to dispense with them is to ask them to do rather more than accept the Roman character. It is to tell them to abolish everything which makes their own revered system of writing the most perfect and elaborate in the world." In answer to this, allow me to say that, though I have been familiar with the Sanskṛit alphabet for nearly thirty years, this is the first time I have heard that "conjunct consonants are essential" to that alphabet. Professor Williams knows full well that by using the *viráma* all such "monograms" may be avoided; and in a note to his letter he supplies the strongest possible argument against their use. He there says: "As to the Nágarí alphabet, my own experience of teaching it to 600 or 700 students at Haileybury enables me to affirm that it requires at least two months for the most apt scholar to read it fluently; that the majority do not master it in twice that time, and that some, though they know all the letters, never acquire the power to read it without hesitation." Surely this statement is enough to prove that these monograms merit the fate of those Greek contractions that formerly puzzled ingenious youth. If they are thus laid aside, I venture to predict that a week will be ample time for any youth of average talent to learn to read Sanskṛit words with fluency.

With reference to the Arabic alphabet, as enlarged by diacritical points, Professor Williams accuses me of maintaining a most untenable proposition, in saying that Hindústání ought to be written either in that character or Sanskṛit. As a matter of fact, it is written sometimes in one and sometimes in the other. It is true that additional diacritical points are needed to express certain modifications of t, d, and r, and it is also true that double letters are required to express by the Arabic alphabet the Sanskṛit aspirates; but it is equally true that Professor Williams needs both these contrivances to express Hindústání sounds by Roman characters. If, then, the Muslims of India will cease from "developing æsthetical tendencies in the direction of calligraphy," and confine themselves to writing a plain hand on a uniform model; and if this is rigorously exacted in official documents, we shall hear little more of the difficulty of reading Hindústání when written in the native character.

I am, Sir,
Your faithful servant,
THOMAS JARRETT.

Ely, January 4, 1859.

(35.)

SECOND LETTER OF PROFESSOR MONIER WILLIAMS.

To the Editor of the Times.

Sir,—I had hoped that, a long interval having elapsed since the publication of Professor Jarrett's first letters on the alphabets of India, my own communication might have been regarded as a general review of the question, rather than as an opening for further controversy, especially as I carefully abstained from mentioning names. Your readers are doubtless weary of the topic, and I feel reluctant to trespass further on your indulgence and their patience. Nevertheless, it is only due to the vast importance of this inquiry to attempt to clear the ground of the perplexity in which it has become involved by Professor Jarrett's last letter. I must, therefore, crave permission to recapitulate in a few words my former statements.

1. There are five quite distinct characters current in India, viz. the Nágarí, the Arabic, the Telugu, the Tamil, and the Malayálam.

2. The corruptions of these, and especially of the Nágarí, which are also current in various provinces, depart so widely from their first models, that a large number of additional alphabets are created, practically distinct from the original five.

3. One and all of these alphabets (and especially the two principal), from the peculiar structure of the letters, from the number of compound forms, from the absence of punctuation, and other considerations, are quite unadapted to meet the demands of advancing knowledge for a supply of cheap, clearly printed, readable books.

4. The Roman alphabet, however inferior in beauty and elaboration to the native systems, possesses manifest advantages in compactness, clearness, simplicity, cheapness, and an ample equipment of stops and other modern appliances.

5. Hindústání, which is the mixed dialect used all over India as a common medium of communication, is written with as much suitableness in the Roman character as in the Arabic, Persian, or Nágarí, and has been so written increasingly for the last 25 years.

6. To advance the cause of Christianity and civilisation, to promote intercourse between the mixed races of India, and to bring their languages into some sort of community with each other and with our own, every means should be taken to familiarise the natives with our simple alphabet, by allowing them to write their petitions in this character, by employing it in Government documents, by teaching it in missionary and other schools, by circulating vernacular books printed in English type throughout the length and breadth of the land.

Such is the substance of what I advanced in my first letter, and to these propositions, with all deference to Professor

Jarrett, whose opinion is entitled to respect, I still adhere. In replying to them, Professor Jarrett has, in fact, confined himself to the first, to that part of the third which relates to the Nágarí, and to the fifth.

As to the first, if Professor Jarrett wished to prove to the satisfaction of the public that the Telugu, Tamil, and Malayálam alphabets are all three merely modifications of the Deva-nágarí, he ought to have pointed out in what respects they resemble that character and each other; instead of which he has first quoted a passage from *Mr. Caldwell's Comparative Grammar*, and then, by a reference to a table in my *Sanskṛit Grammar*, attempted to show that I am inconsistent with myself. It must strike every one as unsatisfactory that he should found all his arguments against me on a detached passage, separated from its context. Heresies of all kinds have been supported in a similar manner. I could of course just as easily extract a sentence or two from Mr. Caldwell's book in corroboration of my own views. As it happens, however, I had the very passage quoted by Professor Jarrett in my mind when I wrote in my first letter, "Whatever may be said about remote affinities, each of the five alphabets (of India) has an individuality of its own so decided, that a knowledge of any one of the five would not lessen the amount of labour required for the mastery of any one of the others." What does it signify that four alphabets are said to have had a primeval relationship, or to have started from a common source, if they are known to have diverged in opposite directions, and settled down into shapes as wide asunder as the four quarters of the compass? Let comparative philologists, if they will, trace all the languages and all the alphabets of the world to a common origin. We practical Englishmen look only to present differences. It is enough for us that the five alphabets of India are now as distinct in shape as any five alphabets can be. What consolation is it to poor matter of fact students, who have to toil up five separate steep and rugged paths, to be told that they all have a common point of departure? The differences to us are real, whatever philologists may say. We know the story of Dr. Johnson, who, when he was told by a philosopher that matter had no real existence, kicked his foot against some hard substance, proving thereby that, to himself at least, it had. In like manner, let every one who doubts the real distinction of the five Indian alphabets satisfy himself by merely using his eyes and examining them.

But Professor Jarrett appeals to a table in my Sanskṛit Grammar. This table is not mine, but Mr. James Prinsep's, as stated in my note. It was originally procured to illustrate an elaborate edition of Mr. Prinsep's Essays, by Mr. Thomas, and was lent to me by the editor and publisher of that work. Its use in my book is to show that the modern perfect Nágarí is generally quite distinct in shape from the old imperfect inscription characters, and that its corruptions also are so distinct as to constitute nearly separate systems. This is consistent with what I formerly asserted, and as the Telugu, Tamil, and Malayálam alphabets have no place in the table, I do not see what the table has to do with the question. It is true that the South-Indian characters, especially the Telugu, are said to be derived from the inscription symbols; but if these latter bear no direct resemblance to the modern Nágarí, that can only prove that the South-Indian and Devanágarí are distinct.

The fact is, that as the South-Indian languages have no essential community with the Sanskṛit, so the characters which express them are essentially different. It may be safely affirmed that a native of India, who only knew any one of the South-Indian alphabets, would have far more difficulty in learning to write Nágarí than our Roman letters. If, then, he is to be compelled to give up his own system for an alphabet quite different in shape, he had better adopt the simple Roman than the complex Sanskṛit. Professor Jarrett reminds me that I said the Sanskṛit was "perfect;" let me also remind him that I added that it was too perfect and too elaborate for the wants of a workday age.

As to the part of my third statement which is explanatory of the Sanskṛit alphabetical system, Professor Jarrett says that "it is the first time he has heard that conjunct consonants are essential to the Sanskṛit alphabet." I submit that I made no such assertion. What I said was that conjunct consonants are essential to the integrity of the Devanágarí system, and this I still maintain. It is a mere confusion of the question to compare the Nágarí compound letters with the Greek contractions. They have no real analogy. The Sanskṛit conjunct consonants (which, indeed, are not always contractions *) arose out of what I described as a main feature of the Nágarí system, viz. the inherence of the vowel *a* in every consonant. They may be said to constitute the very backbone of that system, because without them the rules for the conjunction of letters (called Sandhi) could not hold together with consistency. Professor Jarrett alleges that the mark called *virâma* might always be employed to prevent the use of these conjunct letters. Let me explain that the *virâma* is a stroke like one of our stops, placed under a consonant to denote that no vowel is pronounced after it. The natives, however, only use it as a stop at the end of a sentence terminating in a consonant. In printing Oriental books in England we have sometimes applied this symbol, with what Pundits would consider undue license, to separate words whose final and initial consonants are strictly in conjunction. Even in this country, however, we have never gone the length of perverting the *vir·îma* to the abolition of all compound letters. This would be, in the eyes of a Pundit, to destroy the very vertebræ of the Sanskṛit system of Sandhi. What would a Brahmin think of being made to write *kártsnya* (*Anglicè*, "the whole") with four *virâmas* or stops in the middle of the word? His prejudices would be less shocked by asking him to write it in the Roman character. Let the Brahmin, then, keep his Sanskṛit and his Sandhi intact. Why mutilate and disfigure his venerated alphabet? We cannot bring life out of a dead thing by cutting it in pieces. This "rigorous exaction" of stops in the middle of words would only offend the educated natives, without adapting their alphabet to the requirements of living tongues in an age of rapidly advancing knowledge.

I now come to the only other proposition disputed by Professor Jarrett. In order to prove that Hindústání, or the

* In many compounds (such as dw, nk, kk, khw) there is no contraction, the letters being merely placed one above the other.

mixed dialect, cannot suitably be expressed by English letters, he says that diacritical points are needed in the Roman type just as much as in the Arabic and Nágarí. Granted. But this does not place the Roman type in a worse position than the others. They all three labour alike under this disadvantage; but let any one note the advantages which I have described as possessed by the Roman alphabet over the Arabic and Nágarí in other respects, especially in its better adaptation to English, Nágarí, and Persian words, than either the Nágarí to English and Persian, or the Persian to English and Nágarí. The other day a copy of the Queen's proclamation in Hindústání or Urdú (i.e. the mixed language of the camp), published in an Indian Government gazette, and printed in Persian characters, came in my way. I found that a considerable portion of the words (such as "governor-general," "government," "council," "East India Company," &c.) introduced into the Urdú were English. All these words would have been far more suitably expressed in Roman type than in Persian; and when our permanent Urdú, or camp, of 80,000 soldiers shall have settled down in different parts of India, will not the Urdú, or camp language, which is meant to supply a medium of communication between the English soldiers and the natives, have a greater claim than ever to be expressed in English letters?

The inquiry may be thus summed up. A perfect maze of alphabets exists in India. They may be compared to a confusion of roads, leading in opposite directions, crossing and recrossing each other and branching into a complication of by-paths. They are all, however, so hilly, so circuitous, so blocked up with thorns and surrounded with difficulties, that traffic and intercourse are much impeded. Two remedies are proposed for this state of things. Professor Jarrett's proposition is that nothing new should be introduced. He would take the means of communication already existing, and merge them all into two broad trunk roads (which we may call the Arabic and Nágarí). Not a single other road would he allow, and all cross-paths he would utterly abolish.

"Indophilus," on the other hand, proposes to leave all the existing highways and cross-roads undisturbed. They are revered by the natives, and the very hills over which they lead are held sacred. Moreover, we cannot level mountains, or make a labyrinth anything but perplexing. But what we can do he considers should be done. Side by side with the native highways, but piercing instead of traversing the hills, we may introduce the simple, straight, level English railroad. We have no need to force the natives to abandon their old means of intercourse. We have only to commend our own greater facilities to their use, and in the end we may be sure they will adopt that method of communication (that alphabet, I mean) which combines the several requisites of simplicity, ease, rapidity, cheapness, and adaptation to the necessities of a growing civilisation.

Enough, then, of controversy. Let a discriminating public decide which of these courses is the most judicious and practicable.

I am, Sir,

Your faithful and obliged servant,

MONIER WILLIAMS.

Cheltenham, Jan. 8th, 1859.

(36.)

The following letter, from Sir Charles Trevelyan and Sir John Login to the Secretaries of the Bible Society, contains a good summary of the leading objects of the movement, and the appendix marks the practical results to which it has led in this country.

Treasury, 2nd December, 1857.

Reverend Gentlemen,

We beg to recommend to the Committee of the Bible Society, the publication of two editions of the New Testament in the Roman character, — one of them in Hindústání only, and the other in Hindústání and English in parallel columns; the orthography to be that of Sir William Jones as modified by the result of the discussions which took place at Calcutta in the year 1834, and now generally adopted by the missionary bodies in the Bengal and Agra Presidencies.

The Rev. Cotton Mather, who is editing for the Society the complete Hindústání Bible with notes and references according to the same orthography, informs us that he is ready to undertake to pass these separate editions of the New Testament through the press, without delaying the progress of the principal work.

Independently of the general advantages of the application of the Roman character to the numerous languages and dialects of India —(which may be summed up as follows: that it substitutes a cheap and legible, for an expensive and indistinct, character; that it facilitates the acquisition of the native languages by the English, and of the English language by the natives; and that, by making one character serve for many languages and dialects which have already more or less in common, it will greatly assist general intercourse, and create a *tendency* towards a common Indian language, of which English will be the connecting link, and the Christian religion the source of inspiration),—the extraordinary circumstances of the present time appear in an especial manner to require that all Europeans of whatever rank, proceeding to India to reside there, should be enabled at the smallest possible cost of time and money to become acquainted with the native languages, of which Hindústání is the most generally diffused, forming already to a great extent a common medium of communication among all classes of persons in India; and, for many obvious reasons, no instrument could be had recourse to for this purpose, which would be so replete with benefits of various kinds as the New Testament.

We have the honour to be,

Reverend Gentlemen,

Your faithful and obedient Servants,

(Signed) C. E. TREVELYAN.

(Signed) J. LOGIN.

The Rev. The Secretaries
of the Bible Society.

[The Bible Society answered this appeal by determining to print 30,000 copies of the Anglo-Hindústání New Testament,—20,000 in English and Hindústání in parallel columns, and 10,000 in Hindústání only,—all in the Roman character. These will soon be ready, and will be sold at a very moderate price.

The following works in the Roman character have also just issued from the press in this country, or are about to appear:—

1. An Easy Introduction to the Study of Hindústání, accompanied by a full Syntax, Selections, Vocabulary, and Dialogues. Price 2*s.* 6*d.* Now ready.

2. A Hindústání and English Clavis to the New Testament and Psalms.

3. The Bág-o-Bahár, carefully revised, with Preface and Notes. Price about 4*s.* or 5*s.*—This is the standard Hindústání class-book.

4. An English Translation of the Bág-o-Bahár.

5. The Gulistán, or Rose Garden, by Shaiḳh Sa'dí.—This is the well-known Persian class-book.

6. An English translation of the Gulistán.

7. The Prem Ságar.—This is the Hindí class-book, and considered a model of correct Hindí.

8. A translation of the Prem Ságar.

All published by Messrs. LONGMAN and Co., of Paternoster Row, and all in Roman type.

It is also in contemplation to publish a very simple Hindústání Grammar, for the use of English soldiers in India, to be called "The English Soldier's Hindústání Primer." This will soon, it is hoped, be followed by similar primers in Bengálí and the other vernaculars.]

THE END.